HN 59.2 .W37 1999
OCLC: 39733217
Legitimate differences

P9-CAX-494

THE RICHARD STOCKTON COLLEGE
OF NEW JERSEY LIBRARY
POMONA, NEW JERSEY 08240

Legitimate Differences

Legitimate Differences

Interpretation in the Abortion Controversy and Other Public Debates

Georgia Warnke

THE RICHARD STOCKTON COLLEGE
OF NEW JERSEY LIBRARY
POMONA, NEW JERSEY 08240

UNIVERSITY OF CALIFORNIA PRESS
Berkeley · *Los Angeles* · *London*

University of California Press
Berkeley and Los Angeles, California

University of California Press, Ltd.
London, England

© 1999 by the Regents of the University of California

Library of Congress Cataloging-in-Publication Data

Warnke, Georgia.
    Legitimate differences : interpretation in the
abortion controversy and other public debates /
by Georgia Warnke.
        p.   cm.
    Includes bibliographical references and index.
    ISBN 0-520-21633-4 (alk. paper).
    1. Social ethics—United States.   2. Social
values—United States.   3. United States—Social
policy—Moral and ethical aspects.
4. Hermeneutics.   I. Title.
HN59.2.W37   1999
303.3'72'0973—DC21   98-41409
                                                      CIP

Manufactured in the United States of America

9 8 7 6 5 4 3 2 1

The paper used in this publication meets the mini-
mum requirements of American National Standard
for Information Sciences—Permanence of Paper for
Printed Library Materials, ANSI Z39.48-1984.

To Maggie, Tom, Stephen, and Benjamin

Contents

Preface and Acknowledgments

"When democratic citizens morally disagree about public policy, what should they do? They should deliberate with one another, seeking moral agreement when they can, and maintaining mutual respect when they cannot."[1] So conclude two prominent political theorists with regard to sensitive current issues in American life such as abortion, affirmative action, welfare, surrogate mothering, and the distribution of medical care. This book takes up some of these same issues and tries to articulate a deliberative approach to them. Yet it asks two additional questions. First, are our disagreements over such issues as abortion and affirmative action best conceived of as moral disagreements? Second, why should we deliberate with those who disagree with us or, indeed, maintain respect for them? To the first question this study offers a negative answer that I hope provides an answer to the second.

As citizens and theorists, we typically proceed as if our public debates were debates over principle: debates over whether a principle of life or a principle of liberty should govern abortion policy, debates over which principle, that of merit or that of diversity, has priority in admission to schools and professions, for example. But as Americans we share principles of life, liberty, and equal opportunity. We are not diverse cultures with alien principles in our disagreements but rather, I shall suggest, different interpretive communities[2] with different concerns, histories, and interests that serve to illuminate different dimensions of the principles we share. To this extent, our public debates can be understood as analogues of our discussions of texts. Just as we share the plays of Shakespeare as part of our collective heritage, we share our principles. And just as we can legitimately understand *King Lear* or *Hamlet* in different ways, depending on our interests, associations, and experiences, we can legitimately understand our principles differently as well. But if we acknowledge differences in the legitimate ways we can understand both our texts and our principles, then we can also understand the grounds for respecting one another even as we differ. Just as we respect and relish the range of legitimate interpretations that we possess of *King Lear,* we can appreciate legitimate understandings of equality, life, or liberty that differ from our own.

I shall not be suggesting that any way we interpret our shared principles is as good as any other. I shall be suggesting only that more than one way might be legitimate. Nor do I want to suggest that those skilled or interested in the interpretation of texts are also the best participants in our public discussions of how to interpret our principles.[3] Still, I do want to suggest that if we were to acknowledge the interpretive character of our public debates over some of the issues that concern us, we would secure a firm foundation for a deliberative form of democracy. For we would then talk and listen to one another with mutual respect, not simply because political theorists encourage us to do so, but because we recognize the interpretive status of our own positions. We could then no more close our minds to alternative understandings of life and liberty than we can to alternative understandings of our texts. It follows that we could no longer close our minds to the different understandings of our practices with which different understandings of our principles are allied. How we are ever to resolve our debates under these interpretive conditions is a crucial question, of course. I shall be recommending forms of compromise and accommodation that eschew any dogmatic interpretation of our principles without, I hope, risking an intolerable relativism.

The influences that Hans-Georg Gadamer and Jürgen Habermas have exerted on the way this study tries to work out these suggestions, sometimes in opposite theoretical directions, will be obvious. No less obvious will be the influences of Michael Walzer and Thomas McCarthy, although neither would necessarily endorse the conclusions I draw and although, again, their respective influences often pull in different directions. In addition, I would like to thank the Philosophy Departments of the University of California at Irvine and Riverside, Denison University, Stanford University, The State University of New York at Buffalo, and the University of Oregon for allowing me to try out various parts of this book on them and for helpful comments. I would also like to thank Paul Hoffman, Larry Jones, Sarah Stage, Paul Stern, Steve Vogel, the students in the "Hermeneutics and Public Debate" seminar at the University of California, Riverside, and my editor, Ed Dimendberg for helpful, if not always welcome, criticisms. I am grateful to my sons for tolerating my attempts to work on this book, and to my sister, brothers, and parents I owe more than I can say.

Part of Chapter One appeared in the *Yale Journal of Law and the Humanities* (Summer 1997), and a short analysis of the material in Chapter Two appeared in *Dissent* (Fall 1994). A version of Chapter Three appeared in the *Journal of Social Philosophy* (vol. 29, no. 3, Winter 1998). I have treated some of the material in Chapters Four, Five, and Six in portions of essays in the *Cardozo Law Review* (vol. 16, no. 6, April 1995), *Laval théologique et philosophique* (vol. 53, no. 1, February 1997), and *Philosophy and Social Criticism* (vol. 22, no. 2, 1996).

CHAPTER ONE

Interpretation
and Social Issues

Current public debates over social issues in the United States are often pursued and portrayed as though they were arguments over competing moral principles. Thus, the abortion debate is depicted by its participants and commentators as a struggle that opposes principles of life to principles of liberty. So-called pro-life groups argue against a woman's right to terminate a pregnancy on the basis that abortion violates a moral principle of respect for the sanctity of human life. Conversely, pro-choice groups support the right to an abortion on the basis that any restriction of abortion rights violates a moral principle of liberty insofar as it is also a restriction of woman's freedom to decide when or if she is to be a parent. Similarly, discussion over affirmative action is viewed as a debate setting principles of equality against those of fairness or diversity. Those who advocate an end to America's affirmative action policies argue that they violate the principle of equality in granting preferential treatment to certain groups on the basis of their ethnicity, race, or gender. Just as adamantly, those who advocate the continuation of affirmative action policies argue that principles of fairness require preferential treatment to compensate for the effects of past discrimination against certain groups while a principle of diversity requires the spreading of privileges and career opportunities over a wider spectrum of the American public.

Differences on moral principle also seem to divide those who defend the production and consumption of pornography as part of their defense of the principle of free speech from those who attack pornography as a violation of the principle of equality with regard to women. And, finally, the moral principles involved in supporting the integrity of the family and denying the place of market values in it seems to pit those who criticize the practice of surrogate motherhood against those who defend it by appealing to principles involving the rational autonomy of women and the freedom of contract.[1]

Such apparently moral differences are particularly troubling to us Americans because we assume that we *share* moral principles. At least we assume that if we do not share *all* our moral principles, we share certain founding principles that speak to the sanctity of life and to the importance of liberty and equality. Moreover, we assume that we can appeal to our Constitution and ultimately to the Supreme Court's interpretation of it to resolve any disagreements we may have over how and whether disputed practices conform to our principles. Hence, we are dismayed when Supreme Court decisions only increase the acrimony and bitterness in our disagreements as they have in the controversy over abortion and in various cases involving affirmative action.

We are supposed to agree that individual human life is intrinsically valuable and that each individual is to be granted as much individual liberty as is compatible with a similar liberty on the part of all others. We are supposed to agree, then, that each person is to be guaranteed a right to life, the freedom of speech and contract (among other freedoms), and the liberty to pursue his or her own life's projects and conceptions of the good. Americans are also meant to agree that men, women, and children are to enjoy a right to equal concern and respect as well as to careers, offices, and opportunities that are equally open to all on the basis of individual merit and hard work. But if we so completely disagree at least on the four issues I have mentioned—abortion, affirmative action, pornography, and surrogate mothering—then perhaps we only appear to agree on the validity of shared fundamental principles. Moreover, perhaps our presumption that we ought to share an allegiance to the same moral principles aggravates the hostility each side in our debates bears toward the other. Each uses the principles we are meant to share to convict the other side of violating ideals fundamental to our moral identity.

Attempts to resolve such conflicts often try either to narrow the scope of moral disagreement or to dig further down below the principles on which we seem to disagree to a deeper core of moral agreement. The idea here is that the contrasts I have sketched, those that oppose a principle of life to that of liberty, a principle of equality to those of fairness and diversity, a principle of free speech to that of equality, and a principle of family integrity to that of freedom of contract, are all relatively superficial contrasts that can be resolved by uncovering a more fundamental ground of principled agreement. Lawrence Tribe has thus characterized the debate over abortion, for example, as only apparently a "clash of absolutes,"[2] one that can be resolved by considering views Americans continue to share on the value of family life and the proper scope of technological intrusions into it. I want to look briefly at his resolution for two reasons: to support his effort to remove our conflicts from the domain of clashing absolutes and to indicate potential problems in all attempts to minimize our differences by simply invoking more fundamental or more widely shared principles. I shall be arguing that these attempts fail to recognize both the depth of our differences and what I shall be calling their interpretive character. Moreover, I shall argue that only by acknowledging their interpretive character can we begin to find ways to deal with them.

TRIBE'S SOLUTION TO THE DEBATE OVER ABORTION

Suppose, as is likely, that technological advance makes it possible for doctors to remove fetuses from their mothers' wombs at an early point in their pregnancies and to grow the fetuses in surrogate mothers or test tubes. Such a procedure would seem to offer a solution to the conflict over abortion if that conflict pits a fetus's alleged right to life against a woman's alleged liberty to choose when and if she is to become a parent. Without causing the death of the fetus, a woman could liberate herself from both the need to endure a nine-month pregnancy and all responsibility for the fetus or child by simply allowing the fetus to be transferred from her womb to another woman's womb or to an artificial one. But suppose a pregnant woman decides she does not want either to bear a child at this point in her life or to have a fetus removed from her body and brought to term in another place. Does she still have the right to demand an abortion in circumstances in which technology can absolve her of all responsibility for bearing and raising the child she conceived? Can she insist that the life of the fetus be terminated if another woman or the state is willing to bring it to term? She would no longer be compelled to bear or raise the child. But does she have an additional right to insist not only that she be released from the necessity of bearing the fetus but, further, that the fetus's life be ended, that no child genetically related to her be born into the world at this time?

Tribe admits that a woman might reasonably object to the notion that she could discharge her responsibility for a fetus simply by giving it up to another family or to the state to gestate and raise. For many women, it would remain psychologically devastating to think that children genetically related to them were to be born to, and raised by, unknown families or by the state and that these children might be abused, unhappy, or neglected without their biological mothers' knowing or being in any situation to help. Hence, one might argue that even under future technological conditions a woman must still have a right to choose to have an abortion since the state must not be permitted to compel her to allow for the continuation of a pregnancy or for the birth of a child over whose fate she is to have no control. But Tribe also points out that men who impregnate women do not have the right to require them to undergo abortions so that the men involved are not burdened with the potential agony of wondering about the fate of their children. The same might hold for a woman's right to ask that a fetus be aborted rather than simply transferred to a different womb and mother. As Tribe writes, "When one fights for the abortion right in the name of something less than the liberty not to be molded physically and psychologically into a mother, one stands on shaky ground." [3]

Still, if technological advances allow a pregnant woman to separate her life from that of the fetus without terminating its life, and if these technological advances eradicate the right to an abortion, who will be responsible for fetuses transferred to artificial wombs or wombs under the control of the state? Presumably some fetuses would be transferred to the wombs of women who wanted to raise a child. But what about unwanted fetuses? Tribe points out that American systems of foster care and adoption are already badly equipped to deal with unwanted children, special-needs children, and older or abused children. The advance of technology with no right to abortion raises the prospect not only of increasing the population of unwanted children but of state-run fetus factories in which children are manufactured by the state in total disregard for their own parents' feelings or wishes and, moreover, in total disregard for any sense of what might be valuable about both pregnancy and parenthood.

Tribe insists that this futuristic nightmare serves to disclose substantial agreement between pro-life and pro-choice groups below the absolutist clash of a principle of life against that of liberty. Most of us, he insists, "would intuitively feel the force of any . . . fetus's claim to life" if it "could be saved without sacrificing the woman's freedom to end her pregnancy." At the same time, he supposes, most of us would also understand that "that claim to life ... must be offset by the potential evils, real, even if ill defined, of state-run fetus factories." Hence, he concludes, both supporters and opponents of a right to an abortion will finally agree on principles to prevent the intrusion of the state into procreative decisions. Pro-life groups will have to modify their opposition to abortion to avoid the danger of a technologically based, state-controlled production of children that would, in their own view, subvert the nature and value of pregnancy, maternity, and the family. As Tribe writes, "it may be that the right-to-life impulse and the pro-choice impulse may yet find common cause—in the desire to avoid government manipulation of technologies to save or preserve life, but only at the expense of sacrificing what we sense to be most natural."[4]

Yet why should pro-life advocates be dismayed at the idea of growing fetuses outside their genetic mothers' wombs if doing so saved those fetuses' lives? Alternatively, if they would be dismayed, as Tribe assumes they would, why is it not plausible to assume that they would be equally dismayed by both nonnatural birth technologies and abortion rights? Pro-life advocates who oppose abortion often already do so on the basis of a set of beliefs and attitudes about the meaning of life, family, sexual intercourse, God, and mothering in terms of which any artificial intervention into human life-giving processes, including any sort of birth control device other than abstinence or natural family planning, improperly interferes with natural and even sacred processes.[5] The capacity to bring human children into the world, on this view, is a miraculous capacity that attests to a natural or even divine generosity and gives meaning to both marriage and sex, even sex that is not engaged in for strictly procreative purposes. From this perspective, new birth technologies that allow for fetal transfers between wombs are neither a solution to the abortion problem nor a reason to support abortion rights to avoid the greater evil of state-run fetus factories. Rather, fetal transfer and abortion are both points of horror along the same continuum, one that fails to recognize the travesty involved in using artificial means and technologies to interfere with natural and even sacred human life-giving abilities.

The point here is that differences between pro-life and pro-choice groups reach deeper than Tribe imagines. We do not differ only on abortion rights while we continue to agree in our understanding of life, sex, and the meaning of childbirth. Still, Tribe buttresses his own conclusion that pro-life advocates would agree with their pro-choice adversaries in choosing abortion over state-run fetus factories and hence that both sides already agree on what is natural and valuable in family life by citing what he sees as the conservative, traditionalist agenda behind much opposition to abortion rights. Many antiabortion activists, he claims, make exceptions for cases of rape and incest and concede that women should not be forced to give birth to their own rapists' children. But, as he points out, the distinction between these pregnancies and others lies only in the coerced character of the sexual act that leads to them and cannot affect the innocence or the sanctity of the life of the fetus that results. Were the opposition to abortion as exclusively centered on the preservation of human life as its proponents insist, Tribe argues, that opposition would have to maintain the sanctity of life in the case of rape as well as in the case of consensual sex. Instead, in his view, the pro-life idea is that women should not have legal access to an abortion when they have themselves violated prohibitions against sex outside of marriage or against sex for other than procreative reasons. As Tribe concludes, "Rather than center entirely on the protection of 'unborn children' . . . the feeling that abortion should be blocked by government may grow, at least in part, out of a reflexive willingness to enforce traditional sex roles upon women and to impose upon them an unequal and harsh sexual morality." [6]

As Tribe suggests, such a traditionalist, sexually conservative agenda would not be inconsistent with an opposition to state-run fetus factories and the evils of a governmental dismantling of traditional values and natural relationships. Moreover, if, as he claims, the opposition to abortion rights is directed in part at enforcing traditional gender roles, then pro-life groups might be willing to sacrifice this aim to protect against what they might see as a greater evil, namely, all use of birth technologies such as fetal transfers. Yet, it remains unclear why opponents of a right to an abortion would not or could not simply condemn, as the Catholic church already does, both the practice of abortion and all "unnatural" or artificial birth technologies. Why must the pro-life view oppose only one alternative? At bottom, it is not clear that a pro-life opposition to abortion would understand the stakes as Tribe understands them, as a protection of fetal life only at the "expense of sacrificing what we sense to be most natural." Surely, a traditionalist opposition to both abortion and fetal transfers rests on precisely the same foundation: an opposition to sacrificing in either case "what we sense to be most natural" and hence an opposition to all artificial interventions into natural, valuable, and even sacred processes, whether these interventions involve aborting fetuses, removing them to new or artificial wombs, or, indeed, rape.

The common ground on which Tribe thinks the abortion debate can be resolved turns out, instead, to constitute an important dimension of the difference between pro-life and pro-choice groups. They differ not only on the acceptability of abortion rights but on the acceptability of other birth technologies as well. For a pro-choice group, the option of transferring fetuses to different wombs might serve as one more area for the freedom of choice for pregnant women, along with the options of aborting a fetus and giving a baby up for adoption. For pro-life groups, however, fetal transfer technologies would seem to reflect simply one more violation of the sanctity of natural or even divine life-giving capacities. In Chapter Four, we shall see that these differences over the way each side understands the possibility of transferring fetuses between wombs involve deeper differences in fundamental orientation: toward women's lives and liberty to choose, toward the meaning of birth and pregnancy, and toward the proper way to show respect for human life. Rather than provide a resolution to the debate, then, new birth technologies seem more likely to reveal the depth of our differences. But if Tribe's common ground does not provide a solution to the abortion debate, two questions I have tried to raise remain. First, do we share moral principles and, if we do, why do we differ so completely on at least the four issues I have mentioned (abortion, surrogate mothering, affirmative action, and pornography)? Second, how should we think of and try to resolve these differences?

The premises behind this book are, first, that the character of our disputes over at least some of the issues that divide us needs to be clearly distinguished from the character of moral debate over competing principles and, second, that as Americans we do indeed share moral principles. Those who are pro-life do not reject the principle of liberty, nor do those who are pro-choice reject the principle of the sanctity of life. Likewise, those who defend affirmative action policies do not reject the principle of equality, and those who criticize affirmative action policies do not ignore all considerations of fairness and diversity that their proponents defend. Those who are against contract pregnancies do not dispute the validity of principles having to do with freedom of contract and those who are in favor of contract pregnancies do not reject either the principle of family integrity or the value of mothering. Finally, those who want to limit pornography do not dispute the validity of a principle of free speech any more than those on the other side necessarily reject the extension of equal rights to women.

If we Americans accept the principles to which each side in our various social disputes appeal, one might think that our differences can be treated as differences over which principles should have priority in which cases. In this case, our controversies would be controversies over the proper priorities of shared principles. But this analysis also seems ill suited to the cases at hand. Pro-choice groups do not generally argue that even though a fetus has a right to life it should sacrifice it to a woman's liberty. Nor do pro-life groups argue that while women have liberty rights they should relinquish them when they become pregnant. Defenders of affirmative action do not argue that principles of historical fairness and diversity are more important in present societal circumstances than the principle of equality, nor do critics of affirmative action argue that equality trumps fairness. The same holds for disputes over surrogate mothering and pornography. In neither case do our positions divide over the priority we give to different principles in particular situations: to autonomy over family integrity or to free speech over equality or the reverse. But if such conflicts do not stem from either differing principles or differing priorities, what is their source?

I shall be arguing that these and similar conflicts are rooted in differences in the meaning we take our principles as well as our practices to have and, hence, that they reflect interpretive differences. What divides the sides in our debates, in other words, is the different ways we can understand both our practices and the moral and legal principles we share. We do not disagree on the validity of fundamental principles of life, liberty, and equality or on their applications to particular cases. Yet we do disagree in our orientation to these cases and the principles we think they involve; moreover, we do so, I shall argue, because what is at stake are not the moral principles themselves but our understanding of their meaning. Our debates are not moral debates over which principles we should adopt but rather interpretive debates over the meaning of the principles we already possess. I shall also argue that, were we to acknowledge the interpretive character of our debates, we would open up options for resolving them—options that are foreclosed when we persist in believing that we are arguing over principle.

Debates over the interpretation of meaning have their original home in discussions of literature and works of art. In these cases, we assume that our interpretations are just that: interpretations. Moreover, such interpretations have a twofold character. First, we put them forward because we think they are valid and because we can argue for them. We think we possess standards for constructing good or adequate interpretations of texts and works of art, and we think we can appeal to these standards to criticize some interpretations while defending our own. Second, however, we do not think the validity of our own interpretations precludes the validity of at least some alternative interpretations. Rather, we assume that different interpretations of a work can reveal dimensions of the meaning of the work that were previously obscured or hidden to us, just as the dimensions on which we focus might have been obscured to others. Further, we assume that these new dimensions of the work can appear because different interpreters approach it with different experiences and concerns, view it from within different contexts, and come at it from the vantage point of different interpretive traditions. We assume that we can learn from these interpretations and, indeed, that we can learn in a distinctive sense: not in the sense that we approach the one true or real meaning of the text or work of art but rather in the sense simply that we come to understand new dimensions of its meaning and thus to understand it in an expanded way.[7]

While literary critics have not always viewed their interpretations as contributions rather than complete truths, it seems equally clear that literary discussions of texts do not typically end in canonical, finished understanding. They rather reveal dimensions of meaning. In the best interpretations, we are enriched in our understanding of the text and our own concerns and situation. Rather than conceiving of our debates over social issues as arguments over principle in which one—namely, our—side must be right, I suggest we take seriously the idea that our understanding of our principle and practices is interpretive, that its legitimacy does not preclude the legitimacy of some other interpretations, that these other legitimate interpretations can serve to expand our own understanding of meaning, and that while certain interpretations of our principles and practices may be invalid, none is ever finished or finally canonical.

This suggestion implies that our understandings of the meaning of both texts and text-analogues such as moral principles and social practices have their roots in what Hans-Georg Gadamer calls interpretive "horizons" and that different interpretive horizons are suited to revealing different dimensions of meaning.[8] Before attempting to show what this situation implies for our conflicts over abortion, affirmative action, pornography, and surrogate mothering, I want to examine more concretely some of the conditions of literary interpretation that I think are basic to our understanding of the meaning of our practices and principles as well. To do so, I shall concentrate on Emma Thompson's cinematic interpretation of Jane Austen's *Sense and Sensibility*.[9]

INTERPRETIVE DEBATES

What is striking to Thompson in her 1995 film adaptation of Austen's novel is the propriety with which the woman Thompson sees as the main character, Elinor Dashwood, acts. This propriety is, as Thompson understands it, not simply a superficial conformity to established conventions, but rather an attempt to act in a way that is most conscious of one's ethical duties toward others. In particular, Elinor's sense of propriety requires her to be sensitive to the feelings of her family and friends by not overwhelming them with her own feelings if she thinks those feelings would sadden or worry them. Hence, she tells no one when she discovers that Edward Ferrars, whom she loves, is already secretly betrothed to Lucy Steele. Because of Edward's own ethical propriety, Elinor knows that he is committed to marrying Lucy even though he now loves Elinor. Moreover, it is partially because of his ethical propriety that Elinor loves him. Hence, the situation is not one that can be helped and, for this reason, Elinor refuses to burden her family with her despair over it.

The film version of the novel emphasizes the contrast between this sort of behavior and the self-absorbed exuberance with which Elinor's sister, Marianne, attempts both to witness, feel, and express her life in all its emotional range and to have her family and friends witness, feel, and express it with her. But the film also emphasizes the effort an ethical propriety requires. It inserts a scene at Marianne's bedside in which Elinor begs her ill sister not to die since Elinor does not think she will be able to bear what she envisions as a life without Edward if she must lose Marianne as well. In addition, the film treats with sympathy and even indulgence a scene depicting a rare deviation from propriety in which Elinor bursts into uncontrollable and public tears upon discovering that Edward has not married Lucy after all and has, moreover, been released from the engagement through no act of betrayal of his own.

The film's emphasis on the effort involved in Elinor's struggle to maintain her self-restraint is not one that Austen herself would necessarily share. In the novel itself, Elinor never weeps at her sister's bedside. Further, when Edward announces that Lucy has broken their engagement to marry his brother, Elinor is able to control herself until she has left the room and she weeps only in private. But the movie's interpretive license in highlighting both the strength of Elinor's feelings and the strain involved in her heroic struggle to hide them from those who can do nothing to help alleviate them does reveal for a contemporary audience a facet of Austen's work that is important for us: namely, the idea that an ethically grounded propriety is not the same as a simple, unthinking conventionality and that our own assumptions as to the value of emotional expression have their limits. If other epochs do not share our sense of the meaning of Austen's novel, this divergence does not mean that our understanding is any less legitimate for us.

But what is meant by this sort of legitimacy? Thompson's cinematic version of *Sense and Sensibility* both admires Elinor's efforts at self-restraint and smiles at the lengths to which she assumes she ought to take them. Why not, thinks a contemporary sensibility, express your emotions, especially those that threaten to debilitate you, even if they embarrass others or burden them with matters they cannot resolve? Do our friends and family not owe us sympathy even if they cannot alleviate our pain? What Austen considers ethical propriety in general and tries to legitimize against Marianne's expressive emotionalism, we recognize as a peculiarly English version of propriety and, indeed, as a somewhat sweet and old-fashioned ethnic trait. Therefore, even if Thompson shows us that English propriety can teach us to question our own emotional excess and self-absorption, the way we understand this propriety necessarily differs from the way in which Austen understood it. Where Austen contrasts sense to sensibility, we understand a contrast between a still compelling, if old-fashioned, ethical stance and our own assumptions that our friends and family owe us a kind of emotional solidarity even if they can offer us little else.

Here the equal legitimacy of our understanding and Austen's own depends upon history. We have come to admire other so-called ethnic traits besides self-restraint, and we consider ourselves as individuals with rights as seriously as we take ourselves as parts of family and community networks to whom we have certain sorts of obligations. Moreover, the twentieth century has publicly witnessed events to which a self-restrained response would seem to be inhuman. To tie a legitimate understanding of *Sense and Sensibility* to its original audience's or Austen's own understanding would thus be a fruitless exercise in trying to get out of our own skin, as Richard Rorty has put the point.[10] Moreover, to limit our education into the ethical force of propriety for us to what we take as the eighteenth-century's authentic concerns would limit what we can learn from the centuries and cultures that preceded our own.

The point here is not that we cannot or ought not be interested in how Austen or her first readers understood *Sense and Sensibility*. Nor is the point that we ought always to try to "modernize" a text by consciously relating it to our own situation and trying to understand its relevance to us.[11] Instead, the point is that even if we want to understand how an author or her original audience understood a text and even if we are not explicitly concerned with its contemporary relevance, we still understand from out of a particular hermeneutic horizon. Conscious efforts at reconstructing intentions and conscious efforts at modernizing a text are both historically situated. They approach their texts with certain expectations, interests, and assumptions, and these serve to orient an understanding of a text or an author's intentions, to highlight certain features of it as interesting and important, and to cast a particular light on it. As Gadamer puts the point, "Every age has to understand a transmitted text in its own way, for the text belongs to the whole tradition whose content interests the age and in which it seeks to understand itself."[12]

At work here is what Gadamer calls a "fusion of horizons."[13] On the one hand, Austen's text provides an object of interpretation common to Emma Thompson and to other interpreters. On the other hand, Thompson's interpretation fuses with the text as the meaning the text has for her and perhaps for us. One might follow E. D. Hirsch and claim that the differences between Thompson's interpretation and that of Austen's contemporaneous audience speaks not to the meaning of Austen's text but to its significance. Textual meaning, Hirsch insists, must be determinate, and this determinacy can be guaranteed only by identifying its meaning with its author's intention.[14] That which can change historically is not meaning, then, but the importance or relevance of a text for different generations of interpreters. But this distinction between meaning and significance misses the point. For the question Thompson seeks to answer is what the book says, not what the significance of what it says may be for us. Put otherwise, if the book says anything at all, it must say something to us, but because we are historically situated, what it says to us in our circumstances and given our attitudes, culture, and experience will reflect a fusion of our historical horizon and that of the book as the book's meaning for us.

Yet legitimate differences in interpretation extend beyond the historical differences on which Gadamer focuses. While each generation must understand a given text in its own way, not all parts of a single generation need understand those texts in the same way. If historical distance explains the possible legitimacy of different interpretations of the same text, the factors that explain these differences also explain our nonhistorical differences. We differ in the experiences we have had, in the concerns and interests we possess, in the motives and expectations we bring to a given work, and in the cultural assumptions and interpretive traditions that provide our context for understanding. Thompson's understanding of *Sense and Sensibility* is not the only understanding that can make sense to a modern consciousness, nor is it the only one from which it might learn. An alternative interpretation might focus on Marianne's behavior and fate, for example, and try to make sense out of the circumstances under which the excesses of a first love could almost kill one. In pursuing just such an interpretation, Tony Tanner and George Haggerty both appeal to Foucault's account of the idea of nervous diseases in the later part of the eighteenth century.[15] In doing so, Tanner understands Austen to be commenting on the sort of society where social form and masquerade dominate and where the sincere expression of feeling must give rise to both physical and mental illness.[16] In his interpretation of the text, Haggerty stresses the way in which Marianne's move from emotional excess to a quieter propriety expresses Austen's own attempts to "establish a form of narrative that could express feeling without giving way to hysteria." [17] Both Marianne and Austen learn how to connect private meaning to a public context and the Age of Sensibility becomes the Age of the Female Novelist.[18]

An interpretation of *Sense and Sensibility* that focuses on Marianne will thus be importantly different from, and even opposed to, one that focuses on Elinor. While one teaches us to respect and even perhaps emulate an ethical propriety our culture has lost, the other asks us to explore certain relations between form and feeling, between madness and the constraints of civilization, on the one hand, and private emotion and public language, on the other. Whereas one sees Elinor as an ethical exemplar, the other looks to Marianne and sees her learned conformity to public models as somewhat of a sacrifice. Nonetheless, the difference and even opposition between the two sets of interpretations renders neither illegitimate. Rather, we look forward to different interpretations of the texts of our tradition just because of the different light a new interpretation might shed on them and because of the way attention to a different part of the text allows us to rethink our understanding of both the text and ourselves. We might synthesize both interpretations into a new understanding that emphasizes the need to balance the virtues of self-restraint and those of individual expression. Still, our interpretive differences are what keep the discussion of the novel going, revealing new dimensions of it and ourselves and requiring us to reach for new syntheses in a way that discussion will never exhaust. To quote Gadamer again: "the discovery of the true meaning of a text or work of art is never finished; it is in fact an infinite process. Not only are fresh sources of error constantly excluded, so that all kinds of things are filtered out that obscure the true meaning; but new sources of understanding are continually emerging that reveal unsuspected elements of meaning." [19]

VALIDITY IN INTERPRETATION

To appreciate Thompson's interpretation of *Sense and Sensibility,* we need not think it reveals all of its meaning, even for us. Rather, we assume that alternative interpretations will reveal other aspects of the text and, moreover, other aspects of ourselves. From Thompson's interpretation we learn to question some of what we are used to viewing as our emotional prerogatives, while from Tanner's and Haggerty's we learn to recognize the constraints of public forms. In any case, we assume that interpretations can differ, that these differences stem from different experiences and sources of understanding, and, most important, that they enrich our understanding of textual meaning and ourselves. We can incorporate other interpretations (or aspects of them) into our own and learn from one another. Even when we do not agree with a particular interpretation of a text or work of art, we nonetheless try to understand why we differ in our understanding and what we might learn about both the text and ourselves from it. To this extent, differences among interpretations of texts can be as valid as the different perspectives from which we might view a landscape, for example, each of which might reveal the whole of it from the point of a view of concentration on a different aspect of it.

Still, even if one adopts this view of interpretation, it does not entail that all attempts at understanding are equally successful or that all sources of understanding are equally valid. In the literary domain, we appeal to standards that serve to show the inadequacy of certain interpretations even as they allow for the adequacy of more than one understanding of the text at issue. In what follows, I want briefly to present what I take to be Gadamer's version of these standards, not because his version is the only way they can be formulated, but rather because his account helps to bring out two features of textual interpretation that will be important for the suggestions I want to make about our current controversies over social issues.

Following Schleiermacher, Gadamer links the legitimacy of interpretive understanding to the hermeneutic circle, according to which "the anticipation of meaning in which the whole is envisaged becomes actual understanding when the parts that are determined by the whole determine the whole."[20] An adequate understanding of the whole of a text works piecemeal, by fitting new parts or dimensions of it together as coherent parts of a whole that an interpreter is constructing. At the same time, the interpreter must also project an understanding of the meaning of the whole as an orientation to the meaning of the particular parts. In other words, the interpreter understands the meaning of the first chapter of a book in a certain way that depends in part on the way he or she projects the meaning of the whole. The interpreter then tries to find an interpretation for the second chapter that will cohere with the meaning he or she found in the first, according to the same anticipation of the whole. If the interpreter cannot find such an interpretation, he or she has to revise the original understanding of the first chapter and the whole to find an interpretation that fits both it and the subsequent chapters. Understanding, on this analysis, is a circular movement in which the understanding of the meaning of new chapters proceeds on the basis of the understanding the interpreter has constructed of the meaning and unity of previous chapters, while at the same time his or her understanding of the new chapter may require revising the understanding of those previous parts. For Schleiermacher, the end point of this process is the "harmony of the details with the whole," a harmony that is also, for him, the criterion of correct understanding.[21]

Gadamer suggests that this criterion works to expose the illegitimacy of certain understandings of meaning. An interpretation of a text is at least presumptively illegitimate, in other words, if it does not admit of a unity between part and whole. Moreover, it is incumbent upon the interpreter to continue to revise an interpretation until he or she finds one that can show how the text forms a coherent whole. Gadamer does concede that certain texts may simply not possess any unity of meaning. Yet in his view it is not clear that such texts can be understood at all since they do not supply a criterion of themselves for distinguishing between legitimate and illegitimate interpretations. Thus, part of Gadamer's conception of what he calls the "anticipation of completeness" is that "only what really constitutes a unity of meaning is intelligible."[22] One must presuppose that a given text composes a unified whole since only its unity can supply a standard for checking one's interpretations of its various parts and either rejecting those that do not fit the whole or revising one's conception of it. Indeed, even if one thinks that a certain feature of the text such as its language or rhetoric undermines its overall unity, one still needs an interpretation of what that unity is meant to be. A given interpretation need not integrate every aspect of a text to be legitimate. Nevertheless, it must integrate enough of what it can show to be the text's important aspects to count as an interpretation of the unity of that particular text. As Gadamer puts the point, "when we read a text we always assume its completeness, and only when this assumption proves mistaken—i.e. the text is not intelligible—do we begin to suspect the text and try to discover how it can be remedied."[23]

Gadamer introduces a second dimension of the "anticipation of completeness." "The prejudice of completeness," he writes, "implies not only this formal element—that a text should completely express its meaning—but also that what it says should be the complete truth."[24] At least part of Gadamer's suggestion is the idea that genuine understanding issues from an assumption or anticipation, not only that a text composes a unity of meaning, but that it has something to say and, indeed, that we might learn from it. That is, when we understand a text, we understand not only how all its parts fit together into a totality but how it speaks to issues and concerns that we take seriously or can learn from the text to take seriously. We understand a text in that we grasp its point and can understand what makes or would make it valid. Put otherwise, we understand a text when we can see how to situate it within or in contrast to the beliefs, values, and assumptions we already have. Thus, we grasp what it has to say about our lives and assumptions and, conversely, what our lives and assumptions say about it. Indeed, Gadamer suggests that when we understand a text in such a way that it seems to have nothing to say, we must provisionally assume that we have, as yet, failed to understand it. This suggestion correlates with his suggestion that when we fail to see a unity between the parts and the whole of a text it may be, again, that we have failed to understand it. Conversely, if we begin with the assumption that the text we are trying to understand might have both internal coherence and something to say, if we demand of it that it address real issues, we also allow for its point to reveal itself. In this way, textual understanding reflects an exercise in questioning: we ask questions of the text that issue from our hermeneutic horizon, and we are in turn questioned by the text in terms of the claims and conditions it takes seriously. We treat it not as an outmoded text but as a partner in dialogue who can answer our questions and raise its own questions about our own views and assumptions.

This second aspect of the anticipation of completeness thus anticipates education, not just coherence. Its foundation is similar to that of the first aspect: if we are to be able to distinguish either between legitimate and illegitimate or between better and worse interpretations of a text, we require nonarbitrary criteria for doing so. Such nonarbitrary criteria are supplied by the text itself since, if we are to understand it at all, we must assume that it constitutes a unity of meaning and will repay our decoding efforts by speaking to us in our hermeneutic situation by challenging or confirming our beliefs and assumptions.

The point here is not that we must concentrate on finding the contemporary relevance of a text or "modernizing" it, as I put the idea earlier. Nevertheless, unless we approach a text with the provisional assumptions that it comprises a unified meaning and that it can address us by possessing a point that we can understand, then it remains unclear what standards we might point to in trying to show the merit of any particular interpretation. Good interpretations, if we are to pick up on Gadamer's suggestions, succeed in illuminating the difference a given text makes to what we thought we knew—either by giving added confirmation to our views or by asking us to rethink or expand them, even if we do so in opposition to the text we are trying to understand. We take the possibility seriously that the text can teach us something, and we therefore put our own views and assumptions into play in trying to understand it.

Here the virtue of Thompson's, Tanner's, and Haggerty's interpretations of *Sense and Sensibility* is that all seem not only competently to unify part and whole but also to speak to issues that bring our own assumptions into play. Genuine attempts to understand allow for a kind of dialogue, between the questions and issues of a text or text-analogue and those of the interpreter, in which each helps to illuminate the other, or, in other words, the text and interpreter sincerely question and probe one another. Thompson's version of *Sense and Sensibility* shows us what we might still learn from an ethical propriety of thought and behavior, while Tanner and Haggerty raise questions about the relations we assume between reason, illness, public, and private. The parts and whole of the text can cohere in different ways depending on what their interpreters emphasize and how they fit the parts with one another. By the same token, what we can learn about ourselves remains inexhaustible. Hence, there will be more than one legitimate and illuminating interpretation of Austen's novel.

For the purposes of this book, then, two suggestions drawn from Gadamer's anticipation of completeness seem especially valuable. First, the concept of truth that Gadamer (following Heidegger) employs is one that he thinks adequately appropriates the Greek conception of *aletheia*, which he understands as "unconcealment," "disconcealment," or disclosure.[25] That is, in understanding the meaning of a text we bring something to light that was previously hidden or concealed and that comes to light because of the perspective and historical horizon we bring to it and the questions to which we find an answer in it. At the same time, this understanding necessarily excludes or obscures other dimensions of meaning, available from within other horizons. A horizon that could unify and encompass all possible horizons would have to have available to it future points of view and issues as well as all the human circumstances to which a given text might speak.[26] Given Gadamer's belief in the historical finitude of human understanding, however, it culminates in an openness to new horizons for understanding rather than in a dogmatic certitude on meaning.

Second, if we are to expect a point and meaning in the texts we read, this same attitude of openness extends to alternative interpretations of those texts. We need to look at other interpretations of the meaning of our texts in the same way as we look at our texts: expecting them to have something to say. As is the case with texts, not every interpretation will be one that has a discernible point as we see it. Still, it is not clear that the burden of interpretation does not fall precisely on the attempt to see whether and how it might have a point. In any case, this aspect of an anticipation of completeness needs special emphasis in our public debates over social issues: in them we might try to remain open to the possibility that alternative interpretations of our principles can be important—and, moreover, important in rethinking and developing our own.

Of course, the idea that we are to find the merit in interpretations of our principles that differ from our own may seem more risky than beneficial. Suppose arguments in favor of human slavery or racial segregation could be formulated as coherent interpretations of our principles and that these interpretations comply with the conditions of the hermeneutic circle. Can it be incumbent upon us to find the point and value in these interpretations? A response to this question can appeal, I think, to the open structure of what I shall be calling interpretive discussion. Before indicating how this appeal might be possible, however, I want to pursue some of the consequences of the appeal to interpretive discussion in general insofar as it uses our discussions of art and literature as a model.

INTERPRETATION AND SOCIAL ISSUES

If the conditions of textual interpretation can be transferred to our interpretations of our principles, then five preliminary aspects of this transfer seem clear. First, our differences on social issues will be the result of our understanding differently the principles we share rather than the result of our holding different principles. Second, we shall sometimes understand the principles we share differently for the same reason that we understand texts differently: because we possess different interpretive perspectives reflecting different concerns, traditions, and frameworks of interpretation. Third, the merit of our different interpretations will depend at least in part on their capacity to show the unified meaning of the principle at stake and to illuminate at least some of its points for us. Fourth, progress in our debates over social issues will depend less on finding the right answer to the meaning of our principles than on recognizing the interpretive character of our own understanding. Our debates will have less the character of strident debates over principle than the character of interpretive debates over the meaning of works of art or literature in which we assume both the validity and the interpretive character of our own understanding. Fifth, because we recognize the interpretive character of our own understanding, we will recognize that we might be educated or edified by other interpretations of our practices and principles. We will examine the interpretations of others with an eye to their "completeness," and we will assume that neither others' interpretations nor our own are ever finally complete such that they cannot be enriched by listening to others.

Still, why should we even begin to suppose that our principles can serve as analogues of our texts? To the extent that principles of life, liberty, and equality are embedded in the American Constitution, they are already part of a text. Moreover, they are subject to the conditions of textual interpretation, as the existence of historical differences in the understanding of the Constitution makes clear. Just as literary critics cannot understand *Sense and Sensibility* the way either Austen or her original audience understood it, judges cannot understand the Constitution according to the "original intent" of its framers. In the first place, they have to apply its principles to issues that could not have come up for those framers: what equality means or requires in a country that now understands itself as multicultural, multiethnic, and multiracial, what respect for the sanctity of life means given new birth technologies and new technological ways of sustaining life, what freedom of speech means with regard to women's equality or, put otherwise, how the First and the Fourteenth Amendments can be made to cohere with one another, and so on. In all these cases, the principles embedded in the Constitution must be applied to new issues or old issues differently understood.

One might claim that judges should decide these issues in terms that the framers could have accepted if they had been aware of them. But this sort of speculation seems obviously to involve interpretive decisions. A judge must try to figure out what aspect of the new issues or situations would have been important to the framers, how it would have been important, and how they would have thought of it if they could have. As Gadamer reminds us, then, application is always already interpretation.[27] We must decide how the principles with which we are concerned are relevant to the new situations in which we find ourselves, but this decision means we must understand the principles themselves in terms of the perspective our situation sheds on them.

Constitutional principles, however, are subject not only to historical differences in interpretation but also to contemporaneous perspectival differences. If judges and Constitutional interpreters must understand Constitutional principles in terms of the new situations to which they must be applied, they do not all understand these situations or the light they shed on those principles in the same way. Just as judges and interpreters cannot share the historical understanding the framers had of the Constitution, they need not share the understanding of their contemporaries. Take the various understandings of the protection the First Amendment offers to the freedom of speech. Some Constitutional interpreters understand this freedom within the context of our experience with McCarthy-era witch hunts and thus understand it as absolute. Any attempt to restrict speech that goes beyond a minimal concession to the "clear and present danger" standard risks the dangers of political repression, censorship, and thought control. For other interpreters, First Amendment protections of free speech must be understood in relation to Fourteenth Amendment protections of equality. On this view, the appropriate experiential context for understanding free speech is not the McCarthy era but the eras of slavery and segregation in which oppression is accomplished in part through words. These two interpretations of free speech have issued in two different attitudes toward the production and circulation of pornographic materials. But it is not obvious that only one experiential context, only one set of worries or concerns, or only one interpretive framework can be the correct perspective from which to understand the issue. Certainly some accounts of how freedom of speech is to be understood will fail. But our differences on pornography may issue simply from different equally legitimate understandings of our history and what we take to be important in it with regard to this issue. Indeed, if we take literary and artistic discussion as our model, we might acknowledge the possibility that both interpretations might legitimately reveal important aspects of our history and ourselves.

Of course, the institutionalization of Constitutional interpretation in the hierarchy of the judicial system seems to render it importantly different from the interpretation of texts or works of art. At least for any given time, the Supreme Court functions as the last arbiter of the meaning of the Constitution in a way that academic departments do not function with regard to the meaning of texts or works of art. Two additional points remain important from the point of view of what might be called an interpretive democracy, however. First, judicial decisions allow for the expression of interpretive differences in the form of the dissents that become part of the judicial record. Second, even Supreme Court decisions do not always end a public debate that can continue in the press and other institutions of public opinion and that can become effective in Congress, state assemblies, and, if need be, in the process of Constitutional amendment. From this point of view, the judiciary is only an important participant in the larger, ongoing interpretation of what the meaning of the Constitution is for us. The virtues of the judiciary lie in the informed and reflective judgment it brings to the task of interpretation and in the stability it lends to policy and legislative decision making by functioning as the formally recognized arbiter of its Constitutional validity. At the same time, public debate continues and, moreover, continues to assume that its voices can influence the decisions and laws that issue from democratic institutions.

Furthermore, the Constitution is already itself an expression of some of the principles we take to be fundamental. Political philosophers such as John Rawls and Michael Walzer emphasize this circumstance by attending to the meaning of our practices, traditions, social goods, and settled convictions.[28] As a society, we possess a set of traditions, practices, struggles, and commitments, all of which have meaning for us and thus constitute the analogue of a text. Social criticism and political philosophy are not a matter of inventing a new moral and political culture, on this view, but of understanding the meaning of the culture we already possess. We look to the history, ideals, and commitments without which we would not be who we are and assess their meaning for who we are

and want to be. Thus, Rawls looks to the meaning of our liberal traditions as they have developed in accordance with settled convictions such
as the prohibition against slavery, while Walzer looks to the meaning that
social goods such as health, education, and welfare must have for us, at
least as articulated by the totality of our practices, policies, and ideals.
In each case, the investigation is a hermeneutic one into the meaning of
the text of our common life. For both Rawls and Walzer, such an investigation answers questions of what we ought to do as a collectivity with
regard to either particular distributive issues we confront or principles
for what Rawls calls the basic structure. In both cases, claims about what
we ought to do are justified by an understanding of what makes sense
for us given who we are and how we understand the practices and ideals
we possess.

But to the extent that our moral and political culture is the analogue
of a text, its meanings are also subject to the conditions of interpretation. That is, they are subject both to standards of adequacy and to
possible *differences* in interpretation. The understandings Rawls and
Walzer have of our history and our goods may thus be important, well-
considered understandings but also, possibly, not the only legitimate
ones. Rather, we may possess more than one understanding of our convictions and goods and our differences may be equally legitimate. Indeed,
if our traditions, convictions, ideals, and commitments together constitute the analogue of a text, then the question of the meaning of this text-
analogue becomes part of an ongoing conversation among democratic
citizens who must assume the possibility that interpretations other than
their own will have something to say. The meaning of the text of our common life becomes inexhaustible. To cut off interpretation of it therefore
forecloses the possibility of opening different dimensions of its meaning
for us.

In the chapters that follow, I shall be concerned to show that our differences over concrete issues are interpretive ones that are not best resolved through dogmatic appeals to principle but that do, conversely,
lend themselves to reinterpretation and hermeneutic discussion. As Tribe
has already pointed out, the debate over abortion cannot be resolved as
long as one side lays sole title to the principle of the sanctity of life while
the other is thought to ignore it in its all-consuming commitment to the
principle of liberty. Nor, however, can it be resolved by simply assuming, as Tribe does, that all sides can understand the virtues of abortion
over the horrors of state-run fetus factories. If, however, both sides recognize the merely interpretive status of their own views, they might be

willing to learn from one another and even to pursue compromises with one another. Moreover, where compromises are not forthcoming, the different groups might be able to reconcile themselves to legislative policies and judicial opinions about abortion that conflict with their own interpretations of the principles and practices involved since they can now understand those policies and decisions as ones based on legitimate, if alternative, interpretations. Such a reconciliation may be provisional only, a nod to another plausible interpretation even as the opposition continues to articulate its own interpretation as forcefully and compellingly as it can. Still, what no longer seems possible under an interpretive model of our public debate over abortion is the idea that one side is the right or, as pro-life groups sometimes insist, the righteous one.

The same holds for debates over affirmative action, pornography, and surrogate mothering. In these cases, the failure to acknowledge the interpretive status of claims about the meaning of equal opportunity, the freedom of speech, or the freedom of contract hinders just the sort of hermeneutic examination and discussion that might lead to progress on and resolution of the issues. Were we to pursue an interpretive discussion, we would focus on criteria of interpretive adequacy in considering both our positions and those of others, and we would even try to expand our understanding by taking alternative interpretations of our principles seriously as possibly illuminating ones. In short, we would try to learn from one another in our public debates, just as we do in our aesthetic debates. Moreover, as legislators we would try to formulate policies and programs that could accommodate at least some of the different interpretations that were voiced. That is, we would allow for different plausible understandings of the principles involved and, in our political and legislative decisions about these issues, try to encompass or even compromise between these different voices as best we could.

It should be clear that if we take a literary model as a template for public debate and if we therefore encourage openness and mutual education in those debates, this proposal has little in common with one concerned only to encourage respect or toleration for interpretive differences. In the first place, where our differences do not reflect equally adequate interpretations, we will neither tolerate nor respect them. In the second place, where an alternative interpretation does seem to illuminate some part of the unity and point a principle or practice possesses, we will gain new insight into that principle or practice, not by simply respecting or tolerating the alternative interpretation, but by taking it seriously as an interpretation that can be educational for us, that can help us expand our understandings of our principles, practices, and ourselves, even if these understandings can never exhaust what our principles and practices mean or who we are.

Finally, however, it is not clear that we can simply tolerate alternative interpretations of contested issues because we have to arrive at some decision about how to proceed with regard to them. Indeed, this necessity would seem to constitute a crucial difference between social and literary debate: for, while we need never decide what to do about a novel or work of art, social issues require closure or resolution of some sort, even temporary. Whereas we may be able to tolerate and even respect differing interpretations of literature and works of art, the questions our social debates raise require action. Are we to allow for legal abortion or not? Support affirmative action policies or not? If our discussions of literature are to serve as models for public debate, nevertheless our public debate cannot go on forever without at least the temporary closure that legislative and judicial decisions provide. The question, then, is what the relation is between interpretive discussion, on the one hand, and democratic decision making, on the other.

A suggestion of this book is that even at this point our literary debates can claim some purchase on our procedures. In the first place, acknowledging the interpretive dimension of our debates means that, as a public, we can concentrate less on winning these debates or finding the one correct answer to the issue than on the opportunities for expanding our own understanding of the inexhaustible meaning of our principles. Just as we are interested in the light that Thompson's interpretation of *Sense and Sensibility* sheds on the book and ourselves, we might be interested in the light a pro-life view of abortion sheds on both the principle of the sanctity of life and our own account of it. We need not entirely adopt this interpretation as our own. Still, we need not be entirely hostile to it or view it as a threat to principles we share. Just as we learn from Thompson's account of *Sense and Sensibility* to think differently about our view of emotional expression even if we do not and cannot adopt Elinor's complete self-restraint, some of us might learn to think differently about our view of abortion even if we do not and cannot adopt the pro-life insistence on entirely banning it. In both cases, our original assumptions can be modified and moderated by recognizing these assumptions as interpretations of texts, actions, or principles and by admitting the potential plausibility, and even insights, of interpretations other than our own.

In the second place, the question we ask in encountering a plausible interpretation of a text that differs from our own is not only how we might learn from it but also how we might possibly integrate it with our previous view, how an insight into the virtue of self-restraint, motivated by attention to Elinor, can be integrated with an insight into the need for authentic but public self-expression motivated by attention to Marianne. In the same way, a hermeneutic orientation in our public debates can lead both the public and its representatives in democratic institutions to attempt both education and integration, accommodation and compromise. What forms these accommodations take will depend upon the interpretive efforts of those involved, on attempts to work out with those whose interpretations differ a set of rules and regulations that seek to express as far as possible the range of legitimate differences. Such compromises are based not on a sacrifice of principles but rather on the mutual respect that comes from recognizing the interpretive character of one's own understanding and that of others.

To be sure, supporting the ideas of compromise and accommodation seems a queasy prospect. Why not compromise on pro-slavery conceptions of equality if we are going to compromise on pro-choice or pro-life conceptions of liberty and the sanctity of life, for instance? In general, can we assume that the idea that I emphasize—that learning from alternative interpretations of our principles and even history—has only intrinsically progressive possibilities, possibilities of new insight or improved or enriched understanding and accommodation? If we are to anticipate the possible merit of alternative interpretations of who we are and what our principles mean as long as they are able to show the unified meaning of those principles, might we not learn to be or to compromise with racists or sexists as easily as we can learn to surmount these particular prejudices?

I shall first take up this question in Chapter Four and shall have to inquire again into the criteria for distinguishing between legitimate and illegitimate interpretations. My argument will be that the conditions of interpretive discussion already include criteria of openness that exclude those interpretations of our principles, history, and practices that serve to suppress the interpretations of others. We have no access to what we are trying to understand except through our interpretations of it. Insofar as these interpretations are grounded in our previous experiences, cultural heritage, and historical horizons, we also have no access to a critical perspective on our own understanding or the experiences and history that give rise to it except by taking seriously interpretations that differ from our own. Hence, only by opening and maintaining access to alternative interpretations and by guaranteeing the availability of a critical purchase on our own understanding can we assure ourselves of either its continued adequacy to the issues at stake or the ability to develop it in keeping with what those issues and their ongoing history demand. Interpretations that in their content require the suppression of other interpretations preclude just this guarantee. Racist and sexist interpretations preclude the possibility that the interpretive voices of minorities and women can be either expressed or heard. Yet in suppressing alternative interpretive voices racist and sexist interpretations also suppress a range of interpretations through which they might amplify and educate their own understanding. To this extent, they undermine interpretive discussion itself.

The issues raised by abortion, pornography, affirmative action, and surrogate mothering involve fundamental principles of life, liberty, and equality, and I shall concentrate on them in this book for that reason. In each case, our debates also extend beyond the questions of the meaning of the principles themselves to include different approaches to and understandings of the text of our common life. Thus, the debate over abortion is not limited to our different understandings of life or even liberty but includes different orientations toward sexual intercourse in general, motherhood, and women's roles. The debate over surrogate mothering is played out over the context in which we understand the role and autonomy of women and mothers, while the controversy over affirmative action extends to questions of how we understand the history of the civil rights struggle in the United States. Finally, our debate over pornography engages not only the issues of equality and free speech but those of sexual identity and authenticity as well. Our debates over the meaning of shared principles are embedded in sets of orientations, assumptions, and attitudes that indicate that, in simply opposing life and liberty, liberty and essentialism, liberty and equality, and equality and diversity, we may be missing the bulk of what is at stake.

I shall begin, in Chapter Two, with the debate over surrogate mothering since the question of whether or not surrogacy contracts should be treated as legitimate has always been debated in what might be called hermeneutic terms. Questions about surrogacy have been pursued in terms of questions about women: how contractual relations, autonomy, mothering, and the family are related, what mothering is, and what childbirth means or should mean. Yet I shall be arguing that attention to this set of interpretive questions has been misleading to the extent that it assumes mothering and childbirth must have only one meaning and hence must be understood and valued in only one way. In contrast, I think it is important to open up the range of ways we might think about the integrity of the family and I thus want to shift attention away from the interpretive question directed at the meaning of mothering and childbirth and focus, instead, on what I take to be an important dimension of the meaning that participating in a family has for us. In attempting to rethink the debate from this point of view and thereby attending to different dimensions of the idea of mothering and family, I mean to contribute to the ongoing discussion of the issue. I also want to argue that these dimensions show how joint custody can sometimes offer an appropriate way of resolving actual custody disputes that arise when a surrogate mother wants to keep the child to whom she has given birth. Moreover, I shall suggest that the idea of joint custody can serve as a model for resolving our debates over some of our other social issues as well. Just as custody disputes often pit two sets of equally competent parents against one another, our debates over principle often pit equally competent interpretations against one another—which we might try to accommodate.

In Chapter Three I shall take up the debate over affirmative action because I think its defenders have too quickly given up custody of principles of equality and equal opportunity, allowing critics sole rights to these principles and adopting an idea of diversity instead. For opponents of affirmative action, principles of equality and equal opportunity require a commitment to a strict racial, ethnic, and gender neutrality. But this equation of equality and neutrality constitutes a particularly one-sided interpretation of the principles at stake and their history. At least since the beginning of the civil rights movement, our American conception of equal opportunity has also included the idea of the full integration and participation of previously excluded groups in all aspects of American civic, political, and social life. The connection between equality and racial, gender, and ethnic neutrality, a connection on which critics of affirmative action concentrate, does get at some part of the meaning of the principle of equal opportunity for us. But an account that ignores other dimensions of the principle and the historical struggles over its meaning, in particular an account that ignores the link between equality, on the one hand, and integration and participation, on the other, is not an interpretation, I shall argue, that can be adequate for us.

In Chapter Four I shall again take up the debate over abortion. In the case of surrogacy, I shall be offering a new interpretive perspective that is accommodationist in its core and that supports shared custody by equally competent parents. In the case of affirmative action, I shall be trying to retrieve an interpretive voice that I think has been drowned out. Moreover, I shall be arguing that our principle of equal opportunity might be shared by both this retrieved interpretation and those who emphasize neutrality. Do the principles involved in the abortion debate admit of a similar sort of shared custody? The current dispute over abortion pits interpretations of the meaning of life and liberty against one another that are already well, even vociferously, represented in the debate itself. I shall not, then, be retrieving or articulating new perspectives. At the same time, it is not clear that the constant, loud, and articulate expression of the various voices in this debate has induced either side to listen very carefully to the way the other understands the issues at stake. Hence, my purpose in Chapter Four is to show the plausibility of pro-life and pro-choice conceptions of liberty, the sanctity of human life, and the attitudes toward life in general that the debate involves. The way to begin to resolve the debate cannot be for each side to refuse to take seriously the understanding of the other. Rather, if each side treats these understandings as possibly plausible interpretations of the principles and meanings involved, each side might learn from the other to form a more nuanced conception of them and learn, moreover, to try to accommodate one another or even compromise on this issue.

The last controversy I shall consider concerns the feminist debate over pornography. In this case, the equal dogmatism of both liberal and anti-pornography feminists deafens them to the possibility of engaging in an interpretive conversation about the meanings of the freedom of speech, equality, and sexual authenticity, a conversation that might enrich both of their positions. Instead, each side convicts the other of ideologically sexist stereotypes about women. The possibility that we could learn from racist and sexist interpretations of our principles indicates that this issue of ideology is an important one for an interpretive approach to our principles. As noted earlier, it is in part the idea that interpretations of meaning can be ideological attempts to maintain a certain social order that explains the queasiness we feel at the idea of trying to learn from interpretations that differ from our own, and we need, I think, to be certain that such views do not carry with them racist, sexist, or other ideologies that would demean rather than educate us. Indeed, the feminist argument against pornography is important precisely because it suggests an understanding of the principles of free speech, equality, and sexual authenticity that includes a consideration of substantive conditions such as power, money, and ideology that can distort the field in which interpretive voices must speak and be heard. Hence, I shall be suggesting that we might learn from this understanding of our principles even if we reject antipornography feminism's claims about pornography itself. Still, I think the current debate over pornography also indicates what may be lost by too quick a conviction of ideology: namely, the possibility that an alternative interpretation of our principles could hold something of value for our own understanding of them and that we might develop our understanding by learning from this alternative.

With regard to all four issues I consider in this book, then, I shall be advocating a hermeneutic or interpretive approach, one that tries at the very least to remove the debates from the domain of conflicts of principle. In contrast to this interpretive approach, our present debates over these issues can be characterized as mighty attempts by each side to ignore, dismiss, or find arguments against the view promoted by its opponents. But what if this approach is inappropriate at least for certain of the issues we currently confront? What if it is important not to assume that only one side in our debates over abortion, affirmative action, surrogacy, and pornography can be the correct side to take? The point of this book, in any case, is that rather than assuming the illegitimacy of the arguments of others we might take a more hermeneutic approach and assume they have something to say. Perhaps they do not. Not all interpretations of a literary text are plausible or adequate and not all parents are competent. Still, in our discussions of works of art and literature we are eager to find what may be of worth in the different interpretations offered, and we might try to translate this eagerness into our debates over issues that are less about principles than they are about their interpretation.

A crucial question for this sort of attempt remains the transition from mutual education and discussion to decision and policy. In contrast to what we can learn from our interpretive differences over literary texts, the idea behind a hermeneutic approach to our public debates is that what we learn from our interpretive differences over our principles should somehow be reflected in our laws and public programs. In pursuing this idea, I shall consider part of Jürgen Habermas's work. Although he has serious reservations about the sort of approach I am advocating here, his consideration of questions of rational public opinion- and will-formation is of value in assessing the plausibility of the sort of claim I want to make.

There is a sense in which the contributions I make to the debates I consider in this book belong to what he calls, with Nancy Fraser, the unregulated, "weak" public sphere, devoted more to the articulation of ethical self-understandings than to questions of morally just social policy.[29] Nevertheless, I shall be arguing that his analysis does not yet give this "weak" public sphere and the articulation of ethical self-understandings the attention they deserve. The question here is whether the only alternative to either rational consensus or violence is the kind of negotiated compromise over interests that Habermas envisages or whether something akin to an accommodation of alternative legitimate understandings is possible.

Bernard Williams raises a similar question of whether recourse to idealized notions of rational consensus is the only path available for modern societies that are aware of alternatives to their own ethical conceptions. In suggesting that such societies require ethical understanding as opposed to ethical knowledge and that attitudes of confidence in one's ethical views are more appropriate than attitudes of conviction, Williams adds to the sorts of claims about interpretive discussion I make. I shall therefore amplify those claims with a consideration of the course he suggests between a moral objectivism that cannot tolerate views other than its own and a moral relativism that thinks it must tolerate all of them. In closing the book, I shall look to other social debates such as the controversy over gun control and try to assess what, in the end, interpretive conversation can and cannot accomplish.

CHAPTER TWO

Surrogate Mothering and the Meaning of Family

Surrogate mothering and *contract pregnancy* are terms that describe one of two arrangements. Either a woman agrees to be artificially inseminated with the sperm of a man in order to bear a child for him and his wife and is compensated for her services. Or eggs are harvested from one woman, fertilized in a petri dish by her husband's sperm, and implanted in the womb of another woman, who brings the resulting fetus to term and is compensated for her services.

How are we to understand such arrangements and the principles or values they reflect? For some commentators, the important fact about surrogate mothering is that it allows women to assert their bodily autonomy and to claim jurisdiction over their own procreative power. Surrogacy contracts thereby enhance the liberty of women. Moreover, in supplying a womb and, in most cases, the egg that grows there, women provide sterile couples with procreative freedom and options they could not have without them. Since these women thereby offer a service similar to what semen donors provide, principles of equality demand that they be compensated in the same way.[1] For others, however, pay for pregnancy, and, indeed, its equation with a particularly alienated form of fatherhood, devalues motherhood. Far from reflecting liberty or equality, surrogacy is a form of exploitation in which middle- and upper-middle-class couples fulfill their most fundamental desires by commodifying the bodies of poorer women and buying their babies as merchandise.[2] For the most part, the debate over surrogacy has thus proceeded as a debate over the meaning of motherhood and the autonomy and equality of women. For critics of the practice, surrogate mothering violates principles of equality and liberty because of the exploitation and commodification it involves of both women and children. Moreover, its attitudes toward childbirth ignore the special character of women's work and are part of the cultural undervaluing of women's labor in general.[3] For supporters of surrogate mothering arrangements, however, doubts about the practice reflect a patriarchal ideology that itself violates principles of both equality and liberty because its sole purpose is the control of women's sexuality and capacities for reproduction.[4] Moreover, surrogacy presents women with new roles as mothers and nurturers, extending these relations beyond those of biology alone.

Despite these different orientations toward the principles and values involved, however, the presumption in each case is that, once we give women their due as equal and autonomous agents and as mothers, we will also know how to understand surrogate mothering. Either it promotes women's liberty and equality or it obstructs them. Either it encourages women's value as nurturers or it denies it. Yet suppose that there is no one correct or appropriate way to understand mothering or the relation between pregnancy, child birth, and liberty or equality. In this chapter, I want to look at the meanings mothering and women's roles have been thought to have in order to suggest that a resolution to the debate over surrogacy may lie elsewhere. Indeed, I want to suggest that the issue of surrogate mothering may have less to do with autonomy, women, and mothering than with the character of family relationships. By raising this possibility, I do not want to point necessarily to a neoconservative version of family values. Rather, both traditional and nontraditional families seem to me to share a meaning that can shed light on the issue of surrogate mothering, as well as on the issues of custody to which surrogate mothering arrangements often lead. To clarify this meaning, I want first to indicate the problems involved in associating the issue of surrogate mothering solely with a focus on women and the value of mothering. I shall then turn to what seems to me to be a crucial characteristic of family relationships, one that our debates about surrogacy has thus far ignored, I think. Because the question of surrogate mothering is associated for most Americans with the case of "Baby M," I shall begin with it.

SURROGACY AND "BABY M"

In February 1985, Mary Beth Whitehead and her then-husband Richard Whitehead contracted with William Stern to bear a child conceived from Mary Beth Whitehead's egg and William Stern's sperm. According to the terms of the agreement, Whitehead was to be artificially inseminated with semen collected from Mr. Stern. She was to carry any resulting fetus to term and was not to obtain an abortion except at the wishes of Mr. Stern. Neither Whitehead nor her husband were to "form or attempt to form" a parent-child relationship with any child she conceived under the terms of the agreement; both were to terminate all their parental rights upon the birth of such a child and, moreover, "to sign all necessary affidavits prior to and after the birth of the child and voluntarily participate in any paternity proceedings necessary to have William Stern's name entered on said child's birth certificate as the natural or biological father." In return "for services and expenses," William Stern was to pay the Whiteheads $10,000 upon the birth of a live child as well as all medical, hospitalization, and pharmaceutical expenses not covered by the Whiteheads' insurance policy. If Whitehead miscarried before the fifth month of a pregnancy, she was to receive no compensation other than expenses; if a child were stillborn, she was to receive $1,000 in addition to expenses. Finally, if William Stern died either before or after the birth of a child under the terms of the agreement, that child was to be placed in the custody of his wife, Elizabeth Stern.[5]

On March 26, 1986, Whitehead gave birth to a baby girl and decided to keep the child, reneging on the terms of the surrogacy agreement. The Sterns went to court and were granted temporary custody on May 5, 1986. Before they could retrieve the baby, Whitehead left New Jersey with her family and the baby and disappeared for three months, after which time the baby was placed in the Sterns' custody. On March 31, 1987, the New Jersey court upheld the validity of the surrogacy contract. It awarded full custody to the Sterns, allowed Elizabeth Stern legally and immediately to adopt the child, and terminated Whitehead's parental rights. On February 8, 1988, however, the New Jersey Supreme Court reversed the lower court on the legality of the contract. It restored Whitehead's parental rights and also granted her visitation rights but allowed the Sterns to retain custody of Baby M following normal custody disputes' standard consideration, which looks to the best interest of the child.

The New Jersey Supreme Court found "the payment of money to a 'surrogate' mother illegal, perhaps criminal, and potentially degrading to women." The payment, it said, was for the "the sale of a child or, at the very least, the sale of a mother's right to her child, the only mitigating factor being that one of the purchasers is the father." The surrogacy agreement assumed that an agreement on adoption could be made prior to birth, "even prior to conception," and this assumption violated standing adoption law as well as custody practices. As the court continued:

> The surrogacy contract violates the policy of this State that the rights of natural parents are equal concerning their child, the father's right no greater than the mother's. . . . Under the contract, the natural mother is irrevocably committed before she knows the strength of her bond with her child. She never makes a totally voluntary, informed decision, for quite clearly any decision prior to the baby's birth is, in the most important sense, uninformed, and any decision after that, compelled by a pre-existing contractual commitment, the threat of a lawsuit, and the inducement of a $10,000 payment, is less than totally voluntary. . . . Worst of all, however, is the contract's total disregard of the best interests of the child. There is not the slightest suggestion that any inquiry will be made at any time to determine the fitness of the Sterns as custodial parents, of Mrs. Stern as an adoptive parent, their superiority to Mrs. Whitehead or the effect on the child of not living with her natural mother.[6]

The court also considered the longtime effects on a child's discovering that "she is the offspring of someone who gave birth to her only to obtain money." And it discussed Whitehead's predicament: "She was guilty of a breach of contract, and indeed, she did break a very important promise, but we think it is expecting something well beyond normal human capabilities to suggest that this mother should have parted with her newly born infant without a struggle. Other than survival, what stronger force is there?" Moreover, it asked, "how much weight should be given to her nine months of pregnancy, the labor of childbirth, the risk to her life, compared to the payment of money, the anticipation of a child and the donation of sperm?"[7]

Some feminists applauded this decision as a victory for the equality of mothers with fathers and for the right of a mother to keep her children. But for others, it seemed to rest on a stereotypical conception of a woman's biological role, on a particular view of what motherhood involves, and on an attempt to exert ideological control over the significance and scope of women's reproductive capacities. This analysis of the higher court's decision understands it in part in terms of the context of the historical response to artificial insemination by donor (or A.I.D.), of which surrogate mothering remains a species. On reflection, the analysis turns out to be difficult to dismiss.

The worry that A.I.D. elicited at its start was that it was a form of adultery,[8] a crime traditionally considered to be much more significant when perpetrated by a woman than when perpetrated by a man. In Jewish law, for example, an adulterous wife must divorce her husband and must not marry her lover, while a husband's adultery is not by itself grounds upon which a wife can seek a divorce. In England until the mid-twelfth century, a husband was allowed to kill both an adulterous wife and her lover. And even though the passage of the Custody of Infants Law in 1839 in England finally granted women the right to retain custody of children in a divorce, this right could be rescinded if the woman were found guilty of adultery. Indeed, in some states of the nineteenth-century United States adultery was not defined in terms of sexual relations between people of whom at least one was married. It was rather defined more specifically as the sexual relation between a married woman and a man who was not her husband.[9]

Artificial insemination by donor was understood by many as just this sort of relation. In 1921, a Canadian court argued that the real crime of adultery involved "the possibility of introducing into the family of the husband a false strain of blood,"[10] and it decided that, on these grounds, artificial insemination by donor constituted adultery. In 1954, the Superior Court for Cook County, Illinois, agreed, calling A.I.D. "contrary to public policy and good morals" and defining it as adultery on the part of the mother. In 1960, the Feversham Committee in England found A.I.D. to be a threat to the institution of marriage and society as a whole. Any children issuing from the practice were to be considered illegitimate and the entry of the mother's husband's name in the Registry of Births an offense. "Succession through blood descent," the committee argued, "is an important element of family life and as such is at the basis of our society. On it depend the peerage and other titles of honour and the Monarchy itself."[11]

Given this general understanding of the disproportionate crime of a woman's adultery and the relation between it and A.I.D., doctors who artificially inseminated women usually did so under the condition that the insemination remain a secret. In his analysis of the practice in 1957, A. M. C. M. Schellen explicitly recommended that sperm donors remain anonymous. Moreover, he insisted that doctors performing inseminations should make concerted efforts to match a donor's physical characteristics with those of the mother's husband and that any children conceived through A.I.D. should never be informed about the way or by whom they were conceived.[12] Schellen claimed that his recommendations followed at least in part from the continuing ambiguity about the legal status of the procedure, as well as from fears by donors that they would be held legally responsible for any children born by A.I.D. unless their contributions remained secret.

Still, in part Schellen's recommendations also followed simply from the adulterous connotations he seemed to think the procedure possessed. For instance, with other medical ethicists he argued that if a donor's identification were not kept secret a woman undergoing artificial insemination by donor might transfer her affections to the donor or, alternatively, her husband might pursue him in a jealous rage because he thought she *had* transferred her affections.[13] Opponents of A.I.D. in fact argued that "the true human love of a woman expressed itself in wanting her husband's child," while the desire for "just a child" reflected an animal urge.[14] Accordingly, Schellen calls any *unmarried* woman who wants a child through artificial insemination "guilty of ruthless selfishness" since, by definition, she cannot be motivated by the desire to have her husband's child. Moreover, he claimed, such a woman "can have little true love in her heart." [15]

What does this set of reactions to artificial insemination by donor mean for the case of surrogate mothering? If the desire to bear any child, as opposed to the desire to bear one's husband's child, is evidence of an animal urge, what must be evidenced by the desire to bear a child one does not intend even to keep? If the artificial insemination of a married woman who wants to bear and keep a child is tainted with the connotation of adultery, how must the artificial insemination of a surrogate be considered? Finally, if a woman willing to undergo A.I.D. to bear a child "can have little true love in her heart," what must be said about the woman who is willing to undergo A.I.D. for money? Schellen himself called surrogate mothering "artificial prostitution," an "ugly" word, he admitted, but one, he thought, well suited to the practice.[16]

The flip side of understanding surrogate mothering as artificial prostitution is defining what are to count as the legitimate feelings and desires of what might be called "real" women and mothers. If a woman wanting a child with no genetic relation to her husband betrays an animal urge, then real or properly human women and mothers are those who are solely interested in bearing their husband's children; they are certainly not those who are interested in bearing the children of someone else's husband. Moreover, real women and mothers are those who serve as the fountain of familial affection to whom all instrumental rationality and monetary considerations are foreign. Real women cannot want to enter into agreements that affect the most tender aspect of their being just for the sake of money, and if they are forced into such agreements by circumstances beyond their control it would be unreasonable to expect them to abide by any promises they made.

Such reasoning betrays clearly essentialist assumptions about what a "real woman" is. She is one who defines herself as her husband's wife, his children's mother, and the source of family love and care. But this reasoning also bears a suspicious similarity to that of the New Jersey Supreme Court. In a sense, by being unable to comply with the terms of the surrogacy contract Whitehead redeemed herself as a legitimate woman and mother. The payment Whitehead was to receive was payment for the sale of a mother's right to her child. Yet a natural mother cannot know "the strength of her bond with her child" before it is born. Indeed, no force is stronger. Hence, a woman cannot make an "informed decision" in consenting to the sale of her rights prior to the birth of her child, and if she does so consent she must do so only under duress, financial hardship, or emotional self-delusion. The promise Whitehead broke is a promise neither she nor any real or legitimate woman or mother could be expected to keep. Instead, it is one only artificial prostitutes incapable of true human love could keep, and by showing herself unable to do likewise Whitehead merely proved her status as a woman and mother, as incapable of alienating her nurturing responses as natural mothers in general must be.

In part, because they thought the New Jersey Supreme Court's decision contained these sorts of presumptions about women and mothers, some feminists firmly rejected it and supported the lower court's ruling instead. In their estimation, while the higher court focused on the emotional responses of women and dismissed the ability of women to take responsibility for their contractual commitments,[17] the lower court upheld both the personal liberty of a couple who sponsors a pregnancy to form a family and the surrogate's freedom to choose to perform her services under a contract. If a surrogate father is allowed under the law to sell his sperm, a surrogate mother must, as a matter of equal protection of the law, be allowed to sell her reproductive services. Moreover, the lower court ruled, monetary damages could not possibly compensate William Stern for the loss of his child, and therefore the court was within the law in ordering specific performance of the original contract.

The lower court may have found no reason to assume that surrendering a child is necessarily more emotionally painful for women than giving up a child born of their sperm is for sperm donors. Alternatively, it may have thought that surrendering his particular child was as emotionally painful for William Stern as surrendering hers was for Mary Beth Whitehead. Yet, despite the support this appeal to principles of equality received from certain feminists, the lower court's reasoning can also be understood to follow from ideas about the autonomy and responsibility of women, the character of real mothers, the thrust of A.I.D., and the meaning of surrogacy similar to those from which the New Jersey Supreme Court's decision can be understood to have issued. Surrogate mothers typically describe their motivations for entering into pregnancy contracts with childless couples as, at least in part, altruistic ones. They depict their actions as attempts to do a good deed for others and to give something of themselves, in the light of which the monetary gain is entirely secondary. As one surrogate mother describes her motivation, "I'm not going to cure cancer or become Mother Theresa, but a baby is one thing I can sort of give back, something I can give to someone who couldn't have it any other way." [18] Such self-descriptions might be seen as attempts to lift surrogate mothering out of the subhuman domain of artificial prostitution and into the more respectable domain in which women's traditional tenderness and concern for others holds rule. To be sure, these self-descriptions might themselves be understood as evidence of a patriarchal ideology that buys into a specific idea of what women and mothers are supposed to be. Rather than simply representing themselves as autonomous agents with desired services to sell, then, surrogate mothers must themselves hold onto traditional conceptions of women's social role and psychology. They must understand themselves as generously giving of themselves to others rather than as attempting to earn money for purposes of their own.

But the outrage the lower court in the Baby M case evinced when Whitehead tried to renege on the surrogacy contract seems to follow from this same understanding of what constitutes a real woman and mother. The court did not simply uphold the validity of the surrogacy contract. It also vilified Whitehead's mothering capacities and questioned her child-rearing methods, her relations to her other children, and her sanity. In these respects, it relied on the expert testimony of psychologists such as Dr. Marshall Schecter who attributes to Whitehead a "mixed personality disorder." She suffered from a "borderline personality disorder," he claimed, as evidenced in part by her handing the baby out a window to her husband to avoid the baby's being taken by the Sterns, from a "narcissistic personality disorder," as evidenced in part by her dyeing her prematurely white hair, from a "histrionic personality disorder," as evidenced in part by her functioning as the dominant force in her marriage, and from a "schizotypal personality disorder," as evidenced in part by her talking about paying off debts that, in Schecter's opinion, she could not possibly pay off given her and her husband's "present vocational and educational training." When Schecter also claimed that she played "patty cake" incorrectly and mistakenly gave the baby stuffed animals to play with instead of pots and pans, a group of women and feminists released a letter to the press declaring that "by these standards we are all unfit mothers." [19]

Nevertheless, the vitriolic response of the court, its expert witnesses, and even the press to Whitehead's actions may have stemmed in part from the surprising selfishness those actions seemed to reflect. If surrogates in particular and women in general are meant to be selfless, giving people to whom the monetary compensation for their services is a secondary good, then a surrogate's selfishness in trying to keep the child she bore is deeply troubling. In making an arrangement with a surrogate, a contracting couple implicitly relies not simply on her desire to earn money but on her willingness to help and on her traditional tendency to sacrifice her interests for the best interests of others, particularly her children. Yet in trying to keep the child, a surrogate simultaneously indicates that she really is not interested in the money and also that she is not interested in helping or sacrificing her own interests. Her actions thus cannot be considered those of a legitimate woman and mother but only as the acts of a selfish impostor.

The surrogate mother is thus demonized both coming and going. On the view of women and mothers that both court decisions seem to adopt, a woman's function lies in creating the conditions for the good of others. If she is willing to be artificially inseminated with the sperm of someone other than her husband and if she does not even intend to keep the child thus conceived, then two interpretations of this willingness seem to predominate. On one interpretation, it is evidence of an unseemly and even adulterous economic interest and the woman's status as a respectable being can be rehabilitated only if she reneges on the surrogacy agreement. A woman's connection to her child is not only sacred but socially required. If she can so easily give it up, if she is interested in not only bearing the child of a man other than her husband but also giving the child up to this other man, she must be something less than a woman and certainly not a real mother.

According to the other interpretation, a surrogate who reneges on her pregnancy contract is doubly damned. She has entered into a slightly adulterous relationship and now selfishly wants to keep the product of that union, although she had promised it to others. Hence, if a surrogacy contract is upheld, it may not be for the reasons feminists could support, because it enhances what they understand as women's freedom and autonomy, but rather because the traditional role of women and mothers in providing for the good of others requires that they sacrifice their interests in this instance, as in most others. Indeed, Phyllis Chesler suggests that this notion of women's role is behind many cases besides surrogacy in which biological mothers give up their children because they are told that, given their circumstances and the best interests of their children, they would be selfish if they did not.[20]

"IN A DIFFERENT VOICE"

A particular interpretation of women's natural role, emotional character, and capacity for autonomous choice, together with a particular view of what mothering is, lies, then, at the bottom of the prosurrogacy view of the lower court and the antisurrogacy argument of the higher one in the Baby M case. Either we condemn the practice of surrogate mothering and the couples who seek to gain children through it as an attempt to suspend the natural feelings of women and mothers toward their own children and the meaning of childbirth in general. Or we condemn as unnaturally selfish surrogate mothers who try to keep their children in violation of both their children's own best interests and the strongest expectations and hopes of the couple who initiated the surrogate arrangement. In the first case, a surrogate's autonomy lies in recapturing and acting on the tender feelings of natural women. In the second case, it lies in the voluntary character of a gift relation in which she does her best for others. Still, at the heart of both court decisions is a similar assumption that there is one canonical and proper way to understand women and mothering and one proper and canonical way for women and mothers to be.

An interpretive dogmatism similar to that of the courts seems to pervade the feminist surrogacy debate that looks to women's moral voice.

What has come to be called "difference feminism" tries to show the way in which women's roles as mothers and nurturers serve as a source of moral strength rather than solely as the ground of an emotional weakness impervious to the claims of reason, autonomy, or contractual agreement. Yet this second idea of women and the meaning of real mothering leads to the same attempt to establish a canonical view of who women and mothers are or ought to be as the first view taken by the courts. Moreover, it leads to the same opposition between prosurrogacy and antisurrogacy arguments.

The idea that women's traditional social roles and emotional psychology might be sources of moral strength rather than weakness is the conception most famously connected with Carol Gilligan's *In a Different Voice.*[21] Beginning with Nancy Chodorow's account of typical child-rearing practices in which women function as the primary parent for young children,[22] Gilligan argues that this circumstance means that little boys must model themselves on a largely absent father and in opposition to their primary parent, while little girls model themselves on the primary, mothering parent and grow up in connection with her. Hence, issues for the self-identity of little boys and, later, men are their autonomy and rights as independent agents, while issues for little girls, and later women, are separation and loss of connection.

This difference issues in a difference in the structure of moral thinking. For what Gilligan calls an ethics of justice, which she associates with a masculine form of thought, central questions concern what rights are due to individuals and how the equality between individuals can be preserved. On Lawrence Kohlberg's moral scale, this form of moral thinking occupies the highest rank and women typically score much lower. But Gilligan contends that women simply tend to think about moral issues in a different way: not in terms of preserving individual rights and equality but in terms of preserving human connection. In considering moral dilemmas, women tend to think less about rights than about their responsibilities to both self and others, less about abstract principles of justice than about the good of the concrete other.

In a well-known example of this difference, Gilligan considers the dissimilarities in the answers two children, Amy and Jake, give to the "Heinz dilemma." According to the terms of the dilemma, Heinz's wife is critically ill, but the druggist who is selling the drug that can cure her is selling it at a price too high for Heinz to afford. The question the psychologist poses to the two children is whether Heinz should steal the drug. Jake answers yes and continues, "For one thing, a human life is

worth more than money, and if the druggist only makes $1,000, he is
still going to live, but if Heinz doesn't steal the drug, his wife is going to
die." Amy, however, answers no. "I think there might be other ways besides stealing it, like if he could borrow the money or make a loan or
something, but he really shouldn't steal the drug—but his wife shouldn't
die either."[23]

According to Gilligan, the situation presents itself to Jake as a mathe-
matical problem in which the possible death of Heinz's wife outweighs
the druggist's monetary gain. But the horror of the situation for Amy lies
not as much in the inequality of possible outcomes as in the druggist's
lack of responsiveness to and solidarity with Heinz. "Her belief in the
restorative activity of care . . . lead[s] her to see the actors in the dilemma
arrayed not as opponents in a context of rights but as members of a network of relationships on whose continuation they all depend."[24] For
this reason, Amy's solution to the problem is one that does not involve
restoring the proper relation between life and profit but rather one that
involves continued communication, a feel for the complexity of the situation, and a willingness to be both responsible and responsive to all the
individuals involved. "The truths of relationship . . . return in the re-
discovery of connection, in the realization that self and other are inter-
dependent and that life, however valuable in itself, can only be sustained
by care in relationships."[25]

How does this analysis affect the attempt to understand the meaning
of surrogate mothering? At first glance, it may seem to tip the balance of
argument against a prosurrogacy position. According to an ethics of
care, the traditional role women possess in functioning as the reservoir
of emotional connection in families and relationships is not to be considered proof that they are impervious to reason or incapable of maintaining voluntarily initiated contractual agreements. Rather, it is proof
of a different voice in morality. This voice, moreover, is one that would
seem to strike out against severing a gestational or a genetic mother's
bond to her child or indeed demanding, as the Stern–Whitehead surrogacy contract demanded, that she not even form such a bond. Rather,
sustaining and strengthening human bonds lies at the core of women's
general ethical response to others and holds, as well, of her relation to
the fetuses she carries to term.

From this point of view, what is crucial to any pregnancy is the way in
which a pregnant woman becomes what Mary Shanley calls a "person-
in-relationship." This characterization holds, for her, of all gestational
mothers, whether they are also the genetic mother of the fetus or not. The

"embodied" relationship is one of which no one can predict the course and which is "stronger than that between the commissioning parent(s) and fetus or between [the surrogate mother's] own 'intentional self' and the fetus prior to conception." Hence, according to Shanley, a legal rule enforcing a pregnancy contract "would reinforce notions of human separateness and insularity rather than recognize that the development of individuality and autonomy takes place through sustained and intimate human relationship."[26] As Elizabeth Anderson puts the point in an echo of the New Jersey Supreme Court:

> The demand to deliberately alienate oneself from one's love for one's own child is a demand which can reasonably and decently be made of no one. Unless we were to remake pregnancy into a form of drudgery many women who do sign a surrogate contract will, despite this fact, form a loving attachment to the child they bear. . . . Treating women's labor as just another kind of commercial production process violates the precious emotional ties which the mother may rightly and properly establish with her "product," the child.[27]

On this view, the care and concern that distinguish women's moral voice act against any commodification of pregnancy or, indeed, children and also against those considerations of autonomy and justice embodied in the notion of contract. Children "enter the world in a relationship," Barbara Katz Rothman writes, "a physical and social and emotional relationship with the woman in whose body they have been nurtured."[28] This relationship does not rule out the possibility of abortion. Rather, for both Shanley and Rothman, the relationship between fetus and gestational mother is the relevant relationship with regard to either a decision to abort or a decision to carry a fetus to term. The decision-making capacity of the mother, just because she is the person-in-relationship, cannot be rescinded by the state, the father, or the "commissioning" parents. Still, the relationship of care and concern that a mother has for her child does rule out the commercial values associated with surrogate mothering. As Thomas H. Murray writes,

> If adults flourish best in enduring, warm relationships, and if caring for children also contributes to the flourishing of adults, then we should encourage practices and policies that support such relationships. To the extent that the dry view of human flourishing implicit in market place values shrinks our perceptions and undermines our support for family life, it threatens not merely children but adults as well.[29]

But if an ethics of care thus seems unequivocally to oppose the validity of pregnancy contracts, it is noteworthy that the legal scholar Carmel

Shalev turns to Gilligan in her case *for* the validity of surrogacy contracts. The linchpin of an ethics of care, in her understanding of it, is responsibility for self and others. It is a concern with the network of relationships for which one is responsible and not simply a concern with individual rights. But responsibility includes responsibility for one's decisions in the social context in which they are made. If one takes both notions of responsibility together—responsibility for others and responsibility for commitments made—then surrogacy contracts must, in Shalev's view, be understood as results of the responsible decisions of responsible agents thinking through and in the context of a network of relationships. For their part, the rights involved or the determination of what can and cannot be properly established can be determined only in terms of the responsibilities the contracting parties have adopted:

> In the ethic of passion and care, interest is the correlative of responsibility, which focuses on the decision-making process of the person whose contemplated action may affect the interests of others. . . . Autonomy replaces liberty to denote the act of choosing responsibly, acknowledging the social context in which a choice is made and the decision maker's ability to affect others as much as self through any chosen action.[30]

The feminist controversy over surrogate mothering thus seems to result in the same two positions with regard to surrogacy as the legal one. Moreover, it does so because of a common view of what women's moral voice and relationship to motherhood mean. The association of women with an ethics of care is either the result of an unreflective and even essentialist understanding of women's natural function as mothers or the result of a feminist and reflective understanding of an important moral voice. In either case, however, there remain two alternatives. Either surrogacy arrangements devalue the proper attachment of natural mother and child, as Anderson and the New Jersey Supreme Court believe, or they adequately represent women's responsiveness to the good of others who can therefore rely on their contractual integrity, as Shalev and the New Jersey lower court argue. Either surrogacy arrangements undermine women's moral voice by subordinating an ethics of care to the marketplace equivalencies of an ethics of justice or they enhance women's moral voice by showing the way an ethics of care undergirds relations of responsibility. Both sides appeal to what they take as a canonical conception of women's nature and moral voice. Significantly, however, this appeal does not seem to decide the issue of surrogacy one way or the other. In the remainder of this chapter, I would therefore like to move away from this exclusive understanding of women and mothers to look at the character of family relationships in general. My idea here is that the debate over surrogacy might be amenable to a kind of resolution if we no longer assume that mothering has only one meaning and, moreover, expand our horizon to consider a dimension of family participation that encompasses mothers, fathers, and children.

SURROGACY CONTRACTS

In her defense of surrogacy, Shalev rejects any equation of an ethics of care with what she considers sentimental notions of motherhood or attachment and associates it, instead, with a conception of responsibility to self and others. Fundamental to this conception, in her view, is the expression of intent. Those individuals who express the intention to become parents—whether through traditional means or through adoption, contracting with a surrogate, or agreeing to artificial insemination—count as the real parents of the child in question and the responsible parties in the web of relationships they create. They must be the decision makers, and their intentions and decisions are the ones that must be supported by law. Because what counts here is the intention to become a parent, responsibility must be decided at conception or as close to the time of conception as possible. In the case of adoption, this requirement means that women who agree to give their children up must abide by their original decisions to do so without the customary option of changing their minds within a certain period of time. In the case of surrogate mothering, the requirement means that pregnancy contracts must be considered valid and courts can require specific compliance.

In this latter case, what Shalev calls the "sponsoring couple" takes over responsibility for the pregnancy itself, as well as for any children resulting from the surrogacy agreement. This stipulation means that in cases in which a fetal abnormality is detected it is the sponsoring couple's decision as to whether or not the pregnancy should be terminated. Shalev denies that this stipulation, one written into the Stern–Whitehead surrogacy contract, violates a woman's constitutional right to an abortion. According to her interpretation of Gilligan, rights can follow only from responsibilities, and responsibilities turn on the network of relevant relationships. These relationships differ crucially enough in the case of surrogacy from those in the case of a nonsurrogate pregnancy to alter the constitutional issues at stake:

> The surrogate's constitutional privacy consists in her personal authority to make a reproductive decision that specifically anticipates the dissociation of

biological from social motherhood, supplemented by her capacity to enter legally effective contractual relations that determine the allocation of the child-rearing responsibility, regardless of gender and biological connection. The sponsoring parents have similar authority to make reproductive decisions and effectuate them by means of contract.[31]

It is a consequence of Shalev's view that sponsoring parents cannot themselves renege on pregnancy contracts in the event that a baby is born with significant deformities. They can, of course, give the child up for adoption, as can any couple with regard to an infant they do not want, but the sponsoring couple remains legally responsible for the child until that time.[32] Still, it also seems to be a consequence of Shalev's view that a biological father cannot be required financially to support a child he has fathered unless he specifically agrees to or intends to function as the child's father. Child support might be legitimately required of fathers (or "deadbeat dads") who initially have either explicitly or tacitly expressed their intentions to enter into a father–child relation. Nonetheless, under a "consent–intent" conception of parenthood it does not seem that fathers can be legally compelled, as they are under some current law, to support children whom they fathered through sexual intercourse with their mothers but never intended to father.

But such laws illuminate an important aspect of our understanding of the meaning of a family. The idea is that, in the absence of an explicit agreement that transfers legal and financial responsibility from one parent to the spouse of the other, biological parents should help support their children once they have them, whether or not they wanted or intended to have them. Moreover, this idea seems to rest on the notion that families, even nontraditional families, constitute sets of relations that are not always intended or chosen. We do not choose our children or our parents any more than we choose the person with whom we fall in or out of love. We do not become pregnant just because we decide or intend to do so; nor can we yet either control the sex of our children or pick their personalities. To be sure, we are able to realize some intentions with regard to some of these factors, and emerging birth technologies promise even more intentional control than we have had thus far. To a certain extent, we can decide when not to be pregnant by using various methods of birth control or by having an abortion. We can even abort fetuses if their sex is not the one we wanted. We can decide to have little to do with the people who turn out to be our parents, and we can narrow the range of possibilities for falling in love. We can also take positive action to fall in love or become pregnant, and we can rely on the medical profession or singles associations to help if we are having trouble. Finally, we can even choose to have a child without becoming pregnant.

Still, none of these strategies results in or even promises total control over the situation. And this lack of ultimate control seems, in fact, to correspond to a significant aspect of our understanding of family. For while Shalev's conception of contracting to be a parent rests on the intentions and control of sponsoring parties, at least part of what it seems to mean to have or belong to a family is just to lose control. Families are less things that we create or contract into than relationships or the consequences of relationships that happen to us both as parents and, perhaps more obviously, as children.[33] As parents, our responsibility for our children, whether we discharge it by raising them as best we can or by trying to secure a better home for them than the one we can supply, does not depend on our original intention to have or not to have them. It depends only on the children's existence and this seems to be the state of families in general. Whether we intend them or not, exercise our procreative rights or not, give birth to the children we imagined or not, the salient fact about a family is not the intentions—and thus not the contractual control—that may or may not initiate it. Rather, the salient fact about a family relationship is the fact that it simply exists.

It is important to be clear about what sort of consideration is being advanced here. Anderson's opposition to surrogate mothering arrangements condemns the forms of valuation such arrangements impose on women's reproductive labor and children. On her view, surrogacy commodifies women's labor because it both subsumes it under production-line values appropriate to the creation of salable merchandise and underestimates the value owed to the ongoing relationship between mother and fetus. Hence, surrogates are supposed not to form the kinds of attachments to their fetuses that are proper and part of our social practices surrounding pregnancy. For their part, the children of surrogates are denied what is due them: namely to be loved and cherished by their parents. As Anderson puts her point, "the fundamental calling of parents to their children is to love them. . . . Parental love can be understood as a passionate, unconditional commitment to nurture one's child, providing it with the care, affection, and guidance it needs to develop its capacities to maturity."[34] A surrogate mother, in contrast, uses her child only for "personal advantage" while the commissioning parents treat it as a commercial product.

But if families are relationships that happen to us rather than entities that we intend or can contractually control, as Shalev assumes, it seems

equally odd to legislate the proper form those relationships are supposed
to take. Certainly, a mother cannot know what her bond to her child
will be before it is born, as the New Jersey Supreme Court argued. But
the bond with her infant seems only the beginning of what a person cannot know. She cannot know how the existence of the child will change
her relationship to its father, her work or career, her parents, or herself.
Nor can she know that changes in these relationships will be determined
by the strength of her attachment to the child. It may be the opposite. If
a surrogate mother cannot know that she will not feel a powerful bond
with the fetus she is carrying or with the child to whom she gives birth,
neither can a mother who intends to keep her child know that she will
feel such a powerful bond.

Of course, she may "intend" to feel a connection, and it may be either
"proper and correct" that she does, as Anderson maintains, or specifically proscribed, as the Stern–Whitehead pregnancy contract demanded.
In neither case, however, are family relationships dictated by what philosophers or contracts find proper and correct. Rather, it seems to be a
crucial aspect of their meaning that they spill out beyond anything we
can control, intend, or imagine. In one case, the strength of a surrogate's
bond with her newborn infant may make it impossible for her to surrender it as agreed upon in a preexisting pregnancy contract. In another
case, the continuing strength of the surrogate's commitment to other
goals may mean that it is not difficult at all.[35] But if at least part of the
meaning of family relationships is that they go beyond our intentions,
then these results would seem to be consistent with that meaning and to
preclude the law or philosophy from issuing any one set of criteria for
the appropriate content of the relationships at stake.

In the conflicting attitudes we have explored toward surrogacy and
mothering, the proper relation of a natural or birth mother to her child
has been understood to be one of four different possibilities: (1) an attachment that cannot be sundered even under contract because of the
proper feelings of real women and mothers; (2) an attachment that requires sundering under certain situations, among which surrogacy is included, for the good of the child to which a proper mother is committed; (3) an attachment that, even in a surrogacy arrangement, attests to
a pregnant woman's ethics of care and sense of self-in-relationship; or
(4) a lack of attachment in a surrogacy arrangement that attests to the
pregnant woman's ethics of care and sense of self, autonomy, and responsibility. But if by family we mean a set of relationships that happens
to us, then why must mothering have only one meaning? Rather, all four

of these possibilities would seem to be possible permutations of human relationships and possible interpretations of the meaning of motherhood, our sense of self, and the ideas of autonomy and responsibility. None of the permutations can be foreseen or prohibited by philosophy or contract, just as none of the interpretations can be excluded by philosophical or legal principle.

Are we mothers only if we can take up a certain social and emotional relation to our fetuses (and even abort them only because we know what is best for our "relationship")? Are we mothers only if we value our children in some proper way and know how to guide them to maturity? Is there a difference between these pronouncements and those of a Schellen according to whom only certain kinds of motherly love are human or of a Schecter according to whom only certain ways of playing children's games are expressions of adequate mothering? There seems to be an obvious danger in pronouncements such as those that Anderson and Shalev make that only certain feelings and relations will qualify as motherly or womanly and that, if one does not have these, one is either the artificial prostitute that Schellen originally condemned or simply irresponsible. Anderson writes:

> Children are properly loved by parents and respected by others. Since children are valued as mere use-objects by the mother and the surrogate agency when they are sold to others, and by the adoptive parents when they seek to conform the child's genetic makeup to their own wishes, commercial surrogacy degrades children insofar as it treats them as commodities.[36]

But parents have children for all sorts of reasons and value them in all sorts of different ways, whether they expected to or not. Was it improper for parents of earlier generations to want children in order to guarantee help on the farm or sustenance in old age? Is it improper to have a child to increase the chance of finding a bone marrow match for another of one's children?[37] And even if these roles counted for or against wanting children, could the parents involved not value them in other ways as well? And might not a woman be a very different kind of mother to the children she lives with, those she gives up for adoption, and those she bears for others?

These considerations seem to confirm the idea that what is importantly at issue in the question of surrogacy is neither the strength nor the proper direction of a woman's or mother's emotions. Nor is the issue one of finding the one conclusive answer to the meaning of mothering or care in general. Rather, the more crucial issue may be the strength, nonintentional nature, and multiple character of family relationships in general.

Because we recognize that these sorts of relationships can evade our intentions, we do not require couples to remain married, even though they have signed a contract to do so. On this ground alone, it is unclear how we could hold surrogate mothers to a higher standard.[38] But it is also unclear how we could prohibit surrogacy contracts as a mode of improper valuation. Certainly some modes of relating to children or to our responsibility toward them are morally and legally unsustainable. Notable here is child abuse. But it is not clear that surrogacy does not reflect one of the many morally sustainable variations in human relationships and family connections.

If we cannot prohibit surrogate mothering on the grounds that it reflects an improper mode of valuing children, nor, for similar reasons, is it adequate to conceive of contract pregnancy as simply an ordinary form of contract. Given the unpredictability of family relationships, any contract pregnancy can spill over the legal barriers with which we surround it. What are we to do, therefore, when a surrogate, whether the biological or gestational mother, tries to keep the child she formerly agreed to relinquish and the "sponsoring parents" refuse to relinquish their intention to have it? What about Baby M? In this case, custody remains with the Sterns but Mary Beth Whitehead has liberal visitation rights. If we begin with the idea that family relationships are unintended and that we must begin with respect for some of the different paths that mothering, family relationships, and nurturing roles can take, then we might take this resolution to be supportable. Indeed, why not admit that the child might have two mothers and even two fathers and that all the parties involved might learn to cope and even flourish with that arrangement? It would not have been one they intended, but they might get on with it nonetheless.

This sort of solution seems to be the one a Vermont court used in settling the adoption case of "Baby Pete." In this case, a woman became pregnant by her husband in the midst of divorcing him. Claiming that her current boyfriend was the father, she severed her parental rights and gave the child up for adoption without the actual, biological father's knowledge. Upon discovering that his former wife had given birth to a son, the father sued to regain custody. The court and the parties involved compromised. The adoptive mother retained physical custody and now shares legal custody with the biological father.[39]

In general, this sort of solution might be our guide, for it seems to comply with much of what we consider a family to be, something, *pace* Shalev, that is either entirely unintended or, in any case, surpasses any intentions we could have had. At the same time, it also takes seriously a conception that Shalev endorses, namely that we need not sever old relationships to guarantee the strength of new ones. What the advent of open adoption, surrogacy, and new birth technologies seem to ask us to reject is not any way of valuing the sanctity of family life but merely that partial account of families according to which they properly consist only of biological parents and their children.[40] Where this situation is not possible it must be outwardly imitated by closing adoption records, keeping semen donor identities secret, and so on. But why might one's family not be defined as that group of people who have a special concern for one, those that do have the "calling" or commitment to one that Anderson thinks anyone bringing a pregnancy to term must have: namely, the "passionate, unconditional commitment" to nurture one and to provide one "with care and affection"? Some part of this idea is certainly involved in our colloquial use of "family" to refer to our closest friends. In the general case, the set of people with a special concern for one may be one's nuclear family, whether biologically related to one or a family "by adoption." Or the set of people might be slightly larger, including both of one's remarried parents with their present partners and assorted former stepparents as well. But in other cases, the set of people might involve one's custodial parents and one's biological parent or one's custodial parents and one's gestational mother who served as their "surrogate," or even one's mother, her partner, and their sperm donor.

The point here is that neither law nor moral philosophy should determine which family relationships we can have to which people, as the lower court tried to do in the Baby M case. Rather, they should be trying to understand and facilitate the family relationships that we already have. That is, our guiding question might be how the laws and principles to which we adhere can help us cope with family relationships we may have never intended but that turn out, for various reasons and in various ways, to be integral to who we are. These relationships may not be those simply between parent and child. Rather, if I am a surrogate mother who wants to maintain a relationship to the child I bore for another couple, a relationship I might not have intended to establish at the outset of the contract pregnancy but which I now take as seriously as I take my life, the function of law in this case might be that of helping me with a relationship with the sponsoring couple and, likewise, helping the sponsoring couple with a relationship to me. If I am the biological father of a child whose mother put it up for adoption without my intending or knowing of its existence, the law might help me deal with the relationship

that has grown up between the child and its adoptive parents, and, likewise, it might help them deal with my relationship to the child so that
all of us are able to retain a place in his or her life. None of these complex relationships between parent and child or sets of parents might have
been intended. But if law or moral principle has any role in this predicament, it would seem to be to help us muddle through the network of
family relationships that has happened to us, since this is both what a
family is and, moreover, what we shall have to do in any case.

Since the publication of Gilligan's book, feminists have wondered
whether its conception of a woman's moral voice does not define what
are to count as normal female attitudes in a way as restrictive for women
as any of the traditional stereotypes. To the extent that critics of surrogate mothering seem to sanction only certain sorts of womanly or motherly sentiments or forms of attachment, this worry seems justified. But if
we emphasize, instead, the notion of an ethics of care as sustaining and
nurturing many different forms of human commitment and solidarity,
then I think we can understand it to concur with the view I am advocating here. Contested surrogacy agreements as well as contested custody
arrangements indicate the extent to which relationships thwart our original expectations. In certain cases such as wife-battering, child abuse,
and parental neglect, we require the legal system to enforce restraining
orders and set restrictions on the possible contact between members of
a family. But the circumstance that the law must restrict relationships in
these cases does not mean it should either restrict them or define them
in all others. Controversies over custody in surrogacy cases, as well as
in divorce and adoption cases, often set two sets of competent parents
against one another. Perhaps what we require of the law (or philosophy
or, indeed, child psychology) in these cases is not some way of deciding
which is the more legitimate relationship. Rather, since both already
exist, although in different ways, what we may need is help in sorting
through their complexity and making them work.

The sort of solution I am advocating for cases in which a surrogate
mother reneges on her contractual agreement with a sponsoring couple
thus also provides a plausible framework, I think, for resolving other recent custody disputes. In the Jessica Deboer case, the Michigan Supreme
Court, after a lengthy and complicated legal battle involving both Iowa
and Michigan courts, decided against the legitimacy of the relationship
between Jessica Deboer and her adoptive parents with whom she had
lived for the two and half years she had been alive. It decided, instead,
for the sole legitimacy of her genetic relationship to her biological par-

ents, even though her biological mother had initially agreed to the adoption.[41] In the Kimberly Mays case, a Florida court decided for the legitimacy of the relationship between Kimberly Mays and her custodial father and against the sole or even compelling legitimacy of her biological parents with whom she had never lived because of a mix up at the hospital where she had been born fourteen years ago. Finally, a Virginia court decided against the legitimacy of the relationship between a boy and his lesbian biological mother, granting custody to the boy's grandmother instead.

What is curious about all of these cases is not only their contradictory outcomes but the idea that the court should be involved in determining which of two relationships is the sole legitimate one in order to bring them under the sort of intentional and contractual control they have already superseded. If we begin instead with the definition of a family relationship as that which is essentially out of intentional or contractual control, then in none of these cases would the function of the legal system be to pass judgment on the legitimacy of one relationship over another. Rather, it would be to find a way of accommodating different legitimate claims, securing the different kinds of genetic and custodial relationships that already exist—as long, of course, as these relationships do not involve a history of neglect or abuse.

In advocating this sort of solution, it is important not to ignore the difficulties it involves. The idea of supporting all the different legitimate family relationships that exist need not extend to cases in which parents have voluntarily surrendered their parental rights and, hence, in the terminology of adoption, "abandoned" their children.[42] Once an adoption has been finalized with the consent of both birth parents, the adopting parents can be secure in the knowledge that it is on the way to establishing a family. Still, a more perplexing problem seems to arise with the idea of joint custody, insofar as it is often hard enough to agree with one's partner—presumably someone one trusts and likes—on what is best for one's children. It will be potentially much more difficult if physical and legal custody are split as they are in the Vermont solution or if "sponsoring" parents must consult or even listen to a surrogate mother they neither trust nor necessarily like. This problem does not seem to admit of a general answer. But a distinction that Jürgen Habermas makes between two functions that law might play seems relevant. One function seems to be illegitimate. This is law as a "system mechanism" under which it invades preexisting relationships by requiring them to conform to general regulations in the interest of an efficient operation of the economy and governmental bureaucracy.[43] Prime examples of this function of law are those parts of the social welfare system that, whatever their benefits, also require the reorganization of family relationships and other group solidarities to meet general bureaucratic criteria for dispensing services. But we might also extend this conception of law to cover the way in which family law enters into and defines legitimate family relationships by severing the parental or visitation rights of nonabusive parents and overturning standing adoptions or custodial arrangements without consideration for the family relationships that exist.

The other function of law Habermas terms law as institution. Here, it does not enter into the substance of relationships as much as guarantee their compliance with established legal rights. Hence, it would seem to be a legitimate function of law to promote the safety of women and children in families and to limit visitation rights where they involve child abuse. But it remains an illegitimate function for law to decide what constitutes a family or a compelling relationship. Why should it be the instrument through which we try to regain the control we thought moral theory or contractual agreement would give us? Why should it not, instead, facilitate the variety of relationships in which a child and his or her various sets of "parents" might already be involved?

Attempts to resolve the debate over surrogate mothering start from the assumption that mothering is to be understood in one "correct" way. Real mothers behave only in certain ways, possess only certain attitudes, and are subject only to certain emotions. Philosophical analysis and explicit contracts are to tell us what these correct contours of mothering are, and our analysis of legitimate family relationships will follow from these legal and philosophical determinations. But this account of mothering, philosophy, and the law seems unable to integrate an important part of what we consider a family to be. If families are relationships that overflow our intentions at every turn, then philosophical or contractual determinations can neither produce nor eliminate them. Nor is it clear how they might determine which are legitimate. Rather, family relationships seem to resist the intrusions of philosophy and law because they include a kind of limitless variety and are subject to constraint only at the boundaries of injury, neglect, and risk of death. But if this resistance holds, then law and philosophy might rather help us with the family relationships we have and with the potential joint custody of children with different sets and kinds of family relationships.

In the next three chapters, I want to extend the idea of accommodating legitimate differences from custody disputes over children to disputes over the meaning of principles we share. If the case for accommodation in certain custody disputes rests on the dubious legitimacy of the law's attempts to decide between two sets of equally competent and caring parents, then perhaps the question that arises in some of our other public debates is whether the competing sides in these discussions are also equally legitimate. If they are, can we, in a multicultural, diverse society, sometimes envision joint custody for certain of our norms and values as well as for our children? In Chapter Three I shall be specifically concerned with the meaning of principles of equality and equal opportunity as these principles figure in the current debate over affirmative action policies. While critics of these policies now assert exclusive claims over the meaning of these principles, interpreting them only in terms of a principle of strict racial, gender, and ethnic neutrality, I shall be arguing that their interpretation might, more plausibly, acknowledge the equal legitimacy of an interpretation that stresses the participation and integration of all races, genders, and ethnicities in the institutions and practices of American society.

CHAPTER THREE

Affirmative Action, Neutrality, and Integration

Opponents of affirmative action claim that it is a perversion of anti-discrimination and equal opportunity principles to which Americans have been committed at the latest since the Supreme Court's decision in *Brown v Board of Education*. They argue that, in concert with the civil rights legislation of the early 1960s, this decision meant a commitment to the principle of racial neutrality and the final end to all discrimination based on "an individual's race, color, religion, sex or national origin."[1] Nevertheless, in their critics' view affirmative action policies have progressively eroded just these principles by establishing quotas, timetables, and proportional employment representation based only on race, color, and sex. Herman Belz writes, "Statutory language that was intended to confer an individual right to equal opportunity in employment without distinguishing by color has for many years been interpreted as authorizing government officials and private employers to adopt preferential practices benefiting designated racial and ethnic groups."[2] Lino Graglia concurs. Affirmative action policies mean that "a regime of permissible or compulsory racial discrimination has been established by the court in the name of enforcing constitutional and statutory prohibitions against such discrimination, a judicial feat without parallel in the history of law."[3]

These criticisms, however, depend upon a one-sided account of the meaning of principles of equal opportunity and antidiscrimination. For critics of affirmative action, to be faithful to either principle is to focus only on individuals rather than the group to which they belong and to dismantle all legal and institutional barriers to individual achievement. From the beginning, however, the twentieth-century civil rights movement in the United States has understood the principles of antidiscrimination and equal opportunity in terms of two goals: the legal prohibition of discrimination because of race, color, or, later, sex and the integration or inclusion of African Americans, other minorities, and women into all aspects of American civil, political, and social life. The effort to dismantle barriers to equal opportunity for individuals has always been conjoined not simply with the attempt to ensure racial, ethnic, and gender neutrality but with the attempt to allow for the full participation of blacks, other minorities, and women in all the practices and institutions of the society. And this equation has held because full and common participation has been understood as part of the meaning of the principle of equal opportunity.

In identifying criticisms of affirmative action policies with a one-sided interpretation of equal opportunity, I mean to appeal to the principles of interpretive adequacy that we looked at briefly in Chapter One. The claim that affirmative action violates the principle of equal opportunity because it violates a principle of neutrality fails to take the measure of the whole of the former principle and therefore misses the further connection it has to equal participation and to gender, racial, and ethnic integration. But an interpretation of equal opportunity that simply ignores neutrality is equally one sided. I therefore want, first, to try to show the sense of criticisms of affirmative action insofar as they understand the principle of equal opportunity in connection with an important ideal of racial neutrality. But, second, I want to defend affirmative action in terms of an understanding of the principle that links it also to the goals of integration. I shall then, however, turn to another sort of criticism that opponents of affirmative action raise against it: namely, that even if the principle of equal opportunity can be linked to the ideal of racial integration, affirmative action prevents the attainment of just this ideal. This criticism illuminates an important distinction between integration and inclusion. Furthermore, it raises significant questions about the current emphasis on racial, ethnic, and gender diversity. It is unclear, however, whether the criticism also justifies eradicating affirmative action programs as a whole. I shall begin by reconstructing the meaning of equal opportunity as opponents of affirmative action appear to understand it.

THE CASE AGAINST AFFIRMATIVE ACTION

Critics of affirmative action defend their position by pointing to the Supreme Court's decisions in *Brown v Board of Education* and *Bolling v Sharpe,* both of which stood firmly for the principle that all racial discrimination by the government was unconstitutional. In ending segregation in the District of Columbia's public schools, *Bolling v Sharpe* proclaimed that "classifications based solely upon race must be scrutinized with particular care, since they are contrary to our traditions and hence constitutionally suspect." Moreover, "the Constitution of the United States . . . forbids, so far as civil and political rights are concerned, discrimination by the general government, or by the states, against any citizen because of his race."[4]

In addition, opponents of affirmative action point to the Civil Rights Act of 1964, an act that, in their view, originally stood for a similar principle connecting equal opportunity to racial neutrality and did so by explicitly prohibiting discrimination in large-scale private employment. Thus, section 703(a) made it unlawful:

> (1) to fail or refuse to hire or discharge any individual or otherwise to discriminate against any individual . . . because of such individual's race, color, religion, sex, or national origin; or
> (2) to limit, segregate, or classify his employees or applicants for employment in any way which would deprive any individual of employment opportunities . . . because of such individual's race, color, religion, sex, or national origin.[5]

The act was subsequently modified to include the prohibition of discrimination in public employment. Moreover, it incorporated specific amendments that critics of affirmative action contend were designed to preclude preferential treatment. Employers were permitted to uphold seniority systems and to use professionally developed ability tests as long as neither was the result of an intent to discriminate. In addition, section 703(j) stated that the government could not order an employer to adopt an affirmative action plan.

Belz thus insists that at the root of the Civil Rights Act was the idea that all individuals were to compete for careers and offices open to talent on an equal basis, without regard to those factors of race, color, and, eventually, gender that were beyond the control of individuals. The modern struggle for civil rights was not concerned with preferential treatment, group rights, group interests, or group identity, he claims. Nor was the Civil Rights Act meant either to compensate African Americans for the history of slavery and discrimination or to provide them as a group with the material and social advantages they would have had if they had not suffered this history. Rather, it was forward looking and progressive. It focused on securing equal opportunity for individuals in the present and future by guaranteeing impartial and racially neutral procedures that would treat individuals equally, creating "a situation where they [could] compete on the basis of ability and be judged according to achievement." [6]

Nonetheless, critics of affirmative action argue, precisely this sort of reasoning fell victim to the debilitating effects of policies that emphasized group identity over the achievement of individuals and reinforced racial classification at the expense of the ideal of racial neutrality. By 1968, contractors doing government work were required to "provide in detail for specific steps to guarantee equal employment opportunity keyed to the problems and needs of minority groups, including, when there are deficiencies, the development of specific goals and timetables." [7] In 1970, the Labor Department's guidelines focused on the "underutilization" of minorities where their presence in a particular job class was less "than would reasonably be expected by their availability," [8] and in 1978 the Carter administration further refined the notion of underutilization to specify a hiring rate for any race, sex, or ethnic group that fell below four-fifths that of the group with the highest selection rate, unless this difference was justified by business necessity. [9]

The Supreme Court not only upheld these policies throughout the 1960s but also helped to expand the scope of affirmative action in the 1970s. In the 1971 case of *Griggs v Duke Power Company,* the Court by and large agreed with the lawyers for the plaintiffs that the tests required by the company for purposes of hiring, transfer, and promotion violated the rights of African Americans because they continued the effects of past discrimination and had a disparate impact on black employees as a class. The tests involved either a high school diploma or a passing score on a standardized intelligence test, and the company argued that its policy complied with Title VII's provision for ability tests as long as they were not intended to discriminate against certain groups. But the Court held that the tests could not be shown to have "a manifest relationship to the employment in question." Rather, they served as "built-in headwinds" against the employment of blacks while the Civil Rights Act proscribed "not only overt discrimination but also practices that are fair in form but discriminatory in operation." [10]

Opponents of affirmative action concede that *Griggs* did not completely dispense with the ideas either of qualification or of equality of opportunity for individuals. Still, they argue that it reinterpreted them in ways definitive for the future of employment law. Prior to *Griggs*, an employer could be asked to demonstrate that a given employment practice was not a pretext for discrimination and that it rather rested on legitimate business reasons. After *Griggs*, however, this requirement became a burden on the employer to show the indispensability of any practice that resulted in a disparate racial impact. Moreover, while Chief Justice Burger's opinion in the case referred to equal opportunity and individual job qualifications, he also emphasized that tests for qualification "must measure the person for the job and not the person in the abstract." By doing so, Belz argues, he failed to recognize the difference between "a literacy or intelligence test in voting, which serves little if any purpose in modern government, and an aptitude or ability test in private employment, which serves the purpose of promoting safe and efficient business operation."[11] Graglia condemns the decision in even stronger terms:

> In *Griggs* the Court held that Title VII's prohibition of racial discrimination in employment does not mean that employers must ignore race in setting employment qualifications, but that they must take race into account, and that they may be required to eliminate standard employment criteria that blacks as a group find difficult to meet, even though sufficient numbers of whites meeting the criteria are available.[12]

The Court went even further in the late 1970s. In *Regents of the University of California v Bakke* (1978), it tried to invalidate the idea of absolute racial quotas while still allowing that race could be a factor in admissions decisions. In the case of *United Steelworkers of America v Weber* (1979), the Court upheld an agreement between the steelworkers' union and Kaiser Aluminum and Chemical Corporation to establish a training program in which 50 percent of the trainees would be African Americans until the time at which the percentage of black skilled workers at fifteen Kaiser plants approximated the percentage of blacks in the local workforce. And in *Fullilove v Klutznick* (1982) it upheld set asides for minorities in public contracting authorized by Congress.[13]

At least the *Bakke* decision indicated the extent of the Court's divisions over the legality of affirmative action plans, according to their critics. Five justices voted to uphold Bakke's claim that the admissions policies of the Medical School of the University of California at Davis were discriminatory but disagreed on how. Five justices agreed that race could be used in admissions decisions but disagreed on how. No Justice agreed with Justice Powell's attempt to find a compromise between racial classifications and racial quotas. Still, four joined his majority opinion and did so because it allowed that "racial classification was constitutional." [14] For some critics of affirmative action, then, despite its indication of the contestability of affirmative action plans, the effect of *Bakke* remained a simple disavowal of the principle of racial neutrality. "In the context of widespread adoption of preferential policies . . . Justice Powell's approval of race as a legitimate consideration emerged as the Court's principle teaching on the problem of reverse discrimination." [15]

United Steelworkers of America v Weber and *Fullilove v Klutznick* expanded this teaching. The Court approved the steelworkers' plan for two reasons: first, it was voluntarily adopted by the private parties concerned in order to rectify a "manifest racial imbalance." Second, the plan was conceived of as a temporary measure only, to be discontinued once African Americans composed a more substantial part of the workforce. But Graglia understands the decision somewhat differently: "*Weber*," he writes, "carried . . . affirmative action . . . to its logical conclusion by holding that Title VII does not prohibit racial discrimination against whites." [16] And Belz agrees: "while the Supreme Court might modify disparate impact theory in other cases to make it more reasonable, its explicit approval of racial preference at the expense of universal equal rights promised to have a far more important effect. It legitimized deciding by race in employment and elsewhere." [17]

Critics of affirmative action contend that, since the late 1980s with its new constellation of justices, the Supreme Court has tried to rescind its more radical breaks with principles of equal opportunity and racial neutrality, notably in *Wards Cove v Atonio* (1989) and *City of Richmond v J.A. Croson Company* (1989). Still, in their view the difference that must be continually stressed is the difference between ideals that stress colorblind individual achievement and equal opportunity for all, on the one hand, and the ideal of "a racially balanced society organized on the principles of group rights and equality of result," on the other. [18] Only the first ideal complies with traditional American values: it focuses on the individual over the group, on equality of opportunity rather than racial balance, and on the sort of individual achievement that alone, according to Belz, allows individuals "to gain the rewards of dignity, pride, and self-respect." [19]

Still, there is another way of reading the legislation and case law with which opponents of affirmative action are concerned. In the next section of this chapter, I want to reexamine the history of the Supreme Court's concern with civil rights beginning with the 1950 case of *Sweatt v Painter* up through its decision in *United Steelworkers v Weber* in order to defend affirmative action policies, at least against the absolutism of this first criticism that they have perverted the equal opportunity ideals of the modern civil rights movement. For such ideas cannot be understood in only one way, as demanding only an end to discrimination based on irrelevant characteristics such as sex or skin color. Rather, they also demand the inclusion and integration of those groups previously denied access to most of the opportunities the society has to offer.

THE IDEALS OF INTEGRATION

The case of *Sweatt v Painter* concerned the question of the admission of Heman Marion Sweatt to the University of Texas Law School. To avoid integrating that school, the state had established a separate facility for blacks, first in a makeshift arrangement at Prairie View University, at that time a vocational school for blacks, and then in a basement a few blocks from the regular University of Texas Law School in Austin. Sweatt refused to attend and took the case to the Supreme Court.

In an earlier case involving the University of Oklahoma Law School, the Court had ordered Oklahoma to educate an African American applicant, Ada Sipuel, but had acquiesced in the idea of educating her in a small section of the state capitol roped off for blacks. Civil rights lawyers had attacked this solution and did so, in part, in terms of the unconstitutionality of racial classifications on which critics of affirmative action focus. The NAACP brief thus claimed that "classifications and distinctions based on race or color have no moral or legal validity in our society."[20] In *Sweatt v Painter* an amicus brief submitted by the Committee of Law Teachers against Segregation in Legal Education made the same point: "As soon as laws make a right or responsibility dependent solely on race, they violate the 14th Amendment. Reasonable classifications may be made, but one basis of classification is completely precluded; for the Equal Protection clause makes racial classifications unreasonable per se."[21]

Still, in *Sipuel v Board of Regents of the University of Oklahoma,* the NAACP also argued that the "exclusion of any one group on the basis of race automatically imputes a badge of inferiority to the excluded group."[22] And in *Sweatt v Painter* the Supreme Court agreed. It declared that Sweatt must be admitted to the regular University of Texas Law

School because it could find no "substantial equality in the educational opportunities of white and Negro law students offered by the state."[23] The white law school was not only clearly a better school in terms of the "reputation of the faculty, experience of the administration, position and influence of the alumni, standing in the community, traditions and prestige."[24] Just as important, the black law school excluded 85 percent of the population of Texas, including most of the lawyers, witnesses, judges, and state officials with whom African Americans who were admitted to the bar would have to deal. This form of legal education could not be effective, then, the Court ruled, because it proceeded in isolation from most of the individuals and institutions that the practice of law in Texas concerned.

The Supreme Court decided the case of *McLaurin v Oklahoma State Regents* the same day. Here the issue was whether an African American admitted to graduate school in Oklahoma could nonetheless be segregated from his fellow classmates while there. McLaurin had first been rejected by the university, and when a special three-judge District Court forced the university to admit him, the university devised various stratagems to enforce his continued segregation. It first required him to sit in an anteroom outside the regular classrooms, assigned him a segregated desk in the library, and forced him to eat in an alcove in the dining room at a different hour from the white students. The university subsequently modified these measures so that McLaurin was allowed to sit in the regular classrooms, although behind a railing marked "Reserved for Colored," and, while he could now eat at the same time as the other students, he was forced to do so at a separate table.

The Court ruled that such measures affected his "ability to study, to engage in discussions and exchange views with other students, and in general, to learn his profession."[25] In both *Sweatt* and *McLaurin*, then, the issue was not simply the question of the legitimacy of distinctions based on race but also and simultaneously the question of the connection between equal opportunity and integration, where part of the principle of equal opportunity was understood to involve the capacity to participate in the full life of the enterprise in which one was trying to be engaged. It was not enough to allow blacks to practice law or to educate them with the same legal materials with which white students were educated. Rather, admission to graduate school or to the study or practice of law as an equal was understood to require the integration of African Americans with the whites already established or preparing to be established in the profession. This requirement is even clearer in *Brown v Board of Education,* in which the Court moved beyond the concerns of professional and graduate school education to consider the enterprise of public education.

In overturning laws enforcing racial segregation in southern public schools, *Brown* denied that what it called "tangible" factors of equality—the physical facilities of separate black and white schools, the curricula, and the qualifications and salaries of the teachers in both kinds of schools—could themselves constitute complete equality, even if they existed or, under the threat of a lawsuit, were being brought into existence. Rather, the Court ruled that separate facilities were inherently unequal and were so because of "intangible" considerations. It reiterated its finding in *McLaurin* that these "intangible considerations" included the "ability to study, to engage in discussions and exchange views with other students, and in general, to learn [one's] profession." Moreover, it continued: "Such considerations apply with added force to children in grade and high schools. To separate them from others of similar age and qualifications solely because of their race generates a feeling of inferiority as to their status in the community that may affect their hearts and minds in a way unlikely ever to be undone." [26]

Here the point is not only or even primarily that all racial considerations in public employment, education, transportation, and public life are unconstitutional. The Court did not rule that racial classifications on their own generate feelings of inferiority. Instead, it concentrated on the separation and exclusion of African Americans on the basis of that classification. The decision is directed specifically against the enforced segregation of an African American minority. Depriving Sweatt of the ability to study with whites and McLaurin of the ability to engage in discussions and the exchange of viewpoints with his classmates was a violation of their equal opportunity rights to involve themselves fully in their profession and its associations. In the same way, *Brown* does not merely condemn a policy that assigns schoolchildren to schools on the basis of their race. What is more important, it condemns a policy that assigns African American schoolchildren to segregated schools and thus deprives them of the opportunity to learn and interact with their peers. What *Brown* condemns, in other words, is not the form of thinking about justice and equality that considers race. Rather *Brown* condemns a form of thinking about race and equality that claims not to consider one race unequal to another and yet refuses to include it in its social, political, or civic life.

The subsequent school-desegregation cases reinforce this equation of the principle of equality and equal opportunity with that of integration. By the time the Court lost its patience with its own idea of "all deliberate speed," which it had announced in its second *Brown* decision,[27] urban schools in the South were still segregated. The question the Court addressed in *Swann v Charlotte-Mecklenberg Board of Education,* then, was whether racially neutral assignments of schoolchildren to their neighborhood schools complied with the *Brown* decision if those neighborhood schools remained segregated because of past discrimination in housing or the placement and size of neighborhood schools. The Supreme Court answered the question in the negative, claiming that the community had to invoke a series of measures, including busing schoolchildren, to "counteract the continuing effects of past school segregation resulting from discriminatory location of school sites or distortion of school size in order to achieve or maintain an artificial racial separatism." [28]

From an anti–affirmative action point of view, *Swann* violates the progressive impulses of civil rights reform because it looks to the effects of past discrimination in assessing the degree to which ideals of equality have been realized. Having outlawed the official segregation of schoolchildren, on this analysis of the meaning of the principle of equal opportunity, the Court could and should have ignored the historical segregation of whites and blacks arising from housing patterns and school sites, even if these were themselves the result of discrimination. Still, if we understand the principle of equal opportunity to require not only an end to officially supported discrimination but a commitment to inclusion, then the consequences of past discrimination become more problematic. They continue to contribute to the exclusion of blacks from participation in common endeavors with whites and thereby continue to deny blacks the contacts and opportunities for discussion and influence that are available to whites.

Graglia writes, "in *Swann,* the Court held, incredibly, that 'desegregation' requires that public schoolchildren be excluded from the neighborhood schools because of their race and transported across large school districts to achieve a near-perfect racial balance." [29] The busing that the *Swann* decision required, however, was not a great increase over the amount of busing already in place in either the area or the country (in which 40 percent of schoolchildren were already bused to school). Nor, the Court ruled, was the concept of neighborhood schools sacrosanct. After all, for years in the rural South, African American schoolchildren had been transported across many school districts, passing many white-only schools, to reach their segregated schools. If cities could use busing to enforce Jim Crow laws, it is unclear why they could not use it to promote integration.[30]

The same integrationist reasoning linking the principle of equality to that of inclusion holds for the Court's majority decisions in *Griggs* and *Weber*. Graglia's criticism of the *Griggs* ruling is based on the availability of white applicants who could meet the employment criteria. But if these criteria were, as the Court found, irrelevant to the job and functioned to preclude the employment of significant numbers of African Americans, then they also served as barriers to their equal opportunity understood in its connection to racial integration.

In his dissent to *United Steelworkers v Weber,* Justice Rehnquist interpreted Title VII in terms of an account of the legislative history of the Civil Rights Act that emphasizes the importance of an interpretive memorandum submitted by the bill's floor managers. In the memorandum, the floor managers explicitly denied that Title VII would require employers to maintain any sort of racial balance in their workforce. "On the contrary," they wrote, "any deliberate attempt to maintain a racial balance would require an employer to hire or to refuse to hire on the basis of race," precisely the criterion that, in Rehnquist's reading, Title VII prohibits.[31] In deciding otherwise, he claimed, the Court "introduces into Title VII a tolerance for the very evil that the law was intended to eradicate."[32]

But this is a contestable conclusion. Whatever the thoughts and even intentions of its floor managers, Congress passed the Civil Rights Act as part of the United States' commitment to a principle of equal opportunity, and, as we have seen, this principle has a legitimate connection, not simply to conceptions of racial neutrality, but also to ideals of racial integration. Justice Brennan articulated these connections for the majority in *Weber*, emphasizing the steelworkers' voluntary attempt to reverse the exclusion of African Americans from their worklife and to abolish traditional patterns of racial segregation. Writing for the majority he thus argued that, while section 703(j) of the Civil Rights Act prohibited the government from requiring a business to extend preferential treatment for minorities, it could not prohibit a business from so doing. Indeed, he claimed, "it would be ironic . . . if a law triggered by a Nation's concern over centuries of racial injustice and intended to improve the lot of those who had 'been excluded from an American dream for so long,' constituted the first legislative prohibition of all voluntary, private, race-conscious efforts to abolish traditional patterns of racial segregation and hierarchy." [33]

The *Swann* decision rejected the idea that an equal and inclusive society could emerge from principles of racial neutrality if racial discrimination had already established housing patterns and dictated school sites and sizes. By the same token, *Griggs* and *Weber* suggested that the realization of such a society would also be blocked by forms of education, career aspirations, and employment patterns, themselves created by a history of discrimination. In 1965, Lyndon Johnson famously insisted that "you do not take a person who, for years, has been hobbled by chains and liberate him, bring him to the starting line of a race and then say, 'You are free to compete with all others' and still justly believe that you have been completely fair." [34] Nor, we might add, can you justly believe that you have really included him or her in the competition. Instead, if the descendants of the historically included and the descendants of the previously excluded are now to compete in the same race as equal contestants, affirmative action policies that recognize the effects of lengthy and systematic past discrimination on test scores, educational achievement, career aspirations, and employment patterns are legitimate measures. Such policies are not a perversion of *Brown,* the other school desegregation cases, or the Civil Rights Act. They represent the continuation of the integrationist goals these decisions and the Civil Rights Act announced.

The issue affirmative action seeks to address is the question of how to include as equals into the full life of American society a group that was first enslaved and later systematically and legally excluded by that same society. The extension of affirmative action policies beyond African Americans to other minorities and women depends upon the same premises: that the principle of equal opportunity for all requires the inclusion, integration, and participation of those groups previously subjected to an active, systematic, and historically complete exclusion. In certain areas, most conspicuously major league baseball, the end of racial distinctions also arguably meant full integration. In other, equally important parts of American life, discrimination and segregation had a more disastrous effect. In these cases, the sense of equal opportunity that encompasses the necessity of full inclusion and integration into the society requires more active efforts.

Still, even if affirmative action policies can be justified as part of the integrationist hopes of the struggle for racial equality, opponents can and have claimed that such policies are counterproductive, at least as far as African Americans are concerned. Because affirmative action does not end but promotes the use of racial classifications, and, furthermore, because it often involves the employment of different standards for whites and blacks, it serves, in the view of its critics, only to sustain the prejudice that blacks are less qualified than whites and that they cannot succeed without preferential treatment. In addition, non-black individuals, with no part in the American history of involuntary slavery and discrimination, can legitimately infer that they are paying, unjustly, for the wrongs of the past. By promoting these ideas and prejudices, critics contend, affirmative action undermines its own integrationist goals. It divides American society and erects the same segregating railing around the African Americans admitted into contemporary businesses, institutions, and professions that Oklahoma once erected around George McLaurin. I want to address this issue in the next part of this chapter. For, while critics of affirmative action ignore that aspect of the meaning of our principle of equality that involves the participation of all in the practices and institutions of the society, the restigmatization of African Americans and minorities within these institutions indicates, I think, the equally damaging consequence of ignoring the importance of the connection between equality and neutrality.

AFFIRMATIVE ACTION AND STIGMATIZATION

Shelby Steele writes, "Under affirmative action, the quality that earns us preferential treatment is an implied inferiority. However this inferiority is explained—and it is easily enough explained by the myriad deprivations that grew out of our oppression—it is still inferiority." [35] This sentiment also forms the basis of Stephen L. Carter's suspicions about the meaning of affirmative action policies for African Americans. They stigmatize all African Americans by suggesting that their presence in professions, trades, and universities is typically only the consequence of affirmative action rather than their own merit or qualification. [36] Hence, even those minorities who would have succeeded without the help of racially biased hiring or admissions decisions are assumed to have the places or positions they have only because of their race.

Of course, schools and universities have, for their part, often and uncontroversially factored in differences among students as part of their admissions decisions. [37] As part of their educational mission, they have sought to include students from different countries and different parts of the United States, students with different strengths and talents including athletic, artistic, creative, and purely scholarly abilities, students of both sexes, and students of different ethnic backgrounds. Nor do all applicants compete under the same standards: athletes and children of alumni have notoriously better chances of being accepted to certain institutions than applicants with better records. The presumption in these instances, however, is that all those admitted fall within a certain range of qualification and that completely unqualified athletes or children of alumni cannot win admission even with preferential treatment. Hence, these forms of preferential treatment do not threaten ideals of neutrality to the extent that affirmative action does. For with regard to race, critics of affirmative action insist that the presumption is different. Here the idea is that African Americans are included only because of their race and that they fall outside the range of even slightly or excusably slanted admissions or hiring criteria.

Charles Murray offers two stories that serve to indicate both the price African Americans pay for inclusion in American society under affirmative action premises and the price affirmative action pays when it disregards the relation between equality and neutrality. Drawing on his own observations and statistical evidence, he usefully constructs composites of two African American students, one he calls William, from a middle-class family, whose score of 520 on the mathematics component of the Scholastic Aptitude Test puts him in the 95th percentile of all blacks who took the test, and one he calls Carol, educated at an inner-city school, with the same score. Both are admitted to an ivy league university with separate admissions standards for whites and blacks.

Murray argues that both students would have fared better at institutions where more students had test scores similar to theirs. At these institutions, they would have been treated as equals of the white students and included with them in the various educational enterprises of the university. At the ivy league institution they attend, however, most students consistently outperform them and take from the experience the idea that African Americans are, in general, less able than whites. The consequences of the experience for William and Carol are worse. William works hard during his first semester at the school but receives mediocre grades and eventually stops trying. "He emerges from college with a poor education and is further behind the whites that he was as a freshman."[38] Carol is a student of outstanding abilities, as evidenced by her ability to score well on the Scholastic Aptitude Test despite her inferior education. Still, because she is unprepared for the ivy league school, she is treated condescendingly, and her professors "never push her in the aggressive way they push white students who have her intellectual capacities."[39]

After college, William accepts a position at a corporation that immediately places him on important and visible planning committees, as well as on various teams that present bids to other companies. Meanwhile, white trainees employed with him are given less prestigious assignments and must learn the business of the corporation from the bottom up. The result is that the white trainees learn a great deal about how the business operates and are seen as "go-getters" while "William is perceived to be a bright enough fellow but not much of a detail man and not really much of a self-starter."[40]

Carol suffers an even bleaker fate. She is hired as a reporter by a major newspaper, where it soon becomes clear she cannot write. A white reporter hired at the same time as Carol cannot write either and is let go after a few months. She eventually finds a career that is more suited to her talents and where she is treated as an equal. Carol is, however, kept on at the newspaper because it "cannot afford to have any fewer blacks than it already has."[41] The newspaper gives her some administrative responsibilities and an impressive title to keep her busy. Because of that title she is offered a senior editorial position at another paper, where her now quite noticeable deficiencies become the subject of jokes, most of which "are openly racist."[42]

For Murray, the most tragic aspect of this situation is the fact that Carol, as he constructs her, is an "extremely bright young woman."[43] Had the market been left to govern itself without the intrusions of affirmative action programs, Murray contends that she, as the white woman hired with her as a reporter did, would have found a career more suited to her abilities into which she could have been fully integrated as a person rather than as a black. Indeed, without affirmative action, she would have found a university more apt to take her seriously and to help her develop her abilities in the first place.

Moreover, had either William or Carol attended a less elite institution or started at the appropriate spot in their professions, their intellectual attainments would have been more even with those of white students and their white colleagues, and those whites could not infer from their experience with integration that blacks as a group were less able than whites. To be sure, without affirmative action programs there would be fewer blacks at elite institutions, and blacks would lag behind for "a time." But, Murray insists, "virtually every ethnic group in America has at one time or another lagged behind as a population, and has eventually caught up. In the process . . . the ones who breached the barriers were evidence of the success of that group. Now blacks who breach the barriers tend to be seen as evidence of the inferiority of that group." [44]

While Murray focuses on the impact of affirmative action on black individuals, his analysis also indicates its impact on the ideal of integration. The ideal cannot be met if affirmative action creates the impressions that blacks are less capable than whites and that any achievement by an African American is the result of preferential treatment. Murray's concern in this regard is not a consequence simply of the composites he constructs but is confirmed by an actual controversy in the Piscataway, New Jersey, school district. Due to budget cuts in 1989, the Board of Education decided to eliminate one job in the high school business department. A black teacher was retained and a white teacher with equal qualifications and equal seniority was dismissed for what the school board said were affirmative action purposes. The white teacher sued on the basis of reverse discrimination while the black teacher's actual qualifications for the job were obscured under the premise that she retained her position *only* because she was black.[45] The ideal of integration is also undermined if African American potential is threatened by a system that expects less of blacks and refuses to invest either the time or resources in them that it invests in others. Both considerations can be understood as reasons to continue to take seriously the criticism that deviations from racial neutrality are always problematic for prospects for equality.

For many critics of affirmative action, the second consideration is, in fact, the most telling. Murray claims that the gaps between black scores and white scores on the Scholastic Aptitude Test "clearly mean that we ought to be making an all-out effort to improve elementary and secondary education for blacks." [46] And Carter simply condemns affirmative action as "racial justice on the cheap." [47] Genuine racial justice would require vast improvements in medical care for poor children, skills training, educational improvements "especially at the preschool level," "stable and safe" schools, and improvements in "the social infrastructure of inner-city communities." [48] In contrast, he argues, affirmative action policies have neither decreased the immense differences in the wealth of different individuals and groups in the United States nor created opportunities for the most socially and economically disadvantaged African Americans. Instead, the gap between the median incomes of black families and white families has increased while the primarily middle-class blacks who have received the benefits of affirmative action could have succeeded without them and, what is more important, without the un-warranted and segregating stigmatization they bring with them.

This analysis suggests a more disturbing critique of affirmative action than the original and somewhat simplistic critique that it constitutes a travesty of America's commitment to the principle of equal opportunity, a principle such critics one-sidedly associate solely with the principle of racial neutrality. Rather, this second critique of affirmative action suggests that it constitutes a travesty of America's commitment to equal opportunity even when understood in terms of its connection to racial integration. Thus, if there is an important distinction to be made between the principle of equal opportunity and an end to racial classification, the opposition to affirmative action serves to remind us that there is also an important distinction to be made between inclusion and integration. The implication of stories such as the Piscataway case or those that Murray constructs is that racial classification and race-consciousness in hiring and admissions decisions may perhaps serve to include African Americans in the major institutions, trades, and professions of American society. They do not serve to integrate them, however. Rather, affirmative action includes blacks as blacks or, as Carter puts it, as "the best blacks" rather than the best individuals for the position. And he insists,

> This dichotomy between "best" and "best black" is not merely something manufactured by racists to denigrate the abilities of professionals who are not white. On the contrary . . . it is reinforced . . . every time employers are urged to set aside test scores and to hire from separate lists. . . . It is reinforced every time state pension plans are pressed to invest some of their funds with "minority-controlled" money management firms, even if . . . the competing white firms have superior track records. It is reinforced every time students demand that universities commit to hiring some pre-set number of minority faculty members.[49]

The response of Murray and other critics to the resegregation of African Americans within the institutions and practices into which they are included has been to advocate, again, an end to affirmative action policies. The ground on which this response is based is presumably that racial neutrality not only comprises the better part of the meaning of equal opportunity but also remains the better route to racial integration. On its own, Murray insists, white guilt can serve as a powerful motivation for hiring blacks so that, even without affirmative action laws, businesses and professions would nonetheless seek out truly qualified blacks. "The laws and the court decisions and the continuing intellectual respectability behind preferential treatment," he writes, "are not holding many doors open to qualified blacks that would otherwise be closed." [50]

But the experience of white women seems to belie this expectation. The problem they encountered before affirmative action policies were extended in their directions was not that they were undereducated or unqualified on paper. Nor did they suffer from debilitating economic circumstances or social neglect. Many women grew up in relatively privileged conditions, went to professional schools, and did as well or better than their male counterparts. Still, the perception persisted that only certain sorts of jobs or careers were suitable for women and that very few of these could be demanding ones because of women's role in the family. Raising the society's consciousness about both the capabilities of women in the public sphere and the capabilities of men in the private sphere might have achieved some progress on its own, without the prodding of courts and governments. But it is by no means clear that all of Murray's optimism with regard to the consequences of either racial or gender neutrality is justified.

If the consequence of affirmative action has been to single out rather than to integrate African Americans within American institutions, a second response to this form of resegregation has been, I think, a subtle shift in the justification of affirmative action by those who defend it. Indeed, while this chapter has stressed the connections between principles of antidiscrimination, equal opportunity, and racial integration, today racial integration appears to be an old-fashioned ideal. Contemporary defenses of affirmative action stress the differences between different groups, differences not only between whites and blacks but between men and women, Latinos and Anglos, heterosexuals and homosexuals, and so on. Hiring and admissions decisions now are not to try to include members of these different groups, so defined, as part of an attempt to integrate the institutions of the United States. Nor need these decisions acknowledge any role for neutrality in our conception of equality. Rather, hiring and admissions decisions are to include members of different groups as a celebration of American diversity.

As the so-called politics of difference tells us, the problem with an integrationist ground for affirmative action is that it is also assimilationist. The vision of the United States as a grand melting pot surreptitiously takes white, male America as the norm and requires all those groups accepted into its public life to conform to standards set by the white males who once monopolized it. White males constitute the standard for the normal employee or citizen and others must cut and prune their identities and commitments to fit this preestablished norm. Female employees, for example, must be willing to treat normal female functions such as pregnancy as disabilities and to work the same hours male employees work, whether or not these hours are strictly necessitated by the nature of the work. By so doing, however, the ideal of integration denies differences in the experiences, orientations, and historical or cultural commitments of different groups and, more important, stifles the unique perspectives they can bring to American civic and political life.

In contrast, the more contemporary view of affirmative action connects it to a concern with the struggle for recognition of different groups. Those who are not white, not male, and not heterosexual challenge the assumption that white, male, heterosexual thought, attitude, and behavior constitute the standards by which others are to be judged. Instead, blacks, women, and minorities demand to be accepted as full parts of important institutions without being assimilated to white, male norms. They are to be accepted as who they are in their particular ethnicity, gender, sexual orientation, and commitments.[51] The vision here is no longer that of a melting pot in which cultural, historical, and traditional differences disappear. It is rather that of a rainbow or multicolored rope that holds a multicultural society up and binds it together.

There are two different foundations for a concern with diversity, however. One concern seems to liken our social and political institutions not as much to a multicolored rope as to a zoo: we are to employ affirmative action programs to admit different specimens of predefined and diverse groups into our public life, and we are to do so to learn about each others' customs, traditions, and interests while experiencing each others' point of view. The former chancellor of the University of California at Berkeley, among others, thus argues that different groups should be admitted to the university to help educate students about the different groups and cultures with whom they will have to live as members of a multicultural society.[52] On this view, the purpose of affirmative action is no longer that of satisfying an integrationist principle of equal opportunity and antidiscrimination. Rather, members of different groups are to be helped to participate in American institutions as representative samples of the talents, attitudes, perspectives, and beliefs of the group to which they belong.

Yet to the extent that this defense of affirmative action focuses on differences in gender, skin color, race, sexual orientation, and the like, it also often assumes a kind of homogenization within the selected groups.[53] All African Americans, other minorities, or women are supposed to be not only different from all other races or groups but also absolutely similar to everyone within their own races or groups. What primarily matters about them as university applicants or job recruits are not the complexities of self-identification, allegiance, and heritage but rather only stereotyped aspects of their identity involving their race, ethnicity, sexual orientation, or gender. Hence, they are to be helped by affirmative action programs not because of the promise they hold but rather because of the types they are presumed to represent. Moreover, if critics of affirmative action such as Carter and Murray are to be believed, the "type" African Americans are meant to represent is one that is typically presumed to include a lack of real merit.

The other foundation for a concern with diversity is more consistent with American ideals of equal opportunity interpreted to include integrationist ideals. Here the point is that certain people were excluded from certain professions, trades, and institutions because of their ethnicity, race, or sex and, moreover, that the exclusion was so systematic and debilitating that it would dictate a continued exclusion of people with a similar ethnicity, race, or sex unless more affirmative steps were taken. In this case, diversity is not the goal of affirmative action as much as it is a happy consequence of trying to rectify a historically devastating and unsustainable practice. Many individuals who are admitted into universities or professions on the basis of integrationist ideals will still bring with them the different perspectives, life experiences, and interests that are the goal of diversity. Moreover, they may well do so because, under current social conditions, their race, sex, or ethnicity has offered them these different perspectives, experiences, and interests. Further, some of these perspectives and interests might help restructure institutions and professions to allow all to participate equally. Hence, for example, because women continue to take on the larger share of domestic and child-rearing duties in the family, admitting women into universities, corporations, and the like raises issues about the structure of work, school, family, and child care that were not previously raised. Nevertheless, there remains a difference between including people in a university or profession because they are different and appreciating or even trying to learn from the differences they bring with them once they are admitted.

To this extent, the challenge that a politics of difference raises against the ideal of integration seems misdirected. The meaning of this ideal comprises more than the simple inclusion of minorities or women into professions, trades, and the like. Rather, it anticipates their full participation as equals and, indeed, connects the realization of principles of equality to full participation. But the meaning of an ideal of integration also differs from that of assimilation. People possess different interests, concerns, assumptions, and views because of the different experiences they have had, the different traditions in which they have been reared, and the different environments in which they have matured. To the extent that these differences have historical links to skin color, race, or gender, blacks, women, white men, and others will also tend to differ from one another in important ways. Members of a multicultural society might learn not only to appreciate these differences but to consider which set of social, political, and economic institutions might best accommodate them.

Still, the concern with accommodating differences need not have a homogenizing thrust. One question the principle of equal opportunity raises for Americans is how to integrate blacks, other minorities, or women into the public, social, and civic life of American society after trying to exclude them for so long. Another question concerns what changes might be required in the structure of work, politics, or society to allow their full participation. But the idea that these questions suggest, that different groups can provide a society with diverse attitudes, views, and perspectives—for example, when women enter the workforce they raise questions about balancing career and family that were not raised in the same way before and that may require a restructuring of corporate culture—should not be confused with a categorizing and even essentializing concern with diversity. In a multicultural society, the principle of equal opportunity for all brings diversity with it, but the principle remains a principle of equal opportunity.

In contrast, the recourse to diversity on the zoo model is the consequence of giving up on the integrationist aims that affirmative action has traditionally included. The idea seems to be that, if affirmative action leads to inclusion without integration, if it is, in fact, complicitous with a new form of segregation, let us simply extol this kind of universal segregation of all by all and call it diversity.[54] Of course, if instead we restore the integrationist goals of affirmative action, we still need an answer to the criticism that it cannot fulfill them. In the final section of this chapter I want to consider what this answer might be.

AFFIRMATIVE ACTION AND INTEGRATION

Even if Murray's and Carter's accounts of the counterproductive side effects of affirmative action, at least for African Americans, are accurate, they need not signal the need to return to strict principles of racial neutrality as the only solution to what Murray calls the new racism. Both theorists are certainly justified not only in pointing to the way in which affirmative action policies seem simply to stigmatize blacks but, in addition, in asking whether, for this reason, they can really substitute for a commitment to social and economic justice. Affirmative action cannot compensate for failing schools, an inadequate health care system, substandard housing, a lack of decent jobs or affordable day care, or crime- and drug-infested inner cities. If the justification of affirmative action lies in the attempt to integrate members of previously excluded groups because such integration is part of the meaning of equal opportunity, then its efforts need to be combined with sincere attempts to end poverty and improve American education and access to it. But if the experience of women is any indication, neither is it clear that a commitment of resources to these ends can substitute for affirmative action. Rather, some effort will continue to be needed to overcome the patterns of aspiration and discrimination that would persist without it.

In this regard, it is not clear that affirmative action has been as abject a failure as Murray concludes. African Americans, minorities, and women have entered trades, police departments, fire departments, and other government services that were traditionally closed to them. They are professors, doctors, and lawyers in clearly increased if still pathetic numbers and the economic mobility of blacks has increased substantially. According to Martin Kilson, stable working-class, middle-class, and upper-middle-class households now compose nearly 65 percent of black households. Blacks now compose 2.1 percent of marketing and public relations managers, 6.3 percent of property and real estate managers, 6.7 percent of computer programmers, 15.5 percent of educational and vocational counselors, 7.6 percent of accountants and auditors, 7.2 percent of therapists, 7.1 percent of registered nurses, and 7.2 percent of engineering technicians. In 1970, just 2 percent of the officers in the armed services were black. In 1990, due in large part to affirmative action pressure, 12 percent were black,[55] including one whom many blacks and whites hoped would run for president of the United States.

To be sure, it appears that affirmative action has done little for the 30 percent of blacks caught in what Kilson calls the "static strata." Nor, crucially, is evidence of the inclusion of African Americans in the institutions of American society simultaneously evidence of their full integration. But it is certainly not clear that they would have made equal strides as quickly without affirmative action. Moreover, it is not clear either that all the blacks, minorities, or women in all trades and professions are considered to be unqualified by their colleagues or even that those colleagues have the definitive conceptions of the meaning of qualification and merit in hiring or acceptance decisions that opponents of affirmative action assume they have. As Cornel West points out, "Most Americans realize that job-hiring choices are made both on reasons of merit and on personal grounds." Since this personal dimension is easily susceptible to consciously racist attitudes or even unconscious preconceptions based on the sorts of individuals who typically fill the position, the relevant question, as West puts it, "is never 'merit vs. race' but whether hiring decisions will be based on merit, influenced by race-bias against blacks, or on merit, influenced by race-bias, but with special consideration for minorities and women, as mandated by law." [56]

In any case, the continuing demonstration by African Americans, women, and other minorities across the spectrum of American institutions that they are more than competent to perform the tasks required of them would seem to be at least as powerful a tool for undermining racism and sexism as it is for reinforcing them. As Randall Kennedy writes, "in the end, the uncertain extent to which affirmative action diminishes the accomplishments of blacks must be balanced against the stigmatization that occurs when blacks are virtually absent from important institutions in the society." [57]

West's and Kennedy's claims seem to suggest that if integration remains a goal of American society, affirmative action should not be charged with all the stigmatization blacks encounter. Kennedy, in fact, insists that the stigmatization of blacks is a mere continuation of the racism that has always plagued American society. It is hard to discount this position since so many Americans seem more outraged at forms of preferential treatment that benefit African Americans or women and other minorities than they are at other forms of preference enjoyed by athletes applying to college or the children of alumni at the institutions their parents attended. But perhaps there is a more important point to be made. Suppose affirmative action has helped to include, if not to integrate, those that were previously excluded from our public life. Suppose, despite the problems it involves in terms of stigmatizing some blacks and irritating some whites, it has helped to bring more African

Americans as well as more minorities and women into more parts of American life. Then analyses of affirmative action should neither be focusing on its failures nor simply celebrating its success in promoting inclusion and diversity. Instead, they should be focusing on the question of how we might now take the next step from inclusion toward full integration.

Despite his worries about affirmative action, Carter, for one, does not think it should be completely dismantled. Rather, he proposes a more moderate approach that, in a way, combines both criticisms and defenses of affirmative action. African Americans who seem, like Carol in Murray's composite, to have achieved a great deal despite inferior schooling and the legacy of racism should, Carter thinks, continue to be given a chance. They should be admitted into universities, the standards of which they may not completely meet on paper, in order to be given the opportunity to demonstrate their abilities. Such candidates will pose more of a risk than candidates who do meet all the qualifications on paper. Still, the risk is justified as a means of assuring that, in the attempt to find the best students, universities do not overlook promising black candidates because of factors of discrimination, schooling, and upbringing beyond their control.

As African Americans move up what Carter calls the affirmative action pyramid, however, this justification becomes less and less telling in his view. Perhaps one cannot catch up completely during one's undergraduate years so that some additional affirmative action is justified for graduate and professional schools. But at a certain point, Carter insists, one has to have demonstrated what one can do, and at that point individuals should compete as individuals. "The time has come, finally to stand or fall on what one has actually achieved. . . . The preferences cannot go on forever. Sooner or later, talent and preparation, rather than skin color must tell." [58] And at this point, Carter suggests that the way to close what I have understood as the gap between inclusion and integration is unquestionable achievement. Those that have benefited from affirmative action are, Carter asserts, *"for the rest of their professional lives* . . . to bend to their work with an energy that will leave competitors and detractors alike gasping in admiration. The way to turn this potential liability [the stigmatization issuing from affirmative action] into a powerful asset is to make our cadre of professionals simply too good to ignore." [59] And as he reiterates:

> If affirmative action opens some doors at the level of college or professional school entry, fine; let us then be unembarrassed about it. Thereafter, our

job—and it is a job, one we should undertake cheerfully on behalf of our people . . . —is to make the most of the opportunities affirmative action creates. . . . Only then will we be able to look boorish interviewers and colleagues (and the genuinely racist ones, too) squarely in the eye and say . . . "Sure, I got into law school because I'm black—so what?" [60]

Of course, this strategy seems to place the burden of transforming inclusion into integration on the blacks, minorities, and women who have been stigmatized, first, by discrimination and, second, by affirmative action. It seems overly optimistic to assume that African Americans or other previously excluded groups might themselves remove the animosity directed at affirmative action policies simply by being too good to ignore. A great many are already too good to ignore. If affirmative action policies structured as a pyramid as Carter suggests were combined with a sincere war on poverty, however, the combination might succeed in preparing blacks, other minorities, and women for the careers they desire without stigmatizing them in their eventual participation in those careers. In other words, there is an obvious way to rid society of the presumption that women, minorities, and particularly blacks are not qualified for the opportunities offered them or, in any case, not as qualified as the white men who were at one time assured exclusive access to those opportunities. That way need not ignore the connection between equality and participation. Nor need it abandon affirmative action as a barrier to racial and gender neutrality. Rather, as citizens we might continue to endorse legislation that opens to women and minorities the opportunities once reserved for white men; but, in addition, we might demand schools that can educate us all well, policies that can stabilize the environments in which we grow up, and programs that offer substantial assistance to families who need it. If the goal of affirmative action is understood to be that of full integration, and if full integration is understood in its connection with the principle of equal opportunity, then preferences aimed at involving members of historically excluded groups as full participants in American society are not a perversion of the principle of equal opportunity. Nor, however, are they sufficient on their own.

The point of affirmative action remains what its supporters have always insisted it was: race, ethnicity, and gender consciousness to achieve race, ethnicity, and gender integration that complies with a respect for neutrality. But the ideals of integration are not realized just because a society either eliminates official restrictions on the education and career paths of certain people or actively includes them in its professions and institutions. Rather, integration requires their full and equal participation in the life of the society. And this goal would seem to necessitate both affirmative action and a commitment of material resources. Sympathetic critics of affirmative action understand it as a "small, flawed" substitute for this commitment of resources, a substitute required by the decline of the American economy in the 1970s.[61] But clearly the United States could establish adequate training programs to educate a workforce for a new sort of economy, could institute serious programs and encourage corporations to help develop its inner cities, could enact procedures to enhance the safety of its citizens, and could decline to assist in creating huge disparities in income and wealth. The fact that it does not is a failure of will, not a failure of either affirmative action itself or the connection it expresses between equality and participation.

CHAPTER FOUR

Interpretive Differences and the Abortion Debate

The argument of the last chapter was that close interpretive attention to the principles of equality and equal opportunity reveals the dogmatism in antiaffirmative action arguments that try to understand their meaning only in terms of an ideal of racial neutrality. Such an understanding of these principles ignores ideals of equal participation and racial, gender, and ethnic integration that also constitute aspects of the principle of equal opportunity. At the same time, to the extent that affirmative action has led to inclusion rather than integration, opponents of affirmative action are justified in remaining skeptical of the challenge it raises to ideals of neutrality. Instead of seeking to scuttle affirmative action programs, however, this skepticism might serve to encourage both governmental and corporate efforts to supplement affirmative action with other programs to ensure the full participation that is part of our understanding of equality.

In this chapter I want to turn to the debate over abortion. In considering both surrogate mothering and affirmative action I have been concerned to open up the discussion of these issues to interpretations of meaning that have not received as much attention as others. By shifting attention away from dogmatic and essentialist views of women in the surrogate mothering debate, I tried to show that our conception of family is one that allows for the legitimacy of very different kinds of family and custody relationships. The controversy over affirmative action also begins to look much more tractable once we allow that our understanding of the principle of equality includes the ideal of full participation. In contrast to these two debates, both sides in the debate over abortion have already received ample attention. Indeed, the debate has proceeded for so long and so noisily that many dimensions of the principles it involves, those of life and liberty, have already been unearthed. Rather than resurrecting dimensions of the meaning of the relevant principles that the debate may have overlooked, in my consideration of the abortion debate I shall be more concerned to reconstruct the pro-life and pro-choice sides of the debate as they already exist and to show what they might learn from one another.

As noted in Chapter One, the American debate over the practice of abortion is generally pursued as a conflict over which of two competing moral principles ought to govern the issue. Those who argue that abortion is morally impermissible appeal to the principle of the sanctity of life, claiming that abortion constitutes the simple destruction of innocent human life. There is no clear line in pregnancy at which a fetus becomes a person, no clear line separating a fetus of eight months' gestation from an infant and no clear line separating an infant from a child. Hence, if it is wrong to kill a child or an infant, it is equally wrong to abort a fetus. In the antiabortion view, this argument also decides the legal question of whether a right to an abortion is guaranteed by a Constitutional principle protecting a right to privacy. If abortion is the destruction of innocent human life, then any attempt to find a right to an abortion in the Constitution violates one of the most basic rights it was written to protect.

Those who argue that abortion must remain legally accessible appeal to moral and legal principles of liberty. In the first place, they argue that "Nothing is more devastating than a life without liberty." [1] Women have certain rights over their persons, and among these rights is the right to decide when to give birth to a child for whom they will be responsible. In the second place, with regard to legal rights they argue that if the state cannot compel a woman to pursue a certain profession, marry a certain person, or live in a certain place, it also cannot compel her to carry a pregnancy to term. Rather, at the point at which a fetus is essentially part of its mother's body, this is a personal and private decision.

To conceive of the debate over abortion in this way is, to use Lawrence Tribe's terms, to consider it a "clash of absolutes." [2] Those who reject or seek to limit access to legal abortions think that those who support it sin against moral principles protecting the sanctity of life while those who support a woman's right to choose to have a legal abortion think that those who want to restrict it sin against principles of freedom. But in this chapter I want to suggest that there is a way out of this impasse once we concede that the controversy is less a clash over competing principles than an interpretive debate over the meaning of both moral and legal principles we already share. As I already suggested in Chapter One, Americans differ on the question of abortion, not because they adhere to different absolute principles pitting life against liberty, but rather because they interpret both principles differently. Moreover, they interpret these principles differently because they understand the meaning of human life, sexuality, and traditional gender differences differently and because these differences are rooted in different life experiences, upbringings, and even existential attitudes. I shall suggest that at least some of the differences are equally legitimate and, further, that rather than selecting one principle—life or liberty—over the other as the appropriate standard to govern the debate we might try to learn from the different ways we can interpret our ideals in this case. If we do so, we might also look for ways of accommodating our differences over abortion, just as we might try to accommodate our differences in custody disputes because we acknowledge different legitimate family relationships and try to accommodate our differences over affirmative action because we acknowledge the place of an ideal of participation in our shared principle of equality. I shall begin to try to encourage a similar accommodation in the abortion debate by considering Ronald Dworkin's analysis in *Life's Dominion: An Argument about Abortion, Euthanasia, and Individual Freedom* since his analysis in part presumes the interpretive turn I have wanted to make in this study as a whole.[3]

DWORKIN'S RESOLUTION OF THE DEBATE

Life's Dominion begins by claiming that there are two different ideas contained in the pro-life claim that the fetus is a person. On the one hand, this claim might be taken to mean that fetuses are creatures with interests of their own, primarily an interest in staying alive, and that as creatures with interests they also have rights, primarily a right to life. Dworkin calls the opposition to abortion that derives from this claim a "derivative" opposition since it rests on claims about the rights and interests of persons in general.[4]

On the other hand, the claim that the fetus is a person might be taken to mean simply that human life has an intrinsic value. On the view of this "detached" opposition to abortion, abortion is morally wrong not because it violates the rights and interests of persons but simply because human life is sacred and inviolable and it remains inviolable whatever the rights and interests of persons. As Dworkin writes, "For just as someone can think it wrong to remove life support from a permanently vegetative patient or to assist a dying cancer patient to kill himself, whether or not death is in the patient's interests, so one can think it wrong to destroy a fetus whether or not a fetus has any interests to protect." [5]

Dworkin dismisses the plausibility of the "derivative" objection to abortion. We cannot argue, he insists, that because something will have rights and interests in the future it has them now or that because I have a right to life now that I could not possess unless I had not been aborted as a fetus then I possessed that right as a fetus. As he puts the point, "it makes no sense to suppose that something has interests of its own—as distinct from its being important what happens to it—unless it has, or has had, some form of consciousness: some mental as well as physical life." But this is just what a fetus does not have until quite late in a woman's pregnancy. Dworkin claims that fetuses cannot even experience pain

> before a connection is made between the fetus's thalamus, into which peripheral nerve receptors flow, and its developing neocortex; and though the timing of that connection is still uncertain, it almost certainly takes place after mid-gestation. . . . These thalamic fibers do not begin to form synapses with cortical neurons until some later time, moreover, which has been estimated to be at about twenty-five weeks. [6]

To be sure, someone can act against my interests without causing me primarily physical pain. But capacities to form emotions, affections, joys, hopes, and expectations that someone might dash or disappoint are even more complex than capacities for pain. Dworkin claims, "it seems very unlikely" that these develop "in primitive or trace or shadowy form" before "the point of cortical maturation, at around thirty weeks of gestational age." [7]

It is important to Dworkin that only about .01 percent of abortions take place in the third trimester, or after the beginning of fetal sentience according to current scientific understanding, and that most of these are necessitated to save the life or health of the mother. But he also thinks that most opponents to abortion rights in fact hold the detached rather than the derivative view. [8] Here he points to the same circumstance to which Tribe also points: that pro-life proponents are willing to make exceptions for cases in which the mother's life is at issue or in which she has been raped. [9] As Tribe does, Dworkin insists that pro-life advocates could not make such exceptions if their concern were really the fetus's right to life since, obviously, fetuses would retain this right whether or not their mother's life was at risk and whether or not she had been raped. But, in contrast to Tribe, Dworkin links these exceptions not to a conservative sexual agenda but to the "detached" idea that the life of a fetus has an intrinsic significance that ought to be respected. Under this idea, the view that the exceptions for rape or the life of the mother are morally sustainable rests on the ability to weigh the biological significance of human life against the value of the mother's life or against the disvalue of the acts of violence and coercion through which the pregnancy occurred.

Yet the idea that human life has a sacred value is not only at the core of most objections to abortion; Dworkin claims that it is an idea that pro-choice advocates share. The "paradigm" pro-choice position, he argues, is not one that defends abortion as, say, the moral equivalent of a tonsillectomy. Rather, it is one that understands the moral gravity of a decision to abort a human life but is equally concerned with the moral gravity of wasting a human life, a price that can be incurred when a young girl must give up her future to care for a baby or when a mother's physical or psychological health or the life prospects of her family are endangered or when the life to be created is one that is so diseased as to be unbearably painful for the child itself.[10] On this paradigm position, abortion is sometimes a morally legitimate choice, not because people have absolute rights over their bodies, but because aborting the fetus appears to those involved to be the most morally responsible alternative in view of the circumstances.

Dworkin concludes that what the two sides on the abortion controversy share is as important as how they differ. They do not differ on the moral principles to which they adhere but rather on "how best to respect a fundamental idea we almost all share in some form: that individual life is sacred."[11] Moreover, they differ on this issue because they understand the source of human life's sacred character differently. For the antiabortion position, it devolves from the natural and, for some, even divine miracle of biological reproduction. Human life is a wonder of either God or the creativity of nature and ought not be brought to a premature end by human beings themselves. For the pro-choice position, in contrast, human life is primarily a human miracle. It is a product of the human investment that conscious, self-interpreting individuals make in their own lives and the lives of others. Human beings have dreams and goals for themselves and for those close to them, as well as a sense of the meaning of their past and the investment they have made in their own and others' futures. In certain cases, it is a violation of this human investment to sacrifice it to merely biological life. Hence, under certain circumstances, sacrificing the human investment a young girl has in her own life or the investment a profoundly diseased child and its family might make in a life destined to be short and unforgivably painful is worse than aborting a fetus.

If the issue that divides Americans is an interpretive one about the meaning of human life, then, according to Dworkin, it is also a religious one, one that addresses "the same issues—about the place of an individual human life in an impersonal and infinite universe—as orthodox religious beliefs do for those who hold them." [12] Dworkin insists that religious convictions need not involve a belief in a supreme being: certain forms of Buddhism and Hinduism do without them, and in deciding legally what is to count as a religious conviction in *United States v Seeger* the U.S. Supreme Court held that a man opposed to all war on general ethical principles need not believe in God to be exempted from military service "by reason of religious training and belief." [13] Beliefs count as religious, for Dworkin, then, if their content addresses fundamental questions about the human condition and about the meaning and purpose of human life.

On this account, pro-choice advocates who think that the value of human life necessitates that women themselves be able to choose the circumstances under which they can accept responsibility for bearing a child are expressing religious convictions no less than those who reject the morality of abortion for reasons more typically recognized as religious. The legal implications, according to Dworkin, of this identity in the grounds of our moral convictions means that access to abortion falls under the protection of the First Amendment to the free exercise of religion.[14] Were abortions not legally available, a family who wanted to abort a severely deformed fetus because of the way giving birth to it would frustrate the family's understanding of the value of human life would be denied the free exercise of their religion. Conversely, those with a different understanding of the same value would not be denied the free exercise of their religion if they chose to bring the fetus to term in a society in which abortions remained legally available.

Yet Dworkin admits that in certain instances the government legitimately imposes a certain conception of inherent value on all its citizens, whether or not they share the same convictions. It collects taxes to support art museums and cultural institutions, for example, and it passes legislation protecting the environment and endangered species. "Why," he asks, "should government not have the power to enforce a much more passionate conviction—that abortion is a desecration of the inherent value that attaches to every human life?"[15] His answer is that impositions of value in the form of views about culture and the environment do not raise Constitutional issues since they do not concern the religious question of the value of human life. Instead, they presumably concern less fundamental convictions about the value of art and nature *for* human life.

But if the right to an abortion is now to be legally protected as part of the principle of the free exercise of religion in which the law recognizes legitimate differences in religious beliefs, do Americans not also differ in their understanding of what counts as religion and its free exercise just as they differ on their understanding of the sanctity of life? Attitudes toward art are not supposed to raise fundamental issues. But might not one take art as one's religion, as an attempt to give value to the human condition and to represent the meaning and purpose of human life in the same way that religion does? If governments support art museums and public art, then why are they not imposing a conception of the value of human life? And if they support certain art museums and certain forms of public art while rejecting others, are they not imposing their specific conception of the value of human life on all their citizens? Conversely, if with Dworkin we assume that the value of art is a secular one, are we not also assuming a shared understanding of the difference between religious and secular ideas?

The same ambiguity extends our understanding of the value of nature. Suppose those opposing environmental legislation do so on the basis of a religious conviction of the greater value of human life over that of endangered species. Many groups do oppose governmental protection of the spotted owl, for example, just because it places the value of an endangered species over that of the ability of loggers to provide food and clothing for their families, pursue their employment opportunities, and live their chosen form of life. If questions about the intrinsic value of human life are to be deemed religious questions, perhaps we will have to support the logging industry over endangered species on the basis of the freedom of religion.

Of course, many environmental groups view animal life as intrinsically just as valuable as human life and, indeed, understand their environmentalism in explicitly religious terms. Indeed, to place more value on human life or, at the very least, not to understand the balance in nature of human and nonhuman life, is a moral, cosmological, and religious blindness of the highest order. Still, just as we must support the right to an abortion, in Dworkin's view, because it does not require those opposed to abortion to have one and thus does not undermine their religious freedom, we shall have to support the logger's view of the intrinsically higher value of human over owl life since doing so does not require religiously oriented environmental groups to log. In sum, it is not clear that we can assume that we agree in our understanding of when a value is a religious one and when it is less fundamental. Indeed, we might have to question government regulations on the right to sell body parts or challenge proposed sanctions against human cloning since the values involved in these prohibitions seem to involve fundamental values about human life and would therefore seem to be subject to the principle of the free exercise of religion. In Dworkin's view, a woman has a right to determine for herself whether or not to have an abortion because her values and her conception of the sanctity of human life are at bottom religious convictions. But it remains unclear why those holding the detached objection to abortion cannot understand the issue in terms akin to those we apply to community support for art, the value of nature, and the disvalue of selling body parts or cloning oneself, issues not reserved for individuals to decide for themselves but open to community decision and regulation.

Dworkin limits our legitimate interpretive differences to our different understandings of the sacred character of human life. The debate over abortion can then be resolved by showing the religious roots of our different positions on this meaning and appealing to a principle on which all Americans agree as to the right to the free exercise of one's religion. But if the range of our different understandings extends to differences over the meaning and scope of what is to count as a religious value, then the solution to the debate is not so easy. We cannot assume that we differ just in our understanding of the sanctity of life while agreeing in our interpretation of what religion or its free exercise is. Rather, we shall have to admit that our differences extend more broadly. The broad sources of our differences over abortion form the focus of studies that both Kristin Luker and Faye Ginsburg pursue. In what follows, I turn to their work.[16]

THE EXTENT OF OUR DIFFERENCES

Both the sociological study that Luker published in 1984 as *Abortion and the Politics of Motherhood* and the socioanthropological study that Ginsburg published in 1989 as *Contested Lives: The Abortion Debate in an American Community* serve, in part, to support and deepen Dworkin's view of the character of the opposition between pro-life and pro-choice views of abortion. As Dworkin does, they both indicate that the debate over abortion contains more and different conflicts than that simply over the question of whether the fetus is a person and hence whether abortion is murder or not. In part, however, the studies suggest that Dworkin's solution remains superficial and his emphasis on the common respect both sides possess for the sacred character of human life conceals at least as much as it reveals. The pro-life and pro-choice women that Luker and Ginsburg study differ not only in their views of human fetuses but in their own lives, their existential attitudes toward life, and their understanding of the point of men's and women's lives. Further, they differ so profoundly that they might be said to inhabit entirely different worlds.

The average, female, pro-life advocate, according to Luker, married quite young and has three or more children. Although she might have some college education, she does not work outside the home or have personal income of her own. Nor did she delay having children to pursue a career. Her husband is typically a small businessman who in the early 1980s made approximately $30,000 a year. The pro-life woman, in addition, is usually Catholic and, in any case, sees organized religion as a large part of her life.[17] The average female pro-choice advocate, in contrast, typically marries somewhat later than her pro-life counterpart, has fewer children, and has some graduate or professional training beyond a B.A. degree. She maintains a regular job or professional career and is married to a professional so that in the early 1980s their family income was above $50,000. Organized religion plays almost no part in her life.[18]

These profiles reflect different life choices, experiences, and attitudes. Quite apart from the question of whether the pro-life advocates Luker studied hold a "derivative" or "detached" view of the immorality of abortion, their idea of what respect for human life means encompasses views about the lives of men and women and the meaning of sexual intercourse that are quite different from the pro-choice account of these matters. For pro-life advocates, not only is human life sacred, so is the act of intercourse through which new life begins. Sexual intercourse is meant primarily for procreation and should therefore be engaged in only when one is married and, moreover, open to the possibility of becoming pregnant. Indeed, pro-life advocates are as typically against artificial means of contraception as they are against abortion. Not only do they consider many forms of contraception abortificants; all forms other than

abstinence undermine a reverence for the act of sexual intercourse, re-
ducing it from an act connected to the potential creation of human life
to something merely healthy or fun. Hence, pro-life advocates tend to
view natural family planning, a method of unassisted birth control in
which couples abstain during fertile parts of the woman's cycle, quite
differently from the way pro-choice advocates typically view various
methods of birth control. What is most important about NFP for those
who are pro-life, according to Luker, is neither its effectiveness nor its
reliability, precisely the characteristics pro-choice couples stress in their
estimation of various birth control techniques.[19] Rather, for pro-life advocates it is because sexual intercourse without highly efficient means of
contraception always involves the possibility of creating life that it possesses a sacred quality it cannot have otherwise. As one of the respon-
dents in Luker's study claims, "the frame of mind in which you know
there might be a conception in the midst of a sexual act is quite different from that in which you know there could not be a conception. . . .
I don't think that people who are constantly using physical, chemical
means of contraception really ever experience the sex act in all of its
beauty."[20]

Consistent with this view of contraception is a view of parenthood
that rejects the idea that it must be planned for, prepared for, or fit into
one's overarching life or career plan. Rather, what pro-choice women
call "unwanted pregnancies" are for pro-life women simply "surprise
pregnancies," and there is always room in one's life for the child that results. For some pro-life advocates, this capacity to accommodate un-
planned pregnancies issues from the contours of a woman's life, at least
if she is married and has children. On this view, a woman's life is one devoted primarily to raising children, managing a household, and attending to the needs of her husband. To refuse to allow room in this scenario
for one more child is to choose career and self over care and concern for
others. As Luker amplifies the point,

> it is obvious that a woman who does not work in the paid labor force, who
> does not have a college degree, whose religion is important to her, and who
> has already committed herself wholeheartedly to marriage and a large fam-
> ily is well equipped to believe that an unanticipated pregnancy usually be-
> comes a beloved child. Her life is arranged so that for her, this belief is true.
> This view is consistent not only with her values, which she has held from ear-
> liest childhood, but with her social resources as well.[21]

Ginsburg's research indicates that the connection pro-life advocates
draw between unanticipated pregnancies and beloved children holds for

them even when a woman's life is not yet arranged so that an unanticipated pregnancy can be easily integrated into it. Rather, many pro-life
advocates take a woman's unwillingness to change her life to accommodate a baby or to struggle through less than optimal circumstances for
raising children as a sign of the low status that the domestic work of caring for and nurturing families has in American life.[22] What is most important, namely raising children, is conceived of as a task to be under-
taken only if it is at least somewhat convenient and fits at least somewhat
comfortably into the rest of one's life. Some pro-life advocates insist that
men and women are simply intrinsically different and suited to different
roles in life. Men naturally occupy the public domain of work, while
women tend to the domestic cares of raising children, managing households, and attending to their husbands' needs. But other pro-life advocates do not think that women cannot work outside the home or that, if
they do so, they should not be paid as well as men. Still, they also insist
that caring for children, husbands, and homes is a full-time job on its
own and, moreover, the most important one. Working outside the home
is thus potentially problematic to the extent that it takes time away from
the nurturing of families and encourages a kind of materialism, selfishness, and careerism that many pro-life advocates tie to demands for the
right to abortion. Indeed, in their view defending the right to abortion
is part of an American reversal of values that creates an emotional desert
where the province of care and concern for others ought to be.[23] To this
extent, as Ginsburg puts the point, abortion signifies "a social denial of
nurturance."[24]

From a pro-choice point of view, of course, the pro-life position on
sexual intercourse is simply "medieval"[25] while its view of pregnancy
and childbirth is irresponsible. Sexual intercourse can be "amative" as
well as procreative, and when it possesses a "transcendent" character it
does so, not because of any potential connection to pregnancy and
childbirth, but because of its actual connection to intimacy.[26] Moreover,
one's responsibility to children means that there is not always "room for
one more" or even for one. Parenthood is no longer part of a supposedly
natural scheme of things but is rather optional and therefore special,
requiring special preparations. Children need the best set of emotional,
psychological, social, and financial resources one can provide for them.
Hence, if one is responsible, one will become a parent only when one is
emotionally, psychologically, socially, and financially ready to be one
and to care for children in an appropriate way.[27] As one pro-choice min-
ister responded to Luker, "I remember giving a talk [in which I said] that

I thought one of my roles was to be an advocate for the fetus, and for the fetus's right not to be born. . . . I think if I had my druthers I'd probably advocate the need for licensing pregnancies."[28]

Both pro-life and pro-choice advocates thus appeal to the values of nurturance and care in appealing, jointly, to a principle of the sanctity of human life. Nonetheless, they understand both the values and principle at stake in very different ways: whereas pro-life advocates link the principle of the sanctity of life to the need to accept, gratefully, new human life in all its forms and in all circumstances, pro-choice women connect the principle to the need to be responsible, careful, and considerate of the human life that already exists. Moreover, whereas pro-life advocates contrast values of nurturance and generosity with support for a right to an abortion, pro-choice advocates insist that nurturance and the choice to abort a fetus can be linked. As in the debate over surrogate mothering, what might be called an ethics of care extends to both sides of this debate and simply leads in different directions.[29]

The same holds for the common appeal pro-choice and pro-life advocates make to a principle of liberty. In the view of the pro-life advocates whom Luker and Ginsburg studied, women are free to choose different sorts of lives, but these lives bring different commitments with them. One cannot accept the responsibility of sex and marriage without assuming also the responsibility for their consequences, a responsibility that ties married women tightly to the domain of domestic concerns. Not surprisingly, pro-choice advocates think that married men and women can occupy the same worlds; both can work and ought to be involved in raising their children. Moreover, they think that married women who do not work are irresponsible insofar as they are only "one man away from disaster" or from a life of poverty in which they cannot care for their children at all, much less subordinate all other parts of their lives to accomplishing this task. For pro-choice women, caring for one's family is only one of the roles women can perform, and, given the capacity to control their reproductive lives, it need not limit their options any more than it limits those of men.[30]

Thus, if pro-life and pro-choice advocates share a respect for the intrinsic value of human life and commonly appeal to a principle of liberty, this agreement lies over a set of differences in terms of which, as Luker points out, their differences over abortion are only "the tip of the iceberg."[31] They differ on the question of abortion because they inhabit different cultures: they differ in their life circumstances and resources, in the choices they have made, in their orientation toward life and liberty,

their attitudes toward parenthood, and their understanding of the meaning of sexual intercourse itself. Not only do they differ; they are also mutually suspicious. From a pro-choice point of view, the pro-life position
is not only medieval but ideologically designed to maintain traditional
gender roles and to eliminate women from public life. From the pro-life
point of view, the pro-choice perspective is equally frightening in its attempt to undermine a way of life that pro-life advocates find not only
satisfying and meaningful but also the last defense against the crass materialism and selfishness of the modern age. For Luker, both factors—
the entirely different cultures in which pro-life and pro-choice advocates
live and the threats to their way of life that each position finds in the
other—make it clear "why the abortion debate is so heated and why the
chances for rational discussion, reasoned arguments, and mutual accommodation are so slim." [32]

But are they so slim? Suppose we consider the full range of our differences over abortion, from the different ways we live to the different
ways we respect human life, understand parenthood and responsibility,
think of women's roles, and interpret the meaning of sexual intercourse.
These differences do not reflect moral differences in the principles to
which we adhere. The pro-life and pro-choice opinions Luker and Ginsburg investigate agree in the norms and values to which they appeal.
Both sides refer to principles of liberty, to norms of responsibility, and
to values that reflect the importance of children and of meaningful sexual relations in constructing a fulfilling life. Nevertheless, they understand what these principles, norms, and values mean in very different
ways. In what follows, I therefore want to ask what prospects for resolving the abortion debate might lie in recognizing our differences as
cultural and interpretive rather than moral. Further, I want to ask what
each side in the abortion debate might have to learn from the other. [33]

INTERPRETATION AND THE ABORTION DEBATE

Despite Dworkin's attempt to resolve the conflict over abortion by
ignoring different possible interpretations of the principle of the free exercise of religion, an account he gives of the relation between legal and
literary interpretation seems to lead in a different direction. Indeed, it
seems to lead in a direction close to the model of legitimate differences
that this book has tried to promote. According to what Dworkin calls
the aesthetic hypothesis, any "interpretation of a piece of literature attempts to show which way of reading . . . the text reveals it as the best

work of art." Here Dworkin picks up on Gadamer's "anticipation of completeness" to argue that part of any genuine attempt to understand a text involves an effort to construe its meaning in such as way that it has as much point or value as possible. To read a detective novel, Dworkin insists, as if it were a philosophical treatise on death is to obscure a point of view from which it can be a piece of literature with value. Still, Dworkin also argues that we can approach texts with different aesthetic hypotheses about what makes a piece of literature a good one. "Different theories or schools or traditions of interpretation," he writes, will "assume significantly different normative theories about what literature is and what it is for and about what makes one work of literature better than another." [34] If our aesthetic hypothesis demands that we interrogate eighteenth-century novels in terms of issues of class, race, and gender, then we will understand and rank their value differently than if our aesthetic hypothesis directs us to look at aesthetic form instead. Hence, our interpretations of texts under different aesthetic hypotheses will differ.

At the same time, Dworkin argues that all interpretations must comply with what he calls constraints of "fit" [35] and what the German hermeneutic tradition of Schleiermacher and Gadamer understands as the coherence of part and whole. In reading the work as the best work of art it can be, interpreters cannot change the work, ignoring large parts of its plot, descriptions, or characterizations. Nor can they fail to show how the various parts of the content of the text fit together as a coherent unity or how its style and tropes are to be integrated with what the interpreter takes to be the text's content. To this extent, considerations of fit constrain questions of how the text is the best it can be: "Perhaps," Dworkin writes, "Shakespeare could have written a better play based on the sources he used for *Hamlet* than he did and in that better play the hero would have been a more forceful man of action. It does not follow that *Hamlet,* the play he wrote, really is like that after all." [36]

Yet if our interpretations of literary texts can differ in their aesthetic hypotheses and still remain constrained by considerations of fit, this analysis suggests that our interpretations of life and liberty in the debate over abortion might similarly differ in constrained and therefore legitimate ways. Luker claims that the "surprise, outrage, and vindictiveness" that characterize the abortion debate are the predictable result of finding that one's world view is not universally shared:

> Individuals are surprised because for most of them this is the first time
> their deepest values have been brought to explicit consciousness, much less

challenged. They are outraged because these values are so taken for granted that people have no vocabulary with which to discuss the fact that what is at odds is a fundamental view of reality. And they are vindictive because denying that one's opponents are decent, honorable people is one way of distancing oneself from the unsettling thought that there could be legitimate differences of opinion on one's most cherished beliefs.[37]

Still, these are not the typical reactions to finding that others do not share one's understanding of a text or work of art. Nor are they part of Luker's or Ginsburg's response to their own investigations of pro-life and pro-choice views. Instead, these responses seem to reflect a willingness to take seriously, as interpretations constrained by considerations of fit, understandings of life, liberty, sex, and abortion that differ from their own. Indeed, they reflect a willingness to see these interpretations in their "best light" and to use them to illuminate the issues at stake.

Suppose we develop these attitudes. Suppose we no longer conceive of the debate over abortion as a clash between different absolute principles, between principles of life and procreative responsibility, on the one hand, and liberty and "amative" sex, on the other. And suppose we no longer conceive of it as a conflict that must end in a consensus on the liberty of all to their own sense of religious or sacred values, as Dworkin claims, where, as Americans, we also agree on what is to count as a religious value. Suppose, instead, we take up his analysis of the possible validity of different interpretations of law and literature that all nonetheless comply with constraints of "fit" and "best light." Suppose, in other words, we construe our differences over abortion in the same way that Dworkin construes our differences over literary texts, as the consequence of different contexts of assumptions and values duly and legitimately constrained by considerations of fit. Moreover, suppose we not only take the alternative views of abortion seriously but actively look for the ways in which they might complement and expand our own.

On this view, it is important to the pro-choice position in the abortion debate not to ask only how it might argue against the "truth" of the pro-life view. Rather, and more important, it might ask how it could expand its own understanding by taking the pro-life view seriously, as both an internally coherent position and as a possibly plausible and appropriately constrained interpretation of the meaning of the values, norms, and principles at stake. It need not adopt a pro-life position. Still, in considering it hermeneutically, a pro-choice position might conclude that it has focused too entirely on a woman's life and liberty and might therefore be led to revise its own understanding of these principles to include a greater appreciation of the value and even potential of different sorts of human lives. As many feminists themselves point out, some women experience feelings of grief after enduring an abortion, even when they have no feelings of regret.[38] That abortion is not the equivalent of a tonsillectomy, that more is at issue than the right to decide what is done with one's own body are parts of what pro-choice advocates can learn (and many already have learned) from the pro-life view. Pro-choice advocates might learn, in addition, to concede that abortion can cause grief without assuming such grief casts suspicion on those decisions or on pro-choice advocates' commitment to principles of autonomy.[39]

Moreover, pro-choice advocates might learn from the pro-life attack on the materialism and consumerism of American life, as well as from the particular existential orientation that many pro-life advocates manifest by accepting life's vicissitudes. From their point of view, pregnancies happen, and one's life adjusts to loving and caring for the children that result. One need not accept all the fatalism this life orientation implies. Still, there is a dimension of it that seems important and that we already met in considering surrogate mothering: namely, that not all of life can be controlled or planned. New technologies, both with regard to giving birth and to preventing it, bring with them a focus on control that can blind us to other possibilities. This blindness seems obvious with regard to new birth technologies, which can lead couples to be so intent on technologically conquering their infertility that they overlook the parenting opportunities that exist through adoption.[40] Some of the same might be said for attempts to control our fertility. We do not have to give up all attempts to control fertility or infertility to see the point that not all aspects of love or life are ones for which we can completely plan, whether through technology or law. Instead, we might hold onto two ideas: first, nurturance is a value that may require us to change our lives while it enriches them and, second, reliance on technological control can imprison our lives as much as it may seem to liberate them.

On the other side, the pro-life position has a similar opportunity to learn once it understands that its claims about liberty and the sanctity of life reflect interpretations of ideas of which other interpretations are possible as well. By taking seriously the pro-choice understanding of liberty, the pro-life view might learn to find dimensions in the meaning of this principle that center on the particularity of different family circumstances. Moreover, in the meaning of the sanctity of human life it might learn to find dimensions that distinguish between different kinds of human life, just as the pro-choice position learns to see connections between them. It might also learn to consider the level of social services required if women and children are to have a decent life, as the pro-life position might come to understand it. One cannot be consistently pro-life only up to the point of birth. Rather, a pro-life position might learn to concern itself with prenatal care, child care, and the poverty in which many families, with their children, live.[41]

On the more existential level, a pro-life advocate might learn from the pro-choice position to be less quiescent in the conduct of his or her life and, more important, in the conduct of his or her children's lives. If those who are pro-choice can learn to modify their technological hubris from the attitude pro-life advocates take toward life, pro-life advocates might learn to modify the imbalance they have struck between control and acceptance as well. They might learn to understand the raising of children as a grave responsibility, not a natural occurrence that one simply accepts, but a journey the implications of which inspire awe and intimidate enough to legitimate some level of emotional, psychological, social, and financial preparation. Indeed, since family relationships seem inevitably to overwhelm the intentions we have with regard to them, it makes all the more sense for individuals to be able to decide for themselves when they are simply not ready for them.

In any case, we might overcome the clash of absolutes in the debate over abortion not by denying our differences or exaggerating them. Instead, we might recognize them as "just" constrained interpretations of the meaning of certain norms and principles that both sides in the debate take seriously. Further, we might ask how each interpretation of these norms might be educated and expanded by the other so that each is helped to a more complex understanding of the meanings our principles, norms, and values might have.

ACCOMMODATING DIFFERENCES

This plea for reciprocal hermeneutic education on the issue of abortion remains problematic as thus far elucidated. In the first place, it leaves largely unanswered the question of what policies might conform to the different interpretive perspectives a pluralistic and hermeneutically oriented society might take on the principles of life and liberty. Even if we recognize the interpretive character of our understanding of our principles, thus allowing us to learn from one another, in no case does it assure that we will learn the same thing. Rather, because of the different lives different interpreters lead and because of the different contexts within which they understand the issues at stake, different interpreters might very well integrate the insights they find in alternate interpretations differently. Hence, supporters of the right to abortion might still claim that access to legal abortion must remain unrestricted, even if the question of abortion now appears to them to involve a more complex conception of the principle of liberty, the value of human life, and the place of technological control within it. Similarly, opponents of a right to abortion might continue to try to restrict such a right even if they recognize new dimensions in the idea of liberty and acknowledge the inherent value of all the lives involved as well as the possibility of a new balance between acceptance and active responsibility for one's life.

A second problem with the account of reciprocal hermeneutic education I have given thus far is that it is oversimplified. The controversy over abortion is not just a debate we carry on with others. It is also a debate we carry on with ourselves. Indeed, with regard to the issue of abortion, it is almost too easy to understand the plausibility and possible legitimacy of perspectives other than our own and to accept different understandings of its meaning at different times of our lives. But this ambivalence seems to compound the problem of action. We cannot agree on principles of action with those whose interpretive perspectives we do not share or cannot come to share no matter how much we may have learned from them. Furthermore, as individuals we are pulled in different directions by different orientations toward our own lives and by the different ways we can understand the meaning of the norms and principles involved.[42]

Yet this second problem may point us in the direction of resolving the first problem posed by the potential that different groups might learn different lessons from their interpretive discussions with one another. In *Life Itself: Abortion in the American Mind,* Roger Rosenblatt cites statistics according to which 73 percent of Americans support the right to abortion while 77 percent think of abortion as murder.[43] This ambivalence, he thinks, means that for us the issue of abortion is irresolvable and that we must learn to live with the irreconcilable. "We must not only accept but embrace a state of tension that requires a tolerance of ambivalent feelings, respect for different values and sensibilities and no small amount of compassion."[44] Yet while such a tension might be unavoidable, why should we embrace it? In my view, we might do so because we recognize the cultural and interpretive dimensions of the debate, because we acknowledge that it concerns norms, values, and principles the meaning of which, even for ourselves, is multidimensional. Furthermore, once we concede that we can understand the meaning of our values, norms, and principles in more than one way, it becomes possible to conceive of the goals of social and political debate differently as well. These cannot be only those in which we succeed in coming to a consensus on meaning either with others or with ourselves. Instead, sometimes we may have to consider forms of compromise and reconciliation that reflect the myriad of constrained, reciprocally educated interpretations we can come to hold as individuals or as a society.

This kind of reciprocal education already appears to have accomplished some narrowing of the interpretive divide on the question of abortion, at least among nonextremists on either side. Pro-choice advocates rarely rest their case on assertions of bodily autonomy while at least some pro-life advocates emphasize more than the months leading up to birth. Indeed, one of the virtues of the debate may be that it has been so extensively pursued that we have become somewhat clear both on what we have learned from one another and on what kinds of considered differences nonetheless remain. With regard to these differences, we might begin to look for solutions that try as best they can to accommodate both sides. We might begin to formulate a policy that, first of all, articulates a respect for the value of human life by addressing such social needs as those for adequate health care for pregnant women, health care for babies and children, child support, paid parental leaves of adequate lengths, good and affordable day care, and flexible work schedules for parents of young children.[45] We might also provide education about parenting responsibilities, encourage teen-age abstinence, assure easy access to birth control products, and reform our adoption policies so that adoption is seen as a viable and, indeed, valuable option in addition to both abortion and fertility treatments. Third, we might accept certain temporal limits on the right to an abortion while at the same time articulate an understanding of the value of women's individual liberty by allowing for purely elective abortions up to a certain point. At the very least, such a compromise (along the lines of Scandinavian solutions) seems able to reflect the ways in which both sides in the American debate may have learned from one another without denying the differences that remain.

To be sure, reorienting our efforts toward this kind of compromise may seem too quickly to abandon the search for a more principled and clear consensus. To make a comparison that is often made in the abortion debate, suppose those opposed to slavery had abandoned the attempt to convince or fight southern slaveholders in favor of retaining one of the various compromises on the issue or supplementing the idea of a parity between free and slave states with legal guarantees ensuring slaves a certain standard and quality of life. Suppose the pro-slavery position could be articulated in a way consistent with a plausible interpretation of our principles of freedom and equality and suppose our hermeneutic efforts were to be directed both toward learning from this interpretation and toward accommodating it in our laws and policies. Of course, the possibility that a pro-slavery interpretation could be valid may seem remote, especially if part of the meaning of the principle of equal opportunity includes the participation of all.[46] Still, the question the issue of slavery seems to raise is how we know when to continue to try to learn from an understanding of the meaning of our norms, values, and principles that differs from our own and when to dismiss that understanding as irredeemable. Are the constraints to which Dworkin and the hermeneutic tradition appeal, those of internal unity or fit and possible truth or best light, sufficient for distinguishing those interpretations to which we need to continue to listen in hermeneutic conversation from those interpretations of meaning to which we need not? Or do these constraints imply that there might always be some point or meaning to an interpretation that we have simply failed to understand?

In my view, the idea of reciprocal hermeneutic education issues its own standards for assessing contributions to our understandings of meaning, standards that require the participation of all those affected. If we stress the idea that a hermeneutic or interpretive discussion of our practices and principles contributes to our own understanding of them, then it is crucial that we prevent the possibility of excluding interpretive voices from our hermeneutic debates or effectively silencing or distorting such voices within them. Rather, the development of our own understanding of meaning will depend upon its capacity to situate itself in relation to other understandings of meaning and to incorporate what it takes to be their insights. But this condition means that we must have open access to these other understandings of meaning. For the sake of the continuing vitality and strength of our own interpretations, we must encourage a rich plurality of interpretive voices. Moreover, any interpretation of the meaning of our norms and principles, even one that is internally consistent, that depends upon the exclusion or suppression of another interpretive voice must be rejected because it threatens or restricts the alternatives only against which we can strengthen and justify our own interpretations. If every account of the meaning of life, responsibility, or liberty remains "just" an interpretation, then it can test its adequacy only by setting itself against others and proving its superiority to them, at least by its own lights. Any interpretation that would prevent the possibility of listening to any other, by excluding this particular voice from public debate, thereby weakens its own position as well as that of all others.

Interpretations of the meaning of liberty or equality that allow for slavery or racial segregation accomplish precisely this sort of self-debilitating exclusion. Insofar as they prevent the interpretive voices of slaves or minorities from entering into the interpretive conversation, they limit the alternatives against which their own adequacy can itself be shown. The failure here is not a failure to agree with the substantive content of what the slaves or minorities might say in interpretive dialogue. Rather, the practices of slavery and racial segregation silence, demean, and distort the articulation of that content in such a way that it cannot even serve as a foil against which to test the adequacy of any other position. Slave and minority voices are not recognized as voices that must be admitted to the conversation as even potentially legitimate interpretations from which we might learn. Hence, versions of the meaning of liberty or equality that allow for slavery or segregation remain devastating to the strength of all contributions to the debate, even the exclusionary interpretation itself.

Of course, antiabortion advocates can insist that fetuses are excluded from the current debate over abortion in just this way. This idea seems to be some of the sense of the pro-life claim to speak for "unborn children," and it implies that any attempt to accommodate a right to an abortion, in the same way as a right to white supremacy, effectively and illegitimately silences an interpretive voice. There is also a second and opposite direction in which the abortion debate might be said to exclude an interpretive voice. By promoting a traditional view of women and women's place in society, the pro-life view might be said to perform the ideological function of excluding women from the public sphere and hence from our hermeneutic dialogue. This is one of the implications of Cass Sunstein's argument in "Neutrality in Constitutional Law (with Special Reference to Pornography, Abortion, and Surrogacy.)"[47] I shall first examine this argument and then return to the pro-life claim to speak for fetuses. If sustainable, either argument would provide a way of avoiding the kind of interpretively based compromise I have proposed to the debate over abortion and, more to the point, perhaps, provide a resolution of it as satisfyingly principled as the resolution of the issue of slavery. A presumption behind the present study, however, is that the case against slavery serves as a misleading model for at least some of the social issues we currently confront, including that of abortion.

ABORTION AND EQUALITY

Dworkin's resolution of the legal controversy over abortion rests, as we have seen, on an understanding of the freedom of religion that protects differences on certain fundamental values, among them the different ways individuals respect the value of human life. For his part, Sunstein abandons arguments that link the right to an abortion to a right to privacy and turns, instead, to considerations of equality: restrictions on abortion rights constitute a form of gender discrimination because they impose burdens on women that they do not impose on men. Pregnancy is a co-optation of a woman's body for the use of a fetus, and, Sunstein writes, "the government cannot impose on women alone the obligation to protect fetuses through a legal act of bodily co-optation." [48]

Of course, under current stages of technology, men cannot become pregnant, so it is unclear how laws either prohibiting or restricting abortion *could* impose obligations on them. But Sunstein's concern is the way in which law can either turn or decline to turn biological capacities into sources of social inequality. In the case of restricting access to abortion, laws would selectively impose on women caretaking functions and "good Samaritan" behaviors they do not impose on either men or governments. In *DeShaney v Winnebago County Department of Social Services,* the court declined to hold the county responsible for the brain damage Joshua DeShaney suffered, even though the department knew he was continually beaten by his parents and did nothing to stop them. [49] As Sunstein points out, governments also do not compel parents to donate their kidneys or bone marrow to save others, even their own children. "It seems clear," he writes, that such an obligation "would be treated as a frightening and unacceptable intrusion on personal autonomy—even where life is at stake and even when death would result from refusal to carry out the relevant duty and even when the people to be protected owe their existence and vulnerability to the people on whom the imposition would be placed." [50]

This argument rests on an understanding of abortion that interprets it, not as the destruction of fetal life, but rather as a simple decision not to allow part of one's body to be used for the protection of another life, just as one might decide not to donate blood or provide a kidney. [51] One might make this decision even if a human life is at stake and even if that life owes its "existence and vulnerability" to its parents—in the case of a contemplated abortion, to the woman carrying the human life but in other cases to any parent who, for genetic or biological reasons, has the capacity to save or nurture the life of a child and declines to do so. Eileen L. McDonagh puts the point more strongly, not in terms of deciding against good Samaritan laws but in terms of arguments against what she calls captive Samaritan ones. "Abortion does not stop the giving activity of the woman as a good samaritan, nor does it present women with the option of being a bad samaritan. . . . Rather abortion stops the fetus from taking the woman's body and liberty without her consent, thereby freeing her from the captive samaritan status imposed by the fetus." [52] If the traditional understanding identifies abortion with murder instead of with a refusal to be either a captive Samaritan or a good Samaritan by donating some portion of one's body to another, Sunstein's claim is that this identification is simply sexist. Women are supposed to be mothers, caretakers, and altruists, and when they decide not to accept these roles their refusal is typically seen in extreme terms. [53] That we typically do not employ similar terms to evaluate men's choices and decisions, even about their own children, reflects, in Sunstein's view, a history of questionable differentiations on the basis of sex.

Sunstein does recognize that a male-only draft selectively imposes on men a requirement to use their bodies to protect others in the case of war. But he sees this selectivity as a confirmation of his point. In both the case of involuntary pregnancy imposed only on women and the case of involuntary military service imposed only on men, the state turns "natural" differences in biological and physical capacities into social distinctions. Moreover, these distinctions reinforce traditional divisions between public and private spheres, divisions that relegate women to the domestic domain while only men are full, publicly oriented citizens:

> The central point is that legal provisions ensuring that only men are drafted are part of a system of sex role stereotyping characterized by a sharp, legally produced split between the domestic and public spheres. . . . Legal restrictions on abortion are an element in the legal creation of a domestic sphere in which women occupy their traditional role, and principally or exclusively that role. Male-only drafts are part of the legal creation of a public sphere in which men occupy their traditional role, and principally or exclusively that role. [54]

This defense of a right to an abortion might seem to avoid hermeneutic difficulties and effectively to connect support for abortion rights with a principled support for civil and political rights. Just as slavery and Jim Crow laws excluded African Americans from American public life and debate, restrictions on abortion rights, on this analysis, seek to relegate women to the domestic sphere of the household and thereby to exclude their voice in our public considerations of who we are and what collective actions we ought to take. According to this argument, the right to an abortion must be defended on as firm a ground as the right of all to political and civic participation. Indeed, the pro-life implication that men and women occupy separate but equal spheres appears as implausible as the corresponding justification of Jim Crow laws to enforce segregation.

Nevertheless, it is not obvious that Sunstein's analogy between pregnancy and kidney donation serves as the only plausible interpretation of the practice of abortion or one that can resolve the debate in a conclusive way. "The permanent sacrifice of a part of the body is in some respects more, and in some respects less, intrusive than enduring an unwanted pregnancy," Amy Gutmann and Dennis Thompson write. "But the differences between preventing the destruction of a fetus and not requiring organ donations to save the life of one's child are great enough to require different moral arguments for each kind of case." [55] Moreover, even if the analogy can be sustained, it remains unclear on Sunstein's analysis why antiabortion advocates could not push the demand for equality in a direction opposite to the one he imagines. Why might they not simply insist for the sake of consistency that the state impose "good Samaritan" and duty-to-rescue laws on men as well as on women? Why not regard all members of a family as Samaritans captive to it? And why not require all family members either to donate parts of their bodies when needed for the protection of another life for which they are responsible or to replace the reserves they use if their own body parts are not compatible with the needs of their children? If the problem with laws restricting or preventing abortion is that they impose caretaking functions on women that they do not impose on men, then it seems that the requirements for a more coherent understanding of equality could be met by imposing these functions on men as well.

Sunstein's appeal to the principle of equality reinforces the condition that at least part of the pro-life movement seems already to have learned from the pro-choice position, namely that if it is going to be pro-life it must be pro-women's and pro-children's lives as well as pro-fetuses' lives. Decisions that restrict women's access to abortion will simply not fit with decisions absolving men and governments of responsibility for the welfare of children. Still, the pro-life position can learn from Sunstein's understanding of equality to be more consistently pro-life while remaining antiabortion. And if this is the case, our best hope of resolving the controversy over abortion might remain that of acknowledging the legitimacy of at least some of our differences and of trying to accommodate them in our laws and policies.

What about the opposite equation, not between pro-life and pro-slavery or prosegregation positions, but between pro-choice and pro-slavery or prosegregation positions? In excluding fetal voices from our hermeneutic dialogue, are we not guilty of the same form of discrimination manifest in debates over the morality and legality of slavery or racial segregation that exclude slaves or minorities? In the case of the controversy over abortion, we might make two points. First, fetuses cannot themselves voice their interpretations of meaning or, therefore, engage in hermeneutic conversation. Slaves and minorities can, and it is arguably because they can that they must be part of our interpretive conversations on the meaning of our principles and values. If our conversations over abortion are to be similarly open, they must also include pro-life interpretations of how human life is to be respected and how we ought to think about our liberty and our human existence. Fetuses themselves, however, do not interpret. To be sure, infants cannot engage in articulate hermeneutic conversation either, and it is certainly not clear that their inability to do so justifies either infanticide or their exclusion from the interpretive discussions that concern them. Yet if infants and very young children do not yet speak, they are quite capable of making their own interpretations of their situation abundantly clear. But, second, the circumstance that fetuses and infants share a lack of language, if not voice, may be part of what makes us pause over the matter of abortion and consider a more differentiated resolution to this case.[56] If fetuses are not possible participants in a hermeneutic conversation over the meaning of our norms and principles, and if they are not participants even in the manner infants are, neither do they lack the capacity to participate in the same way that rocks and appendices do. In a hermeneutic conversation we might learn to acknowledge both sides of this disjunction and to formulate a policy that does its best to accommodate different legitimate interpretations of our principles and ideals.

CHAPTER FIVE

Pornography, Ideology, and Silence

In the previous chapter, I argued that neither pro-life nor pro-choice views of abortion are well served by the effort to dismiss the other as medieval, irresponsible, self-indulgent, or religious. Rather, each side might take a more hermeneutic attitude toward the other. In the case of the abortion controversy, a hermeneutic attitude might allow pro-life proponents to learn to become better advocates for the sorts of social services that would support a woman in her decision both to carry a fetus to term and to raise a child. Pro-choice forces might learn more forthrightly to acknowledge limits on a woman's right to control her body. On a more existential level, pro-choice views might learn to moderate a kind of technological hubris that is so oriented to "fixing things" that it ignores other options, and pro-life views might learn to be less acquiescent in their acceptance of traditional forms of life.

But if the issue of abortion, together with those of surrogate mothering and affirmative action, lends itself to an interpretive approach, are there other issues that currently confront Americans that admit of more decisive and principled resolutions on the order of resolutions to questions of slavery or racial segregation? Are there positions to which we need not lend our hermeneutic charity and from which we need not try to learn because they violate the conditions of hermeneutic conversation, or, in other words, because they silence a legitimate interpretive voice? The current debate over pornography is interesting in this regard because this is precisely the charge that each side raises against the other.

The charge that some feminists currently raise against pornography is that it silences and subordinates women. Moreover, they argue that, to the extent that the First Amendment is employed to defend pornography as free speech, it participates in the ideological justification of women's second-class status. This feminist attack on pornography and the use of the First Amendment to defend it differs from the concern with obscenity that has occupied the U.S. Supreme Court since 1957.[1] While this second concern has focused on the possibility of excluding certain sexually explicit materials from First Amendment protection because of the way they pander to prurient interests, violate community standards, or lack redeeming literary, artistic, political, or scientific value,[2] the recent feminist concern has focused on harms to women. It claims that pornography degrades, dehumanizes, and demeans women in ways that can lead to violence against them and, in any case, prevents their full and equal participation in public life.[3] Moreover, it defines pornography as the "graphic, sexually explicit" subordination of women in pictures and words.

But other feminists have rejected this view of pornography. They argue that the link between pornography and violence against women has yet to be proven and that antipornography feminism in fact participates in reinforcing traditional, stereotypical, and, to this extent, ideological views of women that serve to diminish their voice in public debate. Defining pornography as sexually explicit material that is intended simply to arouse, anti-antipornography feminists point, first, to the tolerance that liberal principles extend to different individual conceptions of the good and, second, to the function pornography serves in undermining fixed conceptions of both women and their sexuality.

In this chapter, I do not want to address the empirical question of whether pornography increases the risks of injury and danger to women. Studies that have tried to answer this question have thus far issued in different and contradictory results.[4] Rather, I want to consider the way in which the feminist debate over pornography reveals a deeper controversy over the meaning of certain of our principles, those of free speech, equality, and sexual authenticity.[5] Antipornography feminists and their liberal or anti-antipornography opponents do not differ simply in what they take pornography to be or to cause; they also differ on what they take principles of free speech, equality, and sexual authenticity to mean. I shall focus in this chapter on reconstructing and examining what I take to be plausible versions of both antipornography and anti-antipornography or liberal feminist positions in order to clarify both what the positions mean for the principles I think the debate involves and what each position might have to learn from the other. I shall begin with the liberal theorist Nadine Strossen's understanding of the principle of free speech enshrined in the First Amendment and then turn to the questions antipornography feminists raise with regard to it.

FREE SPEECH

According to Strossen's book *Defending Pornography: Free Speech, Sex, and the Fight for Women's Rights,* two principles lie at the heart of First Amendment jurisprudence in the United States. The first is that of content neutrality: neither the government nor the courts can restrict speech just because some individuals or groups disagree with its content or find this content hateful. Indeed, as Strossen quotes Oliver Wendell Holmes, "if there is any principle of the Constitution that more imperatively calls for attachment than any other it is the principle of free thought—not free thought for those who agree with us but freedom for the thought we hate." [6] Second, when the government can restrict speech, it must show that the speech in question presents "a clear and present danger" in that it will cause direct and imminent harm to a very important interest and that no other means short of suppressing speech will prevent this harm. Crying "Fire" in a crowded theater is the most notorious instance of the relevant type of harm, and in citing it Strossen insists on the difference between a clear and present danger and what Holmes insisted is merely a bad tendency. We cannot restrict speech just on the basis that it may lead some individuals to perform objectionable acts.

Strossen takes this principle to imply a strong argument against that aspect of antipornography feminism that contends that exposure to pornographic materials can lead some individuals to rape, molest, harass, or otherwise harm women. We cannot suppress pacifist or socialist ideas because they might lead some to resist the draft, Strossen explains. Nor, therefore, can we suppress pornographic ideas just because they might lead some to engage in acts of violence against women. As she quotes Justice Louis Brandeis, "Fear of injury alone cannot justify suppression of free speech and assembly. Men feared witches and burned women." [7]

Brandeis's defense of free speech relies upon Millian ideas about the power of truth to emerge through free discussion. "The fitting remedy for evil counsels is good ones," he claims. And as he continues:

Those who won our independence by revolution were not cowards. . . . They did not exalt order at the cost of liberty. To courageous, self-reliant men, with confidence in the power of free and fearless reasoning applied through the processes of popular government, no danger flowing from speech can be deemed clear and present, unless the incidence of the evil apprehended is so imminent that it may befall before there is opportunity for full discussion. If there be time to expose through discussion the falsehood and fallacies, to avert the evil by the processes of education, the remedy to be applied is more speech, not enforced silence.[8]

But antipornography feminists question just whose silence is enforced by an understanding of the First Amendment that defends pornography. To be sure, women and pornographers appear to possess equal rights to say and write what they want as long as the content does not fall into specifically defined categories of clear and present dangers. But what if the production and consumption of pornography contributes to an environment in which women cannot do what they intend to do even if they can say or write what they want? What if truth cannot emerge through discussion because the very structure of that discussion is skewed by the effects of pornography and, hence, is far from free? Suppose pornography impedes the fullness of "full discussion?"

These sorts of questions are suggested by the use that Jennifer Hornsby, in considering the harms of pornography, makes of J. L. Austin's distinction between illocutionary and locutionary aspects of speech.[9] By the locutionary component of what he called a speech act, Austin referred to its propositional content: "that p." The illocutionary component, however, refers to what the speaker means to do with this propositional content: whether, for example, he or she is asserting that p, denying that p, begging that p, ordering that p, or hoping that p. The condition for the success of such illocutionary acts is what Hornsby calls reciprocity. That is, the force of an illocutionary act depends upon the hearer's recognition of the act as the one the speaker intended, and speaker and hearer can come to an adequate understanding of one another only by recognizing both locutionary and illocutionary components for what they are. Indeed, Hornsby writes, "we can say: x-ing is an illocutionary act if and only if . . . the speaker's attempt at x-ing results in an audience's taking the speaker to x."[10] The problem with pornography, on this view, is that it can distort a woman's attempt to perform a certain speech act, obstruct its illocutionary component, or turn it into its opposite. Hornsby refers to the comments of two judges in rape trials in this regard. In a 1982 trial, Judge David Wild said that "Women who say no do not always mean no. It is not just a question of saying no."[11] And Judge Dean insisted in 1990, "As the gentlemen on the jury will understand, when a woman says 'No' she does not always mean it. Men can't turn their emotions on and off like a tap like some women can." [12]

But even if we accept Austin's theory of speech acts, why should the connection to which Hornsby appeals hold? Why can a speaker perform a certain speech act only if she is taken to perform it? And, even if a speaker can perform it only if she is taken to perform it, does she have a right that her intention to perform it be understood as she intended it? Hornsby's account of reciprocity is marred by its reliance on a problematic equation between an understanding of the meaning of a speech act and an understanding of a speaker's intentions. To the extent that such an equation supposes that one's intentions are always exactly mirrored in one's actions or words and that they can therefore be correctly understood in only one way, the equation cannot survive a hermeneutic investigation of the conditions of understanding meaning. As we have seen, when we try to understand the meaning of a text, we do so from a specific perspective, one that takes certain attitudes and assumptions for granted, relies on a certain vocabulary of understanding, and is oriented by certain questions, interests, and concerns. The same holds for our understanding of speech acts and the intentions behind them. We can understand them only from a particular hermeneutic horizon, and this condition holds even when the speech and intentions are our own and even when the issue is what we meant to do by what we said. As both speakers and hearers, we understand the meaning of our own and others' intentions in terms of a particular horizon of interpretation, one both limited and made possible by our historical, experiential, cultural, and linguistic situation. Why, then, can a judge not understand a woman's speech act in a way that the woman does not?

Hornsby's point about reciprocity can be reconstructed in a different way from the way she articulates it, as a point about standards of interpretive adequacy written into the hermeneutic circle. A speaker and hearer may not initially understand the speaker's speech act in the same way. If the speaker is to encourage the hearer to accept his or her understanding of the speech act, then, he or she must be able to show the context in terms of which he or she thinks the speech act should be understood. Suppose, for example, I take myself to be asking for a certain favor and you take offense because you take me to be commanding you in some way. In this case, we fail to agree on the meaning of my illocutionary act and some repair work becomes necessary. To convince you of what I thought I was doing in saying what I said, I refer to a background context of action, speech, and practice in terms of which my particular speech act could have had the sense I attributed to it. In this case, I might point out that raising my voice at the end of my utterance or qualifying it with "please" could plausibly have been taken in the way I understand it, given the linguistic and communicative traditions to which we both belong, and, moreover, that your understanding of my speech act violates that context in important ways. Hence, I try to accomplish the necessary repair work by stepping back from the original speech act, finding a context of speech and practice with which I assume my hearer to be familiar, and showing how my original utterance fits into this context. If I am not originally understood in the way I think I should have been understood, I can try to articulate my understanding more clearly by referring to a wider context of action and practice of which my speech act forms a part. I may not have a *right* to be understood as asking for a favor instead of commanding, but I can at least refer to a framework of language and action that might allow us to repair our efforts to communicate by showing that my understanding of my speech act was a sincere and legitimate one.

Reconstructed in these terms, Hornsby's suggestion is that pornography undermines or distorts the possible success of these efforts at both initial and background contextual levels. Pornographic materials, antipornography feminists insist, are not simply sexually explicit pictures or obscene descriptions that are intended to arouse, as Strossen and other liberal theorists assume. Rather, they claim that, at best, in their nonviolent, *Playboy*-like form, they depict women as objects for the use and sexual control of others.[13] At worst, pornographic materials celebrate the rape, battery, and sexual harassment of women and depict women as enjoying such violence against them. Suppose, then, that a woman denies that she wants to have sexual intercourse with a man. The locutionary component of her speech act and its content are not at issue here. But she can engage in successful communication only if she can convince the man to understand her illocutionary act as one of denying that she wants to have sex or accomplish the necessary repair work if challenged. Yet if women are not always taken to be rejecting a sexual advance when they understand themselves to be rejecting it, they are not always understood the way they understand themselves when they try to refer to a context of action and practice that would give their particular speech acts the sense they think they have. Instead, speech acts such as rejecting a sexual advance, reiterating one's rejection, and giving the context for why one's rejection should be understood as a rejection are all sometimes understood as invitations to greater force or as attempts to raise the pitch of sexual excitement.

In these instances, the initial attempt at communication and all subsequent attempts at repair work fail from the speaker's point of view or turn into what she sees as their opposite but is powerless to correct. The antipornography feminist position implies that this situation is only to be expected in a society in which women are depicted as they are in pornography. For the context to which women must appeal in trying to show the merit of their own interpretations of their speech acts is one already influenced by the effects of pornography. The distribution and consumption of pornographic materials establish expectations about what women want, as well as contexts for what their dress and behavior mean, antipornography feminists insist. These expectations and contexts allow little chance that a woman can offer contexts to show that she is really rejecting a sexual advance when she wants to do so. Instead, an adequate understanding of her illocutionary aims is distorted and undermined by the social context in which it must proceed. Thus, Susan M. Easton appeals to Mill from the point of view opposite to Strossen's to argue that pornography "stifles the truth. Given the quantity of pornographic material and its wide circulation, the pornography industry may actually prevent the truth about women's nature and abilities."[14]

But why, we might ask, should this social context justify restrictions on the free speech of pornographers? It may be that pornographic images and writing contribute (presumably, *with* other cultural products such as television, children's toys, and advertising) to an environment that prevents the "truth" about women (or suppresses an appreciation of their own self-understanding) and systematically distorts an understanding of what they take as their illocutionary aims. But is this obstruction an abridgment of their right to free speech or, in Brandeis's terms, an enforcement of silence? Surely, a right to speak freely is not the same as a right to be heard as one wants to be heard or as one hears oneself. Nor, if we eliminate a problematic equation of meaning with a speaker's intentions, is it the same as a right to the agreement of others on how one ought to be understood at either the initial or contextual levels.

From the antipornography point of view, this objection overlooks a crucial element of the way in which pornography undermines the ability of women to legitimate their own understanding of their speech acts, namely its defense by First Amendment jurisprudence. While different factors may contribute to distortions in communication, opponents of pornography suggest that pornography accomplishes two extra feats. First, it undermines attempts at repair work as well as the initial attempt at understanding. Hence, it has a kind of global effect on understanding. Second, its global intrusions are protected by an understanding of the First Amendment that, despite Strossen's appeal to Brandeis, is not neutral. Indeed, MacKinnon and others such as Cass Sunstein reject the entire notion of content-neutrality on which Strossen's defense of free speech rests. Rather, as Sunstein argues, the questions on which this notion relies—those asking whether an important interest has been suppressed or whether the speech at issue represents a clear and present danger—reflect partisan values that only appear to be neutral in some cases because the consensus that justifies them seems to be so firm.[15] With regard to commercial speech, advertisements for cigarettes and casinos may be banned from television, although advertisements that warn about the dangers of smoking or gambling may not. Employers are banned from warning employees about what they see as the effects of unionization in the period before a union election if their statement might be interpreted as a threat. Union activists, however, are not banned from warning employees about their employers. Even existing obscenity laws that depend upon community standards of offensiveness and prurience are, Sunstein insists, "not a bit less partisan than anti-pornography legislation."[16] Insofar as the community standards reflect a particular viewpoint about what sort of noncommercial, sexual speech is appropriate, the corresponding regulations are not neutral. In this case, as in others, the government upholds certain values over others.[17]

To be sure, Strossen and other liberals criticize the intrusion of the courts into the sphere of all sexual speech, including that which the courts deem obscene. Still, if the First Amendment defense of pornography takes the important question to be whether women's inability to be heard as they either want to be heard or hear themselves can justify restrictions on the free speech of pornographers, antipornography feminists understand the question differently. Why is the appeal to free speech protections more concerned with protecting pornographers than with protecting other possible elements of free speech such as the right to advertise cigarettes on television? Why should First Amendment jurisprudence take its goal to be reinforcing obstacles to women's abilities to secure compliance with what they take as their illocutionary aims? If people do not have a right to be understood the way they understand themselves, it nonetheless may seem unclear why recourse to the principle of free speech should take as its goal defending the construction of a hostile environment for asserting and defending their self-interpretations.

MacKinnon's explanation for this defense involves what Sunstein has called the problem of the baseline.[18] First Amendment protections have been appealed to as support for the construction of a hostile environment for women's assertion of their self-understanding because those who make this appeal assume the naturalness of the existing social order. Under this assumption, interventions of the courts or government to change existing distributions of goods or to alter social relations of power are taken to be impermissibly partisan, while support for the status quo appears neutral. Thus, with regard to the First Amendment the so-called *Buckley* dictum claims that "the concept that government may restrict the speech of some . . . in order to enhance the relative voice of others is wholly foreign."[19] And with regard to the debate over pornography, this dictum is taken to mean that pornographic speech cannot be restricted in order to enhance the relative voice of women. But, from MacKinnon's point of view, this inference simply means that since men already have the power to depict and hear women as they want, as well as the power to secure what they take as their own illocutionary aims, it is a violation of neutrality and the First Amendment to regulate their speech. But it is no violation of the principle of free speech to ignore the way in which the assertion and reception of women's voices are potentially skewed by a distorted communicative environment or, in general, not to regulate the speech of the powerful to help secure the illocutionary aims of the powerless. As MacKinnon writes, "Speech theory does not disclose or even consider how to deal with power vanquishing powerlessness; it tends to transmute this into truth vanquishing falsehood, meaning what power wins becomes considered true. Speech . . . belongs to those who own it, mainly big corporations."[20]

Of course, *pace* MacKinnon, a different point of view is not completely alien to the history of Supreme Court decisions. This point of view is concerned not only with the so-called participant rights of all citizens to engage in public debate, the right Strossen emphasizes, but also with the rights of an audience of citizens to hear competing positions.[21] Thus, in *Red Lion Broadcasting Co. v FCC,*[22] the Court referred to the rights of viewers and listeners to hear different points of view as against the rights of the broadcaster to monopolize the airwaves. And in *Kleindiest v Mandel,* which upheld a decision to deny Ernest Mandel a visa to enter the United States to participate in a conference at Stanford

University, Justice Marshall's dissent rests the case squarely on the First Amendment rights of Mandel's American audience.[23] One might argue along these lines that the publication and circulation of pornography similarly violates the audience rights of citizens insofar as it helps to obscure or distort an understanding of the content of women's speech acts.

The claim here has to be made somewhat carefully. On this reconstruction of the point of antipornography feminism, the claim is not that pornography gags women's mouths or censors their words. The point is rather that, by affecting their ability to persuade others of what they take to be their illocutionary aims, it also affects the ability of their audience to hear them without what might be called disturbances in the field. Banning a speaker, shouting him or her down, and blowing whistles while she or he is trying to speak are all clearly recognized as violations of both the speaker's participant right to free speech and the right of the audience to hear competing points of view. The antipornography feminist claim appears to be similar: pornography obfuscates a mutual understanding of the illocutionary aims of women by creating the same sorts of disturbances and therefore violates not only women's access to free speech but the audience rights of those who seek to come to agreement with women on their illocutionary aims.

Still, if this sort of reasoning has found its way into the First Amendment reasoning in some cases, it seems to be employed when that reasoning turns to pornography only to defend the audience rights of those who want to receive pornographic materials and hear pornographic ideas.[24] This circumstance can only add fuel to antipornography feminist ire, for it may seem that the idea of audience rights should rather extend to the notion that the publication and circulation of pornography obstructs the ability to hear different ideas of different women's or individual's needs, goals, and desires. Indeed, it might seem only a small step from the rationale of audience rights to a broader principle: the First Amendment is not meant simply to allow for a cacophony of claims, where those that are the loudest or have the most financial clout behind them or can procure the greatest access to communications media therefore survive or win out over those with less power. Rather, a more substantive right to free speech might be concerned with eliminating precisely those conditions that distort or intrude upon social capacities to communicate or to hear and address one another's claims. These include shouting and blowing whistles but also the effects of money and power and, antipornography feminists insist, the pornographic intrusion on an ability to understand what a particular woman takes as her illocutionary aim.

The interpretation of the meaning of the principle of free speech that Strossen defends under the idea of content-neutrality understands it to protect a personal liberty to say and hear what one wants as long as that speech does not present a clear and present danger to an important interest. Under this interpretation, one's beliefs, attitudes, and opinions are one's personal property, and the state cannot intrude upon their expression without very serious reasons. The freedom of speech is the freedom to say and listen to, or not to say and not to listen to, what one chooses, to affirm those beliefs that one wants, and to do so without fear of governmental intrusion or reprisal. The understanding of the freedom of speech to which MacKinnon and others appeal appears to be very different, however. Here the idea is that if we are to have what Holmes called a "free trade in ideas"[25] or an uninhibited domain of free public expression, then it is not enough simply to allow everyone to speak if they can, if the public space of expression is not already filled, or if weightier factors such as money and power do not prohibit them from speaking. Nor is it enough to point to audience rights to hear different points of view. Rather, an unrestricted domain of expression means that individuals are able to hear different points of view and to communicate with one another without those distortions, constraints, and inhibitions that are obviously caused by violence or shouting but are also caused by relations of power, immense differences in wealth, and, antipornography feminists suggest, pornographic contributions to societal attitudes about women.

Antipornography and liberal or pro-pornography do not differ only in their understandings of the meaning of free speech, however; they also differ in their understanding of the meaning of equality. To make this point, I shall first look briefly at Ronald Dworkin's account of the meaning of equality as it pertains to the issue of pornography[26] and then turn to MacKinnon's view.

EQUALITY

As Rae Langton explains, Dworkin's general argumentative strategy with regard to questions of equality has four steps.[27] He begins with what appears to be a straightforward utilitarian argument in favor of a certain policy on the grounds that it conforms to the will of the majority in a society in which each person's vote or preference counts equally with that of every other person. Second, he considers which individuals or set of individuals is likely to be adversely affected by the policy once implemented. Third, he examines the preferences that are meant to ground the policy, to discover whether they are what he calls external preferences or "personal." If they are external, he concludes, fourth, that the rights of those adversely affected have been violated, since they are no longer allowed a moral independence that gives their preferences equal weight with those of all others.

According to Dworkin, then, a simple account of the principle of equality means that the worth of all individuals and the worth of their conceptions of the good must be counted equally with all others. Such an analysis of the principle of equality seems to lead, moreover, to a utilitarian calculus that would support censoring pornography. The principle of equality seems to mean that social and policy decisions should reflect the will of the majority in a society where each citizen counts for one and only one preference with regard to the issue. Hence, if the preferences of the majority lie in banning pornography, then these preferences win out over the preferences of a minority either to produce or to consume it.[28]

But Dworkin claims that such a conclusion actually undermines the egalitarian thrust of the theory on which it is based. The preferences of those citizens who want to prohibit pornography are not simply expressions of their own wants or preferences about the sort of literature they want to read or the films or pictures they want to see. They are also expressions of the worth of other people's wants or preferences about the sort of literature they want to read or the films or pictures they want to see. To this extent, they are preferences about other people's preferences. The antipornography majority is in effect claiming that the minority's account of the good life, its "conceptions of what sexual experience should be like, and of what part fantasy should play in that experience, and of what the character that fantasy should be, are inherently degrading or unwholesome."[29] But this attitude means that the majority's views about the fantasies and sexual experiences it prefers, as well as about the fantasies and sexual experiences other people should or should not prefer, count in the utilitarian calculus. In effect, then, its preferences are counted twice, undermining the egalitarian cast that was meant to be utilitarianism's major asset.

How might this conclusion be avoided? If majority decisions are to reflect the principle that all citizens' preferences count equally, then Dworkin insists that what he calls external preferences or preferences about other people's preferences must be left out of the calculus. This exclusion means that majority decisions must be constrained, or "trumped," by considerations of rights. In other words, only those majority decisions are legitimate that do not undermine the right of each person to a moral independence in which his or her own worth and the worth of his or her conceptions of the good life are accorded equal respect and treatment with all others. The principle of equality turns out to involve a right to moral independence according to which individuals have the right not to "suffer disadvantage . . . just on the ground that their officials or fellow-citizens think their opinions about the right way for them to lead their own lives are ignoble or wrong." [30] In the case of pornography, however, the attempts by the majority to prohibit it fail to accord equal respect and moral independence to a notion of the good that involves its enjoyment. Hence, Dworkin concludes, "the right of moral independence is part of the same collection of rights as the right of political independence, and it is to be justified as a trump over an unrestricted utilitarian defense of prohibitory laws against pornography, in a community of those who find offense just in the idea that their neighbors are reading dirty books." [31]

But where, antipornography feminists might ask, do women figure in this analysis? Suppose the enjoyment of pornography effectively denies women freedom in pursuing their conceptions of the good or undermines principles of equal respect for women by portraying them as objects for the use and control of others. In her own criticism of Dworkin, Langton reverses his premises. Suppose the majority in a given society allows pornography as part of the right to free expression. And suppose that, instead of assuming that pornographers are the relevant affected group, we suppose it is women. Then, Langton claims, Dworkin's analysis must run differently. The question now is whether a policy permitting the production and consumption of pornography violates any of their rights, a question we are to answer by examining the preferences that are meant to ground the policy and determining whether or not they are external ones.

Langton concludes that they are. Following a suggestion by Joel Feinberg, she claims that preferences for pornography reflect "macho social and political convictions" and contempt for the worth of women in general. [32] But this analysis means that, in a society that permits the production and consumption of pornography, the preferences of those who enjoy it are counted twice. Women are not accorded equal treatment and respect because the views of pornography consumers about the fantasies

and sexual experiences they prefer, as well as about the fantasies and sexual experiences they think women should prefer, count in the utilitarian
calculus. The right to moral independence requires that the worth of all
individuals and the worth of their own conceptions of the good life are
accorded equal respect and treatment. But this kind of equality is just
what the production and consumption of pornography denies women.

Langton's account of the principle of equality conforms to Dworkin's
own. For both, the principle of equality is tied to a principle of moral independence, and they differ only on the question of whether it is pornography or its prohibition that violates this principle. MacKinnon's analysis of equality considerations in the debate over pornography is more
startling. Pornography, she insists, poses a problem for the principle of
equality, not only because it denies the equal worth of women and their
conceptions of the good, but also because it does so in the same way Jim
Crow laws enforced the subjugation of African Americans, in a state-
sanctioned way enforced ideologically by calling pornography speech.
At issue in the debate over pornography, in other words, is not simply the
issue of why the First Amendment should protect pornographic speech
over women's speech but the issue of why it should abandon women by
constituting pornography as speech in the first place.

Utterances such as saying "Kill" to a trained attack dog in the presence of another person are clearly defined as actions—in this case, the
act of murder. Telling someone to "Raise your goddamn fare twenty percent, I'll raise mine the next morning" constitutes price fixing, not free
speech.[33] "A sign saying 'Whites Only' is only words," MacKinnon argues, "but it is not legally seen as expressing the viewpoint 'we do not
want Black people in this store,' or as dissenting from the policy view
that both blacks and whites must be served. . . . Segregation cannot happen without someone saying 'get out' or 'you don't belong here' at some
point. Elevation and denigration are all accomplished through meaningful symbols and communicative acts in which saying it is doing it."[34]

Of course, the distinction for which MacKinnon is searching here
would seem to be the difference between the sort of speech or communication that possesses meaning within a context of action and practice
and the sort of speech that does not. A sign that says "Whites Only" becomes the action of discrimination because of a set of social and political practices and legal orders of which it is a part, just as the command
"Kill" to a trained guard dog becomes an act of destruction because of
the set of actions and commands in terms of which the dog has been
trained. But this contextual understanding of the connection between

speech and action can be used to confirm MacKinnon's point. Pornography has the force of subordination because it is part of a sexist context of actions, practices, and beliefs. A sign saying "Whites Only" might not have the force of discrimination in a nonracist society, and pornography, she suggests, might not have the force of subordination in a nonsexist society. In contrast, in a society in which, she contends, 38 percent of women are sexually molested as girls, 24 percent are raped in marriage, and nearly half are victims of rape or attempted rape at least once in their lives,[35] the protection the First Amendment is said to afford pornography takes on an institutional meaning. The subordination it serves to enforce is no different from institutionalized segregation.

Strossen misidentifies MacKinnon's point here, perhaps intentionally, criticizing it as a failure to make the necessary distinction between a clear and present danger, on the one hand, and a mere "bad tendency," on the other. The "Achilles heel"[36] of MacKinnon's argument, Strossen claims, is its focus on the political ideas conveyed by sexual expression—ideas, namely, about gender roles and gender-based discrimination. The content of pornography, according to Strossen's account of MacKinnon, is the political claim that women should be subordinate to men. Hence, Strossen asks the obvious question: "If we should restrict sexually explicit speech because it purveys sexist ideas, as the feminist antipornography faction argues, then why shouldn't we restrict nonsexually explicit speech when it purveys sexist ideas? And if speech conveying sexist ideas can be restricted, then why shouldn't speech be restricted when it conveys racist, heterosexist and other biased ideas?"[37] But this identification of pornography with any ideational content is just the identification MacKinnon tries to explode. Pornography contains no more ideational content than a "Whites Only" sign on a drinking fountain. The sign may imply that whites are superior to other groups, just as pornography may imply that men are superior to women. But each primarily, in MacKinnon's view, performs a function, in the first instance that of cordoning African Americans off from the rest of society and, in the second instance, that of cordoning off women.

In the work of MacKinnon and others, then, the conceptions of the principle of free speech and that of equality differ markedly from the conceptions held by their opponents. For the pro-pornography and liberal position, the freedom of speech means the participant right to say what one wants as well as the audience right to hear or read what one wants, as long as the speech in question does not present a clear and present danger. This position is grounded in a conception of equality that stresses the identical worth of all individuals and their right to express themselves and to pursue the life projects and options they have selected, regardless of the choices of their fellow citizens. For the antipornography position, however, free speech means the freedom to speak in a communicative situation that is free of the distortions caused by implicit or explicit coercion, the effects of power and money, or ideological factors such as sexism or racism. The principle of equality, for its part, also takes account of the social context in which one pursues one's life projects. On this account, we must ask, first, whether that social context allows for the identical worth of women and their projects. Second, we must recognize that if that social context institutionalizes racism or sexism then the extent of one's full participation in public life and the extent of the recognition of the worth of one's choices are severely circumscribed. The principle of equality means more than a merely formal moral independence; it means, in addition, the ability of all to participate on the same basis with others in the life and direction of the society.[38]

The controversy over pornography includes another element in addition to the freedom of speech and the principle of equality—namely, the question of what might be called sexual authenticity. While liberal and pro-pornography feminists insist that pornography can have a positive function in assisting the sexual fantasies and self-images of women, antipornography feminists contend that it can only distort sexual identity and expression. To characterize this aspect of the debate I shall refer to a controversy Strossen mentions in her attack on MacKinnon.

IDEOLOGY AND AUTHENTICITY

The cover of an issue of an erotic magazine called *On Our Backs* depicts an Asian-American woman "fully covered in body paint portraying flames with images of fire all around her."[39] To an antipornography group called Dykes against Pornography (DAP), the photograph is both racist and incendiary since it seems to suggest "that white dykes should be getting off on setting Asian girls on fire." The magazine responded that the image was intended to counter views of Asian-American women as sexually submissive and, moreover, that the idea for the cover came from the Asian-American model herself, who apparently wanted to portray herself as sexually "hot." To this explanation, the DAP spokeswoman responded, "I think she's a fucking sellout and that's all I have to say about it."[40]

The issue this case raises pertains not only to the relation between intentions and interpreted meaning but also to false consciousness. The response of DAP to the magazine's cover condemns it, in essence, as an expression of sexuality that simply displays the effects of pornography, in particular, and racism and sexism, in general. The Asian-American model's statements about her intentions are a sellout or, at the very least, are not to be taken at face value because they embody ideological distortions of which she may not herself be aware. Instead, she has internalized sexist and racist visions of an "authentic" sexuality as her own. Indeed, the antipornography position suggests that what are taken to be natural or given components of sexual identity and assertiveness in general are simply reflections of historically and socially specific constellations of power. These are ideologically sustained and reinforced by the patina of a "second nature" in terms of which that sexual identity appears.[41] Thus, insofar as the magazine's editors and model take scant clothing, large breasts, and certain sorts of poses uncritically to mean sexuality, sexual assertion, or being "hot," the magazine simply produces and reproduces the racist and sexist social reality that oppresses women.

But if this critique of false consciousness serves as the foundation for DAP's position on the magazine cover, then anti-antipornography feminists might remain understandably unconvinced. For, from a pro-pornography perspective, pornography, far from contributing to an ideological defense of female oppression, is revolutionary in both its rejection of sexual repression and its exposure of different modes of sexual being. In advocating sexual adventure, sex without procreative intentions, "casual sex, anonymous sex, group sex, voyeuristic sex, illegal sex, public sex," it hardly victimizes women, pro-pornography feminists argue.[42] Rather, it may help some women to understand the legitimacy and generality of their own fantasies and desires. Such an understanding is particularly important, they suggest, for a young girl with what she may initially consider to represent illegitimate lesbian longings. But Ellen Willis insists that pornography also expresses a "radical impulse" in general "insofar as it is critical of the patriarchal ideology which divides women into 'bad girls' who enjoy violent, emotionless sex and submissive, ladylike 'good girls' who are interested only in romance.[43] To the extent that women find themselves enjoying pornography, Willis insists, they free themselves of distorting myths about female sexuality.

Strossen adds that they may discover aspects of their sexuality about which they can be educated in no other way, and she quotes Myrna

Kostash as follows: "Until there is a revolution in the institutions that regulate sexual relations—the family, the school, the workplace—perhaps the pornographic fantasy is one of the few ways that women and men, captives together of those institutions, victims alike of their alienating procedures are permitted connection."[44] Hence, to the antipornography claim that women-produced pornography displays the effects of ideology or false consciousness, the liberal or anti-antipornography position suggests a two-faceted attack. First, antipornography feminism silences different women's differing sexual self-expressions by condemning those with which it disagrees as false consciousness. Second, it impedes their sexual self-development by promoting legislation that would suppress materials through which women can discover different views of an authentic sexuality and, indeed, different ways of being sexual.

The feminist debate over pornography seems to conclude with two irreconcilable positions.[45] From the point of view of the antipornography movement, pornography oppresses women. By defining it as speech and then using the protections afforded speech to defend pornography, recourse to the First Amendment helps to distort an adequate understanding of women's illocutionary aims and to block their full participation in public life. Hence, if traditional liberal interpretations of the First Amendment take as part of their task that of defending the free speech of pornographers, this goal has the ideological function of maintaining women's subordination. Moreover, if the anti-antipornography movement insists that the antipornography movement itself oppresses women by dismissing their professions of enjoyment and rejecting their explanations of their illocutionary aims, for the antipornography position this insistence performs the ideological function of obstructing the expression of more authentic versions of sexuality.

From the anti-antipornography position, however, it is the antipornography movement that distorts what both women and pornographers say. In claiming that certain assertions of sexuality are the effect of sexism or racism or both, the antipornography movement reinforces existing stereotypes about good and bad "girls," blocking progress that would transform sexual relations, release individuals from an unnecessary prudishness, and even educate them in new possibilities of their sexual being. If, from one point of view, pornography is an expression of power relations that oppress women, from the other it is a subversion of the sexual status quo and the attempt to suppress pornography is an attempt to silence a revolutionary point of view.

LEGITIMATE VOICES

This debate has thus far been pursued with a fair amount of hysteria on both sides. Catherine MacKinnon opens her *Only Words* with a horrific description of an imaginary woman's subordination and degradation through history at the hands of sadistic and dominating men, claiming that "pornography makes the world a pornographic place through its making and use, establishing what women are said to exist as, are seen as, are treated as, constructing the social reality of what a woman is and can be in terms of what can be done to her, and what a man is in terms of doing it." [46] For her part, Nadine Strossen begins her attack on antipornography feminism with a dire warning. "Make no mistake," she writes, "if accepted the feminist pro-censorship analysis would lead inevitably to the suppression of far more than pornography. . . . One might well ask . . . not what expression would be stifled, but rather, what expression would be safe." [47]

While each side thus quickly dismisses the other as a form of oppression, censorship, or ideology, more would appear to be at stake than simply the question of pornography. Also at stake are the more fundamental questions of what we mean by principles of free speech, equality, and sexual authenticity and how we might try to realize them. Suppose we take seriously the hermeneutic turn this study has tried to accomplish, the turn from a "clash of absolutes" to a difference in interpretation on the meaning of principles we share. Then we might also view as peremptory the move each side makes to dismiss the other side as a form of false consciousness. Indeed, instead of talking past one another or dismissing one another as hopeless ideologues, liberal and antipornography feminists might engage in a discussion of their disparate understandings in which each side assumes that the other might have something of value to say. In particular, liberal feminists might adopt a more hermeneutic attitude toward the antipornography position and try to understand the way in which it expands our understanding of certain of our fundamental principles, even if they disagree about the impact of pornography on their realization. At the same time, antipornography feminists might adopt a similarly hermeneutic attitude toward the liberal and pro-pornography feminist position, taking seriously the question of whether legislative and juridical attempts to restrain pornography can realize our ideals as antipornography feminists themselves understand them. In other words, they might begin to take more seriously the cautions against censorship that Holmes and Brandeis expressed. In the remainder of this chapter, I want to pull together the different implications of my analysis thus far to develop these ideas.

The remarks Strossen makes about the educational benefits of pornography in helping women to develop their sexual identities also add a second dimension to her analysis of the freedom of speech. Under this second understanding, the principle of free speech does not only protect a personal right to say and hear what one wants under most circumstances. It also protects a domain of self-development. Here the principle has a more public domain than it does in Strossen's first account, inasmuch as its importance lies in the access it guarantees to those beliefs, opinions, and ideas that help us determine who we are and want to be. The principle of free speech protects a public domain of free expression in which individuals are free to hear and discuss different religious, aesthetic, ethical, and personal ideals to help them define who they are, who they want to be, and what they think. Pornography, on this analysis, must be available since it expresses different possibilities for different modes of sexual self-expression and identification.

An alternative conception of the principle of free speech understands it as a condition of the exercise of political liberties. That is, the point of protecting certain forms of speech is to allow citizens to govern themselves collectively and democratically. To do so, they must be able to express their ideas about political ideals and policies and to listen to those of others to come to a mutual agreement on legitimate courses of action.[48] But neither this interpretation of the meaning of free speech nor the two dimensions that Strossen's work suggests completely corresponds to the sense implied by the antipornography position. Here, the conception of free speech extends to the structure of both the private domain of self-development through which we decide who we are and want to be and the public political domain in which we collectively decide, as equal participants, the laws and policies to which we shall adhere.

This understanding of the principle of free speech is close to the model of practical discourse that Jürgen Habermas has culled from the performative structure of communication oriented to understanding, a model tying the justification of norms of action to the assent of all those affected as free and equal participants in a discourse oriented only by the concern to come to agreement over validity.[49] Here, the freedom of all those affected entails their liberty from explicit or implicit coercion and from the effects of money and power, while their equality is structurally defined as their symmetrical ability to raise and redeem what Habermas calls validity claims—in this case, claims about the rightness of actions or norms. In practical discourse, we assess the validity of claims by examining challenges to and defenses of them under conditions free of all force except the force of the better argument. This ideal of free speech need not be an entirely attainable reality. Instead, it might function as a kind of regulative ideal through which we assess obstacles to approximating, as closely as possible, an ideal of unconstrained communication.

If one gives this account of practical discourse an interpretive focus, the ideal of free speech it and MacKinnon's conception articulates is also already anticipated by the condition that hermeneutic conversation involves. According to this condition, our ability to educate and enrich alternative interpretations depends upon the openness of the conversation to all legitimate understandings, excluding those illegitimate interpretations the content of which involves the silencing and suppression of the interpretations of others. MacKinnon's and Habermas's account would seem to be particularly significant for the hermeneutic conception, however, for if one takes up the understanding of free speech that both suggest, then the issue of open hermeneutic conversation can be seen to involve more than simply the question of whether certain interpretive voices are explicitly excluded. In addition, it involves the question of whether ideological assumptions about the worth of certain people or groups can serve to silence and suppress contributions to public discourse in similar ways. One might argue that the Supreme Court's 1896 *Plessy v Ferguson* decision on racial segregation,[50] accomplished just such an exclusion insofar as it simply ignored African Americans' understanding of segregation because of its ideological assumptions about African Americans and the worth of their contributions. Antipornography feminists, arguably, simply extend these concerns further to include pornography as an element of ideology and to show the way they think it affects our attempts to understand the worth of women's contributions to our political debates, as well as the self-formative discussions in which we investigate with others our conceptions of ourselves and the good.

The consequence of this sort of unrestricted domain of expression need not involve eliminating all differences in the way actors or interpreters understand the situations in which they find themselves or the principles they invoke. If one takes seriously a substantive conception of free speech extracted from Habermas and MacKinnon, then one need not deny that individuals can fail to agree or that communicative agreements are not always forthcoming, even without the sort of systematic disturbances that antipornography feminists attribute to pornography.

Nor need one deny that actors in sexually charged situations may sometimes understand those situations differently. The concern of free speech, understood in this way, is rather directed at external intrusions on attempts to come to an understanding, even if that involves understanding that we understand differently. Thus, on this construction of the antipornography view, the problem with pornography is not only that it makes it difficult for actors to agree on their definition of the situation. Pornography also intrudes upon one group's ability to see that it understands the issue or situation differently from another and hence upon its ability to refrain from acting precipitously upon what it takes as a canonical view of the situation or issue. This analysis does not show that pornography indeed functions as an obstacle to the free rein of interpretive conversation. The point is simply that, if this fourth conception of free speech is a plausible one, then we might investigate the degree to which pornography does or does not function as violence, money, and power do in affecting the public space in which we talk, listen, and attempt to learn from one another.

Antipornography and liberal or pro-pornography feminists also differ in their conceptions of equality as it pertains to the issue of pornography. For Dworkin, Strossen, and others, equality in this case means simply the equal right of those who produce or enjoy pornography to do so in the same way that others enjoy their own projects or conceptions of the good. As Strossen quotes Feminists for Free Expression: "It is the right and responsibility of each woman to read, view or produce the sexual material she chooses without the intervention of the state 'for her own good.' We believe genuine feminism encourages individuals to make these choices for themselves." [51]

But antipornography feminists deny the equation between this position and a defense of pornography. In their view, pornography does not offer but rather denies women freedom in pursuing their choices and undermines principles of equal respect for the worth of women. Pornography subordinates their conceptions of their own worth and that of their life-projects to the conceptions men or pornographers have of what they ought to be, and it portrays them, at best, as objects for the use and control of others. In this regard, legal support for pornography in the form of First Amendment protections does not merely add insult to injury. Rather, it legalizes this subordination of women in the same way that Jim Crow laws legalize the subordination of African Americans. As in the case of free speech, the issue with which antipornography feminism is concerned involves the structure of the public space in which individuals are meant to be equal, and, to this extent, it implies a definition of equality identical to what we explored in defending affirmative action policies, a definition that links equality to the capacity to participate in the common life of the community. Equality on this interpretation pertains to our public lives and, moreover, to the structure of the public domain that must allow for the participation of all. If, instead, this public space is one in which women cannot participate, either because of explicit legal constraints or because of ideological constraints through which they internalize subordinating conceptions of their worth and identity, then their equality remains chimerical.

Again, it remains an open question as to whether pornography does function as an ideological constraint undermining principles of equal worth and participation as an equal for women. Nonetheless, the different understandings of the principle of equality at work here should be clear. If, for critics of the antipornography position such as Dworkin, equality means the equal right to pursue one's own, essentially private conception of the good as long as it does not clearly infringe upon the right of others to pursue their conceptions of the good, for antipornography feminists one problem is that pornographic conceptions of the good do infringe upon the right of women to determine and pursue their conceptions of the good, but they do so in a partially concealed, ideological fashion. They do not forbid them, any longer, to be or do certain things but, rather, enforce a kind of state-sanctioned subordination, affecting their conceptions of themselves, of their worth, and of their social role. But this circumstance means that we cannot understand the principle of equality simply in terms of guaranteeing a right to one's own conception of the good; in addition it must guarantee the open and non-ideological character of the necessarily public domain in which these conceptions are initially developed.

Finally, antipornography and liberal or anti-antipornography feminists differ on their notions of sexual authenticity. Here again, the liberal idea focuses on the individual's conception and expression of what he or she understands as his or her authentic self-identity. Whatever individuals understand as who they are and who they want to be counts as an authentic version of identity, and the same holds for their sexual identity. If pornographic materials teach them how to be "hot" or what desires a rape fantasy can satisfy, then these materials help to develop an authentic sexual self-identity. In matters so completely personal, no one, and particularly not the state, should decide for others what constitutes their own sexuality. But, once again, the antipornography feminist position focuses on the more public domain in which these conceptions are first developed. If the environment in which one must find or create one's identity is one pervaded by sexist, stereotypical, and demeaning options, then in the antipornography view the possibilities of self-identity become a form of false consciousness. What one takes to be an authentic expression of who one really is or what one's sexuality really consists in will in fact simply reinforce existing relations of power.

As in the case of the antipornography feminist interpretations of free speech and equality, this interpretation of sexual authenticity entails no conclusions about whether pornography reinforces conformist and demeaning conceptions of women's sexuality or whether it subverts them. What is important for the present discussion is simply that the idea of authenticity implied by antipornography feminism is, again, more public and structural than the one that liberal and anti-antipornography feminists defend. On this view, the test of whether or not one has managed to create an authentic identity for oneself will involve more than a declaration about what one thinks one wants or needs. It will also involve questions about whether one has understood oneself in a way that is conditioned by imposed views about what one ought to want or need.

An answer to the question of whether pornography does present an obstacle to realizing the principles of free speech, equality, and sexual authenticity, as the antipornography position interprets them, requires the same sort of empirical study that has thus far focused, with contradictory results, on the question of whether pornography promotes physical violence against women. Yet the achievement of the antipornography position has nevertheless been to ask us to reconsider what we mean by these ideals. Moreover, even if we ultimately reject the antipornography position's view of pornography itself, we might still admit that the position helps to enrich and deepen our conceptions of our principles and thereby helps define the criteria against which we must measure obstacles to our ideals.

Still, if the liberal and pro-pornography position can learn to expand its conceptions of certain of our fundamental principles by adopting a more hermeneutic approach to the antipornography position, might the antipornography position not do the same by adopting a more hermeneutic stance to the liberal and anti-antipornography position? The antipornography interpretation of principles of free speech, equality, and sexual authenticity includes decidedly dogmatic suggestions about what pornography is (namely, the abuse of women) and what an authentic sexuality is not (namely, what a male culture says it is). The antipornography position therefore culminates in demands for a form of censorship in legislation designed to provide women with civil rights claims against the producers and sellers of specific pieces of pornography wherever it can be shown that those pieces led to insult, injury, battery, rape, sexual harassment, or lower pay at work.[52] But for Strossen and others this is the crucial mistake in the antipornography program, for it introduces legislative and juridical remedies into the domain of individual choices, conceptions of the good, and attempts to develop one's own sexual identity. For this liberal position, the antiobscenity rulings the Court initiated in 1957 already reflect a significant undermining of the principle of free speech where it pertains to sexual words or pictures. The Court, in this view, would do well, not only to refrain from replacing antiobscenity law with antipornography law, but also to retire from the business of scrutinizing sexual speech altogether. If the antipornography position were to take seriously the point behind this position, it might learn not simply to dismiss the concerns liberal theorists raise about the attempt to engineer an uncontaminated public space through legislative or juridical means. It might develop a greater sensitivity to different forms sexuality can take and to the dangers involved in limiting speech, and it might come to question whether legal interventions are more useful in combating pornography than public education and continued debate.

Of course, this recourse to continuing debate and the education of sexist opinions appears problematic for the reasons antipornography feminists suggest. If we are to try to combat demeaning conceptions of women by continuing to speak out against them, and if we are to try to exclude systematic disturbances in communication on sexual discourse and expression, the question remains as to how this is possible if, as antipornography feminists maintain, the field of discourse remains ideologically distorted by the effects of pornography itself. If our public debates and sexual expression are affected by ideological conceptions of our principles, values, and conceptions of sexuality, and if these ideological conceptions support women's subordination, then how is public debate meant to cut through the static to allow for the education of either pornographers or women?

Here Strossen is quite adamant: women and minorities have never been assisted by ceding the right to determine appropriate limits on free expression to governmental bodies. She points out that *Our Bodies, Ourselves,* a book on women's health and sexuality issues written for women by women, has already been the target of censorship campaigns, as have issues of *Ms.* magazine that focus on contraception and Judy Blume's novels for young adults.[53] Indeed, in Canada where the Canadian Supreme Court adopted MacKinnon's views on pornography in its 1992 decision in *Butler v The Queen,* the ruling is most often used to suppress feminist, gay, and lesbian materials that the predominantly male judges in these cases typically find "degrading and dehumanizing."[54] Were the U.S. government's antiobscenity laws rewritten as antipornography laws, Strossen insists, the chances of such censorship in the United States would only be increased. Brandeis's appeal to more speech, then, might be a weak response in view of ideological obstacles to a mutual understanding of a speaker's illocutionary aims and the intimate connection that speech often has to action, as evidenced by state-supported segregation. Still, the equation on which MacKinnon insists between a Constitutional defense of pornography and Jim Crow laws does not mean that the sort of juridical interventions that ended governmentally enforced segregation are equally appropriate to the case of pornography. In this case, laws regulating the production and consumption of what are seen as pornographic materials might be used to suppress precisely that information women need to express themselves in what the antipornography movement itself understands as an authentic way.

The upshot of these considerations is that if we are to ask Strossen and others genuinely to listen to antipornography claims, we must also ask MacKinnon and other antipornography feminists to listen to more liberal concerns. They might learn to question whether censorship can ever enhance free speech, and they might come to wonder whether people should not be allowed their own notions of sexual authenticity while continuing to educate them as to the possible distorting effects of cultural and sexist influences on these notions. In addition to taking liberal and pro-pornography ideas of free speech and sexual authenticity more seriously, the antipornography position might also take seriously liberal and pro-pornography interpretations of equality. Indeed, it might come to agree that equality requires attentiveness to the worth of different people and protection of the right to different conceptions of the good while still demanding that we acknowledge the way some conceptions of the good may covertly impede this equality.

The conclusion, then, of a reciprocal learning process between anti- and pro-pornography feminists would ask us to keep in sight a robust version of the principles of free speech, equality, and authenticity according to which they require us to work to eliminate disturbances in the field of an unconstrained conversation in which all voices can participate on the same basis. At the same time, we might learn from the liberal and pro-pornography position to question the recourse to legal and legislative attempts to engineer this open field of discourse. To the extent that this field is meant to encourage interpretive conversation and the free flow of different legitimate interpretations of our identity, history, and principles, the liberal position asks us to remember that excluding illegitimate voices from our interpretive conversation is a task for the conversation itself, and not for preexisting censorship rules. With regard to pornography, then we might instead allow for its publication as part both of the right to free speech and of the equality right to one's own conception of oneself and the good while attending vigorously to the task of eliminating stereotypical or demeaning conceptions of certain preconceived groups. More specifically, we might educate citizens about the way pornography and other cultural artifacts may distort women's speech, obscure the character of their desires even to themselves, and promote rigidified ideas about gender. But we might do so without recourse to censorship for those who disagree. In any case, for either side to dismiss the other one without seriously attempting to understand the potential value of its interpretation of fundamental principles might contribute to the mutual animosity between parties to the debate. It will not contribute to its resolution.

This reconstruction of the feminist debate over pornography has brought us to fundamental issues about the structure of free speech and the equal participation of all it is supposed to involve. In so doing, it has brought us to fundamental issues about hermeneutic conversation itself. In the next chapter of this study I would like to explore these issues further by comparing the sort of hermeneutic conversation I have promoted in this study to Habermas's conception of practical discourse, which I introduced in this chapter. In its Habermasian formulation, unconstrained communication provides the idealized context for testing the validity of norms and principles. Only those are legitimate to which all those concerned can agree as participants in an "ideal speech situation" in which no voice is excluded and all have the same chances to raise and challenge validity claims.[55] Yet the question relevant to the present study is not how we are to justify our principles but rather how we are to understand them. Accordingly, the next chapter explores the place Habermas finds for the sort of interpretive conversation with which this study is concerned.

CHAPTER SIX

Hermeneutic Debate and Deliberative Democracy

The model of public debate that has emerged in the previous five chapters stresses an interpretive discussion of the meaning of our moral and legal principles. As Americans, we collectively appeal to principles of life, liberty, and equality, principles that we take to be articulated for us in our Constitution and basic institutional structure and that also form the normative background for our debates over the morality and legality of disputed practices. At the same time, we often disagree in how we understand these principles, the way they are articulated, and the meanings of the practices, history, and ideals that surround them. We also often disagree in the way we understand texts and works of art. In these cases, we assume that some of our different understandings are equally legitimate and, moreover, that as long as we can allow them to be voiced such differences provide the opportunity for learning from each other's interpretations to enrich and expand our understanding of texts and works of art in an ongoing way. If our understanding of our moral and legal principles and their articulation in practices is similarly interpretive, should we not orient our public discussions of the issues that divide us to similar opportunities for learning? Norms of action as well as moral and Constitutional principles can be considered text-analogues insofar as they have meanings we must interpret and are therefore subject to differences in interpretation. If we acknowledge the interpretive character of our understanding of both our principles and their articulations, we can recognize the possible adequacy of some different understandings and learn from our differences continually to enrich our own understanding.

Both critics and defenders of surrogate mothering might learn from an alternative understanding of the meaning of family participation to question some of their presumptions about autonomy, control, and the meaning of mothering. Critics of affirmative action might learn from its defenders to take seriously not only which dimension of our principle of equal opportunity that involves gender, racial, and ethnic neutrality but also that dimension which involves integration and the participation of all. At the same time, defenders of affirmative action might learn the extent to which ignoring the connection between principles of equality and those of neutrality allows women and minorities to be both stigmatized and resegregated within the practices and institutions to which they have been admitted. Critics of abortion rights might learn from their defenders to respect the quality of the lives of women, families, and children as well as fetuses and to take seriously those aspects of liberty and equality that speak to the joint nature of the projects in which men and women are involved. By the same token, pro-choice groups might learn from pro-life groups to reemphasize the sanctity of all human life and to help with the effort to find a place in American life for the virtues of care, nurturance, and support for families. Moreover, they might learn to question settled presumptions as to the connection between liberty and technology and to help restore a balance between controlling all facets of love and life and recognizing the way unanticipated events or relationships might magnify and enrich us.

The discussion of pornography adds another facet to this model of interpretive debate, however. For the debate over pornography speaks to the issue of whether certain conditions might not impede or prevent the possibility of just the sort of learning from other interpretations of meaning on which interpretive discussions depend. One can reconstruct the antipornography position from an interpretive point of view as the claim that pornography introduces disturbances into the field of public discussion that work to silence legitimate interpretive voices and hence to remove them from the interpretive space in which we learn from one another. If it remains questionable whether pornography does effect such silencing, other cases of silencing are not so ambiguous. Slavery and Jim Crow laws, for example, silence the interpretive voices of slaves and African Americans either by simply excluding these voices from the public discussion or by so demeaning those that express them that their interpretations cannot be heard.

But this circumstance means that an interpretive model of public debate needs to be combined with conditions that preserve its open character, conditions that I have argued emerge from the logic of hermeneutic discussion itself. If one's own definition of the meaning of principles Americans share is just an interpretation, then it cannot be held any more dogmatically than can an interpretation of a text. Rather, it must be open to the way different interpretations can reveal different dimensions of the meaning of the principle and to the way those different interpretations may change or revise one's own. But this circumstance indicates that the adequacy of one's own interpretation can be tested and developed only in interpretive discussions; if those discussions exclude legitimate interpretive voices this exclusion exacts a considerable price. One's own interpretation will be denied the enrichment, guidance, and even, in some cases, correction that a suppressed voice might have provided it.

The idea of open public debate is one I have associated with the work of Jürgen Habermas and one in general that is connected with ideas of what has come to be called deliberative democracy.[1] Yet, Habermas's conception of public deliberation itself affords only a small role to explicitly interpretive discussions of meaning. His complex account deals with forms of interpretive discussion in three contexts: in the analysis of the way that what he calls pragmatic, ethical, and moral discourses are featured in the rational opinion- and will-formation of democratic societies, in the account of discourses of application, and in the idea of a "weak" public sphere. In none of these contexts, however, does Habermas think interpretive discussion can suffice on its own to resolve public disputes in adequate and rational ways. Since his account thus provides a significant counterweight to the conception of an interpretive democracy, I want to clarify the conception by exploring the ways in which Habermas restricts the role of interpretive public debate. I shall first look at the limited role Habermas finds for it in collective deliberations over questions of policy, and I shall then turn to the role he finds for it in the other two contexts, that involving the application of justified norms and principles and, finally, that involving the relation of a weak public sphere to the procedures of deliberative democracy.

THE PLACE OF INTERPRETATION IN PUBLIC DISCOURSE

How is a democratic society to decide in a rational manner what it ought to do with regard to matters under dispute in that society? Habermas argues that answering this question necessitates examining the different conditions valid solutions must satisfy. He therefore distinguishes among pragmatic, ethical, and moral discourses; ethical discourses serve as the site Habermas finds for what I have called interpretive discussions.[2] Pragmatic discourses involve questions concerning suitable means for realizing goals or preferences upon which an actor or a society has already decided. Thus, if a collectivity has decided to support its poor and unemployed, pragmatic discourses will center on the issue of the best means of doing so. In such cases, a rationally justified choice of means requires "comparisons and weighings" that the deliberators, "supported by observations and prognoses, can carry out from the standpoint of efficiency or other decision rules."[3] Pragmatic discourses can also assess goals in terms of higher-order purposes or interests. Deliberators might be concerned, for example, with the question of whether certain ways of supporting the poor and unemployed create dependencies that are to be avoided. The question pragmatic discourses take up is how to avoid such dependencies, and they do in terms, again, of agreed-upon decision rules. The decision rules can also become reflective, for instance, in the form of a theory of rational choice. Still, Habermas claims, "practical reflection here proceeds with the horizon of purposive rationality, its goal being to discover appropriate techniques, strategies, or programs"[4] for goals that have already been determined.

The goals and preferences presupposed in pragmatic discourses can themselves be contested, however. In this case, deciding the question of what we ought to do as single actors or as a society involves more than deciding the efficiency of a proposed means to an end within a pragmatic discourse. Rather, Habermas thinks valid decisions require forms of ethical and moral discourse. Ethical matters, as he conceives of them, first of all, are matters that concern the individual interpretive question of "Who am I, and who would I like to be?"[5] To the extent that answers to this question go beyond trivial preferences to address the question of one's identity and self-understanding in general, Habermas connects the answers to a person's ideals and conceptions of the good. For their part, ideals and conceptions of the good are connected to cultural values and intersubjectively shared traditions. We do not come to our values and conceptions of the good as unsocialized creatures, in other words, but rather as individuals who have grown up in certain cultures with certain values, with certain interpretive orientations and as members of certain traditions. Hence, the way we understand our fundamental interests, our conceptions of the good, and ourselves is bound up with our heritage and culture. Our individual self-understanding is thus already linked to a collective self-understanding, and when we review our conceptions and life projects we do so in terms of a collective view. "My identity is shaped by collective identities," Habermas writes. "To that extent the life that is good for me also concerns the forms of life that are common to us."[6]

Two important consequences follow from this relation between individual self-understanding and collective understanding. First, one can assess the adequacy of one's self-understanding in conversations with others within one's culture; these others are, Habermas suggests, able to understand one's ideals and life choices since they share in the traditions and vocabularies to which these ideals and choices belong. Second, we can move from ethical-existential discussions involving our understanding of our individual identities to ethical-political discourses that have as their goal "the clarification of a collective identity."[7] The point here is that ethical-existential discussions or discourses in which we help each other clarify our respective conceptions of the good already themselves depend upon a common cultural framework that sets the parameters for the conceptions and discussions of the good that make sense for us. Hence, we can also discuss this common cultural framework and engage in ethical-political discussions that seek to discover who we are collectively, how we understand ourselves and our ends as a community, and what norms and practices reflect our collective conception of the good and sense of who we are. As Habermas puts the point: "serious value decisions result from, and change with, the politico-cultural self-understanding of a historical community. Enlightenment over this self-understanding is achieved through a hermeneutics that critically appropriates traditions and thereby assists in the intersubjective reassurance or renovation of authentic life orientations and deeply held values."[8]

In pragmatic discourses, as Habermas conceives of them, we try to determine the efficacy of policies or programs in terms of goals upon which we have already decided. In ethical-political discourses, we consider the question of how or whether those goals reflect our collective identity and self-understanding and we engage in hermeneutic or interpretive reflection on what that collective identity is. Moral discourses examine laws and policies from a third perspective, that of justice. Here the question is not only whether a proposed course of action reflects our common conception of who we are but how the matter under deliberation can be decided in a way that is just. Moreover, questions of just policy ultimately involve discourses in which participants show that "the interests embodied in contested norms are unreservedly universalizable:

In moral discourse the ethnocentric perspective of a particular collectivity expands into the comprehensive perspective or an unlimited communication community, all of whose members put themselves in each individual's situation, worldview, and self-understanding, and together practice an ideal role-taking."[9]

As Habermas conceives of what he calls the "discursive formation of a common political will,"[10] then, pragmatic discourses, on their own, serve only to assess the appropriateness of different possible courses of action in light of their efficiency and probable consequences. But we also must decide whether those courses of action that are justified pragmatically conform to who we understand ourselves to be (a determination made in ethical discourses) or satisfy the equal interests of all (a determination made in moral discourses) or both. Further, Habermas claims that whether we can engage in ethical-political discussion alone or must engage in moral discourse as well depends upon "the aspect under which the matter in need of regulation permits further clarification."[11] Where that aspect is a morally relevant one, discourses are required "that submit the contested interests and value orientations to a universalization test within the framework set by the system of rights as it has been constitutionally interpreted and elaborated."[12] Examples of such matters, in his view, include tax law and the organization of educational and health care systems since these matters directly affect the distribution of social wealth, life opportunities, and chances for survival. Where, however, the aspect to be clarified is ethically relevant, discourses are required that "push beyond contested interests and values and engage the participants in a process of self-understanding by which they become reflectively aware of the deeper consonances [*Übereinstimmungen*] in a common form of life."[13] Examples of these matters for Habermas include questions of ecology, city planning, the protection of cultural and ethnic minorities, and immigration policy.

Habermas appears to think that the latter issues are accessible to resolution through ethical-political discourses for two reasons. First, they do not involve questions of rights directly but instead center on the ways we understand ourselves. Ecological questions, for instance, are not questions about how to resolve matters in the equal interests of humans and animals. They are, from Habermas's point of view, questions about how the ways we treat nature reflect upon us, what our actions say about who we are.[14] Similarly, questions of city planning are questions about the lifestyles we want to promote, about the ratio of freeways to public transit, about the ratio of apartments to houses our city ought to have, and so on. Questions of protecting cultural and ethnic minorities are questions such as whether Canada ought to preserve and promote a French-speaking culture within a predominantly English-speaking nation.[15] Here the question is whether doing so comports with Canada's self-understanding or its conception of the good as one that actively encourages diverse forms of life. Finally, to the extent that immigration policy is an ethical question, it is not a question of what rights noncitizens have against citizens. Rather, the question involves what kind of community the citizens collectively take their community to be.

Such issues are appropriately resolved in ethical-political discourse, second, in Habermas's view, because they remain open to an ethical-political consensus. The concern of such discourses is the meaning for the participants of the traditions and forms of life they share, and in clarifying their meaning for each other they can often "push beyond" contested values to discover who they collectively understand themselves to be with regard to a particular issue and what policies and courses of action reflect that self-understanding. But, significantly, this condition also indicates the limits of such discourses for Habermas. In the first place, even though a proposed policy or program may not raise a moral question directly, its compatibility with a community's understanding of itself may not be sufficient on its own to answer whether that community ought to proceed with it, if that self-understanding is incompatible with the equal interests of all. A fundamentalist self-understanding, for example, might well reflect a consensus on who a particular group of fundamentalists takes itself to be but also lead to courses of action antithetical to the equal rights of women or to the equal right of individuals to pursue their own alternative conceptions of the good or ways of life.[16]

This deficiency in ethical-political discourse stems from its ties to particular hermeneutic horizons. Habermas does not deny that a group's or society's self-understanding can be reflective and critical. Indeed, where the substance of collective or individual self-understanding is self-contradictory or self-deluded, ethical and ethical-political discussions can help participants clarify what they really mean and how they really understand themselves. Still, through such discourse participants cannot "work themselves free of the form of life in which they de facto find themselves."[17] Habermas therefore insists that while

discourses aimed at achieving self-understanding are . . . an important component of politics . . . the question that has priority . . . is how a matter can be regulated in the equal interest of all. The making of norms is primarily a justice issue, subject to principles that state what is equally good for all. Unlike ethical questions, questions of justice are not inherently related to a specific collectivity and its form of life. The law of a concrete legal community must, if it is to be legitimate, at least be compatible with moral standards that claim universal validity beyond the legal community.[18]

The scope of ethical-political discourses within the sort of collective decision making that issues in concrete norms and policies is also limited, in Habermas's view, because it is restricted to making those sorts of decisions that *can* express the "authentic collective self-understanding"[19] of the society as a whole, as that collection of individuals that will be subject to the decision. In pluralistic and multicultural societies, however, he suggests, these sorts of decisions will be limited. Different groups will begin from different cultural, religious, ethnic, or gender-defined starting points and will differ from one another in their understanding of themselves, their traditions, and the matters at stake. Thus, as we have seen, pro-life and pro-choice advocates tend to have grown up in different religions and cultures, to lead very different lives, and to have very different conceptions of the good. They also differ on what they understand as our collective identity and how it is reflected in the meaning of our norms and values. The same holds for the various sides in the other debates on which this book has focused. Our resolutions to conflicts over affirmative action, surrogacy, and pornography cannot appeal to a collective self-understanding, on a Habermasian view, because the different sides in these debates differ precisely in how they understand our collective identity. Hence, Habermas gives up on any recourse in considering political and legislative matters to "communitarian" notions of who we are and what we ought to do, notions that he defines as those that restrict political discourse to discovering, "at a given point in time and within the horizon of shared ways of life and traditions, what is best for citizens of a concrete community."[20] Instead, the ability of ethical discourses to achieve consensus in decision making would seem to be limited to smaller groups and subgroups within a society who clarify for themselves how an issue reflects on their particular ideals and conceptions of the good.[21]

Yet is the relevance of ethical-political discussions to collective decision making as restricted as Habermas thinks it is? Does it depend solely upon the limited ability of such discourses to recover a collective self-understanding or to reveal the deeper consonances in value orientation and hermeneutic standpoint between members of a society? Is the scope of such discussions therefore restricted in pluralistic and multicultural societies because no such collective self-understanding or consonance in value orientation exists? Finally, can moral discourses make up for this absence? Habermas's account of the controversy over abortion is telling in answering these questions, for he suggests that the controversy can be understood in only one of two ways. Either it is a question of strictly moral discourse, in which case it is to be resolved on strictly moral grounds, in terms of norms "that can be justified if and only if equal consideration is given to the interest of all those who are possibly involved." Alternatively, the issue might be so interwoven with cultural identities and cultural self-understandings that it can be formulated only as an ethical question and answered by members of different traditions in consonance with their own parochial value orientations, ideals, and collective identities. In this case, Habermas claims, the moral question "would first arise at the more general level of the legitimate ordering of coexisting forms of life. . . . The question would be how the integrity and the coexistence of ways of life and world-views that generate different ethical conceptions of abortion can be secured under conditions of equal rights."[22]

In essence, this two-tiered conclusion projecting moral agreement on one level while allowing for a diversity of ethical self-understandings on another level is the same as the one that Ronald Dworkin promotes in allowing for different religious interpretations of respect for the sanctity of life at the same time that he secures legal consensus in the assent of all those concerned to the principles of liberty and equality.[23] Here, conditions securing equal rights attach to the principle of the free exercise of religion while the legitimacy of differences in cultural self-understanding is secured at the ethical level in terms of the diverse ways different cultural subgroups can respect the intrinsic and even sacred value of human life. Yet both Dworkin and Habermas seem to assume that the principles of freedom and equality raise no interpretive questions and engage no interpretive differences of their own. To be more specific, Dworkin assumes that an appeal to the principle of the freedom of religion resolves the matter in what Habermas would call the equal interests of all. Clearly, however, this appeal presupposes a certain interpretation of the meaning of the freedom of religion, one that assumes that we agree in what we understand religious values and their free or legitimate exercise to be. But these understandings are just as much a focal point for dispute in the abortion debate as considerations of what is meant by the sanctity of life. At issue are precisely what are to count as religious values and what are to count as violations of rights.[24]

Hence, it is not clear that the controversy can be as neatly divided as both Habermas and Dworkin seem to assume between those aspects that admit of a moral consensus over equal rights and those that allow for ethical diversity in value orientations. Rather, our ethical diversity in value orientations grounds differences in how we understand the meaning of our equal rights. Moreover, this worry about the proposed solution to the controversy over abortion seems to raise general questions about the sort of coexistence Habermas envisions of an agreed-upon "legitimate order," on the one hand, and "different ethical conceptions," on the other. For this solution works only if we agree with the characterization of what counts as the legitimate ordering and what counts as the sort of ethical conceptions on which we are allowed to differ. But if we allow that interpretive differences can affect not only our understanding of a respect for human life but also our understanding of the principle of the freedom of religion, then we must allow for interpretive differences in our understanding of a legitimate ordering. The distinction between those aspects of the issue that allow for moral consensus and those that permit ethical differences thus seems to collapse. The controversy over abortion remains an interpretive one, to be resolved or pursued, one might argue, on an interpretive level.

In Habermas's schema of pragmatic, ethical, and moral discourses, discussions of interpretive differences are located in ethical-political discourses, and these discourses are conceived of on the model of ethical-existential discourses, as forms of discussion in which a single person or single collectivity comes to one individual or collective understanding of itself. Consequently, Habermas assumes that the relevance of ethical-political discourse for pluralistic and multicultural societies is limited. Moreover, he assumes that where we cannot find a collective self-understanding in the ethical sphere by becoming "reflectively aware of the deeper consonances in a common form of life," or where, indeed, these consonances are morally problematic, we can nonetheless appeal to a moral consensus at the level of legitimate orderings. But if interpretive differences seep into the way we understand the norms and principles that make up these legitimate orderings, then it is by no means clear that the only purpose we should conceive of for an interpretively focused discussion is that of arriving at a collective self-understanding within small and culturally homogeneous groups. Rather, we might conceive of interpretive discussions on a larger scale as forms of discussions concerned with illuminating for each other the different ways we can legitimately understand the norms and principles that compose our legitimate orderings. Our self-understanding is constituted by the way in which we understand our history and traditions, as well as the norms and principles handed down to us through them. It is plausible to assume, as Habermas does, that members of pluralistic and multicultural societies will understand their history, norms, principles, and traditions differently and that the hermeneutic starting points for their self-understanding will be rooted in cultures, orientations, and experiences that they do not necessarily share with all other members of their society. But it is not clear that this circumstance entails either that interpretive discussion is limited in its scope or that the consequences of our interpretive differences can be minimized because they do not effect the understanding we have of our consensus on moral principles.

Habermas accords a slightly larger place to interpretive discussions in his consideration of the application of norms to specific situations of action. Still, here again, it is not clear he takes them as seriously as he might.

JUSTIFICATION AND APPLICATION

Moral discourses are geared, for Habermas, to the validity of norms: according to the discourse principle, the only valid norms are those that can meet with the assent of all those possibly concerned as free and equal participants in an idealized procedure of raising and redeeming validity claims. Moral discourses also require an abstraction from concrete situations of action. They involve examining the possible validity of a principle in a way that is "relieved of the pressure of action and experience" and in which participants, "in a hypothetical attitude, test with reasons, and only with reasons," whether a norm is acceptable to all of them.[25] Legal norms are subjected to a more complex procedure of justification inasmuch as their legitimacy is determined not only in moral discourses but by the rationality of the political legislation that gives rise to them. Hence, legitimacy in this case is determined not only by the validity of moral judgments but by the validity of the means–ends reasoning of pragmatic discourses and the validity of assessments of the situation and the authenticity of evaluations in ethical-political discourses. It is also determined, Habermas adds, by the fairness of any compromises that are reached and by the rationality of voting decisions.[26] But norms of action, whether moral or legal, must be not only justified as legitimate; they must also be applied in particular situations that require judicial decisions, social decisions, or decisions and actions from individuals or groups of actors. All norms, aside from those that are specifically tailored to particular situations, are according to Habermas indeterminate and only, as he puts it, "prima facie" candidates for application to a specific situation. He therefore follows Klaus Günther's account of moral discourses of application[27] and allows that such application discourses can be used as a model for investigating the application of norms in general. In both the moral and the legal cases, then, the question of whether a norm is valid is replaced with the question of whether it is appropriate to the situation or problem at issue:

> One must . . . enter a discourse of application to test whether [the norms] apply to a given situation (whose details could not have been anticipated in the justification process) or whether, their validity notwithstanding, they must give way to another norm, namely the "appropriate" one. Only if a valid norm proves to be the single appropriate one in the case at hand does that norm ground a singular judgment that can claim to be right. That a norm is *prima facie* valid means merely that it has been impartially justified; only its impartial application leads to a valid decision about a case. The validity of the general norm does not yet guarantee justice in the individual case.[28]

As Günther does, Habermas rules out monological or nondeliberative determinations of appropriateness such as those that he thinks are implied by notions of *phronesis* or by ideas of good judgment or character. Rather, he thinks the determination possesses intersubjective and cognitive dimensions: we determine through application discourses which of the norms we have already found to be valid is the appropriate one to apply to the case at hand, and we also determine through application discourses which descriptions of the facts of the case are important and, indeed, "exhaustive" for interpreting the situation. Habermas acknowledges this procedure's dimensions that invoke the hermeneutic circle of whole and part. Which features of the situation we understand to be important will be at least partially determined by the norm we anticipate applying to the situation, just as that norm that we take to be appropriate will be partially determined by those features of the situation that we understand to be important. "What finally decides the issue," he argues, is "the meaning equivalence between the description of facts making up part of the interpretation of the situation and the description of facts that sets out the descriptive component of the norm, that is, its application conditions."[29] As Günther summarizes the interrelation: "the justification of a singular judgment"—in other words, a judgment that, say, that a woman has a right to an abortion is an appropriate application of the prima facie valid moral principles of freedom and equality—"must be based on the set of all appropriate reasons that happen to be relevant for the case at hand in view of a complete interpretation of the situation."[30]

This conception of discourses of application raises certain questions, however. If a singular judgment can claim to be right only if one valid norm alone proves to be appropriate to the case at hand, we might wonder if a singular judgment can ever prove to be right since more than one would seem to apply to any specific case, depending on how interpreters describe and understand the particular case. If only a correct singular judgment grounds a valid decision, then, it might seem unlikely that any decision could be justified. Might there not be more than one appropriate application of a norm and might we therefore not legitimately disagree? Might we not also disagree on what is to count as the complete interpretation of the situation or on "the set of all appropriate reasons that happen to be relevant for the case at hand?"

With regard to many of the issues that divide multicultural societies, of course, consensus on the complete interpretation of the situation or what the reasons are that happen to be relevant is just what we do not have. That which one group calls freedom of contract, another calls the exploitation of women's bodies; that which one group calls murder, another calls a refusal to let others, even fetuses, use one's body without one's consent. What one group calls equal opportunity, the other calls reverse discrimination. And, finally, what one side calls the subordination of women, another calls sexually explicit material that is intended to arouse. Given these differences, it is not clear that we can anticipate a single complete or exhaustive description of the situation to which every one can agree. Nor is it clear that an appropriate application of norms depends upon such agreement. Why not, instead, allow for a diversity in our descriptions of the situation and focus on what each description might add to the others?

Not only do we often interpret the situation differently, we also apply different principles to it as those that ground our particular judgments. If we understand abortion as murder, for example, we may apply principles to it that speak either to the prohibition against extinguishing innocent life or to exceptions to this prohibition. If we understand it as a refusal to let others use the bodies of women without their consent, however, then the principles we apply may be those of equality and exploitation. If we understand affirmative action as reverse discrimination, we may reject it as a violation of the principle of equality. If we understand it as compensation for the effects of racial injustice, in contrast, we may endorse it as a application of principles of fairness. The same differences hold for the cases of surrogate mothering and pornography. If "what finally decides the issue is the meaning equivalence between the description of facts making up part of the interpretation of the situation and the description of facts that sets out the descriptive component of the norm," then it is not clear how application discourses are to decide this meaning equivalence in only one way. Moreover, it is not clear why the appropriateness of the application depends on their doing so. Instead of assuming that meaning equivalence is exclusive, we might focus on the different meaning equivalences a particular situation and set of principles allow.

If we start at the other "end" of the relation, with principles as opposed to the disputed practices or problematic situations to which they are meant to be applied, we seem to encounter a similar problem. How can we collectively determine which prima facie valid principle or norm is appropriate to deciding how to act in a particular situation or whether a particular practice is acceptable unless, minimally, we agree on how to understand the meaning of the principle itself. Conversely, if we differ in how we understand the meaning of the principle, then we will also differ in our understanding of how we ought to apply it to situations about the meaning of which we may also differ. The different understandings we have of the meaning of equality both affect and are affected by the understanding we have of affirmative action policies. Similarly, differing understandings of the sanctity of life both affect and are affected by differing understandings of the practice of abortion. Depending on how one understands liberty, one might or might not allow for pornography or surrogate mothering, again, depending on how one understands them. In any case, if application is bound up with an understanding of the meaning of both principles and practices, then our differences in how we understand the situation to which the principle is to be applied will be simply multiplied by differences in our understanding of the meaning of the principle and by different combinations of those different understandings. Habermas's account of discourses of application is meant to reduce this multiplicity to the single appropriate judgment, but why should singularity rather than multiplicity be our focus?

It is not clear, in other words, why an analysis of the conditions for the valid application of norms and principles should not look beyond a consensus over their appropriateness to an interpretive discussion of the appropriateness of different applications. Habermas's account of the relation between ethical and moral discourse assumes that interpretive differences can be dealt with by a two-tiered approach that approaches consensus on the level of legitimate orderings and admits ethical and interpretive differences in individual life projects on another level. But this approach ignores the way in which our interpretive differences can overflow their supposed level to drown out agreement on what was supposed to be the separate level of legitimate orderings. Similarly, Habermas's account of discourses of application tries to locate interpretive differences over the meaning of a principle on the level of its application to particular situations and, furthermore, to show that disputes over application are themselves resolvable through discourses of application. But the strategy skims over differences in the ways we can plausibly understand the meaning of our practices, the moral and legal norms on which we agree, and the way practices and norms cohere with one another. If, for Habermas, the appropriate application of a principle depends upon agreement on the correct description of a fact situation, on the one hand, and agreement on the meaning of the principle, on the other, then he seems to minimize the possibility that discourses of application might admit a range of different equally appropriate applications.

Habermas admits that in discussions of application "highly contextualistic interpretations of the situation come to the fore which depend on the different self-understandings of worldviews of the actual participants."[31] Yet these different hermeneutic starting points do not seem to cause him the concern with regard to discourses of application that they cause him with regard to ethical-political discourses. In the latter case, the different hermeneutic starting points that members of pluralistic and multicultural societies can hold limit the ability of such discourses to provide ways of rationally resolving matters under dispute. When Habermas considers the application of norms and principles to specific cases, he does not seem to think that different hermeneutic starting points are as intractable: "participants in an application discourse must work their different interpretations of the same situation into a normatively rich description of the circumstances that does not simply abstract from the existing differences in perception. . . . It is a question of a sensitive, noncoercive coordination of different interpretive perspectives."[32]

But what is this noncoercive coordination of different interpretive perspectives? If it involves an appreciation of the legitimacy or adequacy of different interpretive perspectives, then it might also lead to an appreciation of the different applications to which they might lead. In this case, coordination would be closer to an accommodation of differences than to consensus in our interpretations of both principles and circumstances. Moreover, such a coordination would depend upon a recognition of the legitimacy of our differences and a willingness to learn from them. In short, at work would be the kind of interpretive conversation this study has stressed, the outcome of which is less a commitment to principle or to the singular appropriateness of one's own application of principle than an openness to legitimate differences and a orientation toward accommodating them.

Habermas's own discussion of accommodation looks away from the idea of a noncoercive coordination of different interpretive perspectives to the conditions of valid compromise and to the grounds for legitimacy of the idea that the majority in a democracy by and large rules. With regard to both, he suggests that interpretive discussions can assist only in the discovery of problems and interpretive differences and have no direct importance for the resolution of public disputes. Yet, since the conclusion suggested thus far by an examination of Habermas's attempt to deal with the interpretive differences of a pluralistic and multicultural society is that interpretive discussion has a larger role in public debate than he assumes, the idea that it can assist only in the discovery of issues and differences might be misleading as well. To consider this possibility, I want first briefly to reconsider the model I have proposed for interpretive discussions. I shall then use it to provide a foil against which to examine Habermas's evaluation of compromise and majority rule.

LITERARY AND ARTISTIC DISCUSSION
VERSUS BARGAINING AND MAJORITY RULE

The model for interpretive discussions of our differences is our debates over literature and works of art, the relevance of which can be summarized in terms of three general features. First, while the purpose of literary and artistic discussions is to come to an understanding about the meaning of the texts or works of art under discussion, achieving this purpose does not require unanimity. Instead, in our discussions of art and literature we accept the idea that a text or work of art can be understood in a variety of ways, that no production of a play, for example, is the definitive production of that play and that no reading of a text is the last word on the subject. Rather, we expect different interpreters with different concerns, orientations, and approaches to understand the same texts and works of art differently.

Second, we assume that in discussing our interpretations with others we can each develop our own perspective on the text or work without necessarily abandoning it to adopt another interpretation in its totality.

We focus, rather, on how an alternative interpretation understands the text or work of art in question and on what we can learn from it to expand and enrich our own. We do not try to find in these alternative interpretations only those points at which they break down or are impoverished in comparison with our own. Rather, we approach them with the idea that our own understanding of the meaning of the work can always be deepened, that we might use and integrate insights from other interpretations to develop our own, even if we continue to disagree on the meaning of the text, and that we can always learn new perspectives from which it can be understood. Some interpretations of a given text may ultimately have to be rejected because they fail to make sense out of it or show how it fits together as a unified whole. Still, if we were to dismiss all interpretations other than our own, this dismissal could signal only a dogmatic and self-destructive cutting off of possibilities for insight.

Third, while we may come to possess a more nuanced and differentiated view of the work by engaging with the interpretations of others, we have not replaced the wrong view with the right one. We do not assume that our new view constitutes the truth, nor do we anticipate agreement once and for all on the canonical meaning of a work. We rather continue to expand our conception of a work to encompass what we take to be important and relevant parts of other interpretations of it. In listening to and learning from other interpretations of a book or work of art, we deepen our conception and widen our horizons. We do not suppose that we now understand the text correctly or that if our understanding is legitimate "all those concerned" must agree to it. Consensus does not function here even as a regulative ideal. That which serves as an ideal, instead, is the idea that we may come to new insights about both the text and ourselves and that our insights might contribute to an ongoing interpretive discussion. Interpretive discussions contribute to changing constellations of concerns and themes, to new ways of relating different texts and works of art, and to seeing them and us in new ways. But this ever-changing kaleidoscope does not require fevered argument, nor does the defense of one's own position require demonstrating that all other positions are false. It rather requires situating one's perspective in a context of other perspectives in a way that illuminates the text or work of art at issue and even contributes to our understanding of ourselves.

If we transfer these ideas to the domain of public debate over issues that divide us, then, first, we will acknowledge room for legitimate interpretive differences. We will admit that our understanding of the value of human life, for example, or the meaning of religious liberty in the debate over abortion is an interpretation and that other legitimate interpretations—ones that focus on different dimensions of the practices or principles at issue—are possible. Second, we will expect to learn from these different interpretations just as we learn from different interpretations in the domain of art and literature. Just as we assume that alternative interpretations of *Hamlet* can enrich and expand our understanding even if we continue to understand the play or novels differently, we will also assume that we can learn from alternative interpretations of abortion, pornography, and the principles in terms of which others evaluate them. We will also assume that some interpretations will ultimately prove not to provide illumination for our principles and practices. Either they fail to make sense out of them at all or fail to show how they are consistent with the totality and point of our norms, principles, and practices in general. Still, instead of talking past one another and instead of simply dismissing one another as hopeless ideologues, we will engage in discussions of our disparate understandings in which each side assumes that the other at least might have something of value to say.

Third, we will accept the value of alternative interpretations as interpretations that may contain insights for us whether or not they do so for others. Hence, we will give up on the idea that their legitimacy depends upon their rationally motivated acceptability to all those concerned. Moreover, we will view our understanding of the issues not as a definitive one but rather as a contribution to an ongoing discussion in which, if our understanding proves illuminating at all, it will prove so only as part of a larger constellation capable of illuminating a larger kaleidoscope of meanings.

Still, it might be argued that just this idea of illuminating although not exhaustive contributions to a continuing discussion points up the important difference between public debates and interpretive discussions of art and literature. In the former case, the point of discussion is to determine what a society or community ought to do with regard to a matter under dispute, whereas in the latter case it is not. Indeed, it is arguably for this reason that our discussions of abortion or pornography have a fevered character that our discussions of Jane Austen's novels, for example, do not. In the one case, the polity to which we belong will take some action; in the other case, it will and need not. Furthermore, there seems to be an important difference between, on the one hand, legislative and judicial forms of discussion, the purpose of which is to determine law and policy, and, on the other hand, various noninstitutionalized forms of public debate, the point of which may well be more akin to literary debate, namely to raise questions and offer new perspectives without necessarily looking for either unanimity or closure. These doubts raise the question of what part interpretive debate can actually play in determining law and policy, given that the aim of these discussions remains the achievement of collectively binding decisions while the thrust of interpretive discussion remains that of opening up interpretive horizons. Even if interpretive differences cannot be escaped, and even if they might rather be pursued as opportunities for mutual learning in an interpretively reflective mode, it remains unclear that the differences in understanding and self-understanding they explore easily transfer to public policy.

For his part, Habermas considers hermeneutic or interpretive debate an element of what he calls the informal or weak public sphere, "an open and inclusive network of overlapping, subcultural publics having fluid temporal, social, and substantive boundaries."[33] Such publics are suited to discovering and identifying problems, according to Habermas, and to increasing sensitivity to new and different outlooks on them. They thereby add to the possibility of finding new ways of looking at issues and circumstances. Still, their usefulness in actually setting public policy is limited, Habermas insists, by their vulnerability "to the repressive and exclusionary effects of unequally distributed social power, structural violence, and systematically distorted communication."[34] For this reason, he argues that in complex societies they must be anchored in stronger, procedurally regulated public spheres that ideally filter out these effects because of their ultimate connection to the demands of moral discourse. Forms of valid compromise and the justification for majority rule constitute part of this stronger, procedurally regulated public sphere.

According to Habermas, processes of negotiation and compromise are required when the available proposals for resolving an issue affect different interests and value commitments in different ways. In these cases, moral discourse fails to disclose any generalizable interest that would be risked by choosing one option over the other. Similarly, ethical-political discourses fail to uncover a common self-understanding or even agreement on what the issues and values at stake are. In such cases, Habermas claims, the competing values and interests need to be balanced against one another in some form of compromise. At the same time, compromises must be fair, and they are fair, according to Habermas, only to the extent that the procedures for reaching them can be assented to by all those concerned. Thus, while the settlement of the issue may involve bar-

gaining and interest trade-offs between parties, its legitimacy rests ultimately on the idea of consensus in moral discourse, at least at the level
of procedure:

> From a normative perspective . . . fair compromise formation does not stand
> on its own, for the procedural conditions under which actual compromises
> enjoy the presumption of fairness must be justified in moral discourses. More-
> over, bargaining first becomes permissible and necessary when only particu-
> lar—and no generalizable—interests are involved, something that again can
> be tested only in moral discourses. Fair bargaining, then, does not destroy the
> discourse principle but rather indirectly presupposes it.[35]

Habermas's emphasis here is the extent to which compromise and bargaining procedures, like ethical-political discourses, are tied to moral discourses. If a matter under dispute can be resolved through an ethical discourse that reflects the deeper consonances of the value orientations of
the different members of the society with one another, such consonances
are legitimate only if they do not also conflict with the equal interests of
all. Similarly, where a matter under dispute cannot be resolved through
any form of discourse, participants in the dispute can try to compromise, but, again, such compromises are legitimate only if the rules that
govern the compromise meet with the equal interests of all. In this last
instance, Habermas's conception is, once again, a two-tiered one: we
can differ in our response to disputed practices, norms, and the like, and
sometimes in such cases we will have to compromise. Nevertheless, such
compromises are legitimate only to the extent that they rely in the end
on principles of fairness consensually justified in moral discourse.

Yet this solution to those of our public disagreements that we cannot
resolve through discourse seems to face the same difficulty that Habermas faced in describing discourses of application. To be able to agree that
a given compromise does comply with principles of fairness, we need to
be able to agree on their meaning and application. And if just this agreement is lacking because we understand both the principles and the circumstances at issue in different ways, it is unclear that a given compromise can be deemed fair by all the parties involved. In other words, in
cases where no generalizable interest is at stake and in cases in which no
collective self-understanding on the priority of different values is forthcoming, compromise also may afford no resolution to the issue because
participants in the dispute also differ on how they understand the principle of fairness and on which aspects of the situation they think are
amenable to fair resolution in what particular ways.

Nonetheless, it is not clear that compromise needs always to be understood as Habermas understands it, as the result of bargaining under conditions that all participants recognize as fair and in which they trade off some of their interests to preserve others. Rather, in this instance, again, Habermas seems to overlook the importance of interpretive discussion. For, we might also compromise simply because we recognize the interpretive status of our respective positions—that is, because we recognize our own response to a matter under dispute as an interpretation of the issue or the principles and norms we think are relevant to it or both. In formulating a practical resolution or policy, then, we can recognize the possible legitimacy of alternative interpretations and try to accommodate or compromise between them. We can do so, not because we treat our values and commitments as interests to be given up or traded off to maintain others, but, rather, because we recognize that our own understanding is an interpretive one and therefore partial and perspectival. In other words, our openness to compromise is not a question of giving up or trying to accomplish as much as we can, given the contested circumstances in which we find ourselves. Rather, our openness stems from a recognition that our analysis of the circumstances as well as our understanding of the principles at issue is an interpretive one, only. Moreover, insofar as it is interpretive, it allows for the legitimacy of other interpretations as well. Hence, we substitute a kind of hermeneutic openness for argumentative victory and interpretive identity while we acknowledge the legitimacy of the myriad of reciprocally educated interpretations we can come to hold as a society and, moreover, look for differentiated solutions that do their best to reflect these differences.

Of course, this account of the interpretive presuppositions of valid compromise leads back to familiar questions. Even if we acknowledge the legitimacy of alternative interpretations of our norms and principles and our practices, democratic politics would seem to differ from interpretive debate in at least two crucial ways. First, we must come to at least a temporary decision about what we ought to do in discussing principles and practices while interpretive conversation encourages, instead, an ongoing openness to different illuminating interpretations. Second, when we cannot reach a mutually agreeable decision about what to do in the political domain, either through moral or ethical discourse or through a negotiated compromise that all participants recognize as fair, we can recur to the rule of the majority. The idea of majority rule is neither necessary nor appropriate in trying to understand meaning: whether that of texts or works of art or that of principles and practices. Nevertheless, since it seems both necessary and appropriate to legitimate decisions in a democratic society, the relevance or importance of interpretive discussion may seem as limited as Habermas assumes it is.

For Habermas, the legitimacy of majority rule relies on the idea of fallibilism. Different groups can rationally accept the legitimacy of decisions that are not acceptable to them in their substance because and to the extent that they take the decision or policy to be a temporary one, open to revision in the course of public debate and decision making. As he writes, "majority rule retains an internal relation to the search for truth inasmuch as the decision reached by the majority only represents a caesura in an ongoing discussion; the decision records, so to speak, the interim result of a discursive opinion-forming process."[36] This conception of the presuppositions of majority rule could thus not contrast more completely with the presuppositions of literary and artistic debate. While the premise behind these latter conversations is that they might go on forever and that a final consensus is neither necessary nor probable, the justification Habermas gives for majority rule rests on the idea that disagreement is temporary and that the majority decision is only an interim step to a final accord. Moreover, whereas the presupposition behind our participation in literary and artistic discussion and in interpretive discussion in general is that we might learn to understand the works or issues in question in a new way, the presupposition behind our participation in political discussion remains, for Habermas, the idea that we can ultimately convince others of the rightness of our opinion and the validity of our claims. Indeed, the supposition that rationally motivated consensus is possible must, on Habermas's view, remain the premise of our political discussions if they are not to become what Thomas McCarthy calls "more or less refined forms of symbolic manipulation."[37] "If we were (*per impossibile*) to drop the pragmatic presupposition that we could convince others of the validity of claims by offering good reasons in support of them, most of our rational practices would lose their sense, and this, it goes without saying, would entail far-reaching changes in our form of life."[38]

Nevertheless, McCarthy also distinguishes between two perspectives he identifies: that of the participant and that of the observer. Habermas aims to reconstruct the presuppositions of the former, presuppositions that involve the anticipation that we can justify our claims in a way that convinces others. The observer's perspective, however, in certain cases reveals an "irreducible plurality of evaluative and interpretive standpoints." Sophisticated participants in political debates, McCarthy thinks, learn to combine participant and observer perspectives into a form of "reflective participation" that is "informed by the knowledge that irreducible value differences regularly give rise to intractable disagreements on normative questions." In other words, reflective participation involves the idea that, while we presuppose our ability ultimately to convince others of the validity of our claims by offering good reasons, we also recognize differences in our hermeneutic starting points. We are both convinced we can ultimately be shown to be right and aware of our historical and cultural premises and prejudices.

This notion of reflective participation indicates that political debate and interpretive debate are not as radically different as Habermas's remarks imply. Indeed, McCarthy's account seems well suited to characterizing a central feature of our discussions of interpretive matters. In discussions of texts and works of art, we are simultaneously convinced of the merit of our own interpretation and open to the value of others; we participate in our interpretations, in other words, in an eminently reflective way. We want to convince others; but we want to convince them, not of the exclusive correctness of our point of view, but rather of its ability to make a contribution to the discussion and understanding of the text. We do not assume that our position could be assented to by all those concerned under ideal conditions. Rather, we assume that it can change, expand, and further the discussion in which we participate. In the same way, in the political sphere sophisticated participants will presuppose both the adequacy of their own interpretations of norms, principles, and issues and their ability to lead others to reassess their own interpretations. At the same time, they will themselves be open to the possible adequacy of other interpretations, and they will see their own efforts as illuminating although not exhaustive contributions to a continuing discussion.

To be sure, if we are to emphasize the illumination different voices can contribute to our public discussions, we must also be able to differentiate between those interpretations that are legitimate and those that are not, or, in Habermas's terms, between those interpretations that reflect "the repressive and exclusionary effects of unequally distributed social power, structural violence, and systematically distorted communication," on the one hand, and those that do not, on the other. For this reason, the ideal conditions that Habermas writes into rational discourse must play a crucial role in interpretive discussion. Nevertheless, these conditions are rooted in the presuppositions of hermeneutic conversation itself, as we have seen. If our understandings of meaning are interpretations of complex conceptions of which other interpretations are possible as well, then the adequacy of our own interpretations depends upon their capacity to situate themselves in relation to other understandings of meaning and to develop themselves through them. But this condition means that we must have open access to these other understandings of meaning. For the sake of the continuing vitality of our own interpretations, then, we must encourage a rich plurality of interpretive voices in order to test and deepen our own. In contrast, any interpretation of the meaning of our norms the content of which leads to the exclusion or silencing of another interpretive voice must be rejected because it threatens or restricts the alternatives only against which we can continue to develop our own interpretations.

Yet if we encourage hermeneutic discussion of our principles, practices, and norms, and if we do so under conditions that are informal, perhaps, but rigorously cleaned of systematic disturbances, then we might also look for ways of accommodating our differences or compromising with one another. Political debate under presuppositions of reflective participation, McCarthy insists, "might well involve elements of conciliation, compromise, consent, accommodation and the like." [39] If we stress the affinities between reflective participation in aesthetic and political interpretive spheres, then these elements become all the more prominent. In the aesthetic sphere, a hermeneutic openness often leads to the integration and accommodation of diverse understandings; in the political sphere it might do the same. Moreover, in cases in which we cannot accommodate all legitimate interpretations of our principles and practices in our decisions and policies, we can at least look to institutions and practices for keeping the discussion open to a continuing reciprocal education. In such cases, decisions made through legitimate procedures of majority rule will be temporary, as Habermas supposes, and temporary as a "caesura in an ongoing discussion." Still, this ongoing discussion will be an interpretive one, the aim of which is not necessarily truth but simply interpretive accommodation. Under these premises, perhaps most important, we can give up on the embittering idea that only one side can be right. The effort to find solutions to divisive issues that all parties can accept as legitimate need not depend on ideals of unanimity and argumentative closure. It might look, instead, to the way in which democratic institutions and procedures in a pluralistic and multicultural society can accommodate legitimate differences and promote an interpretive openness. That is, it might take as its goal the integration of or compromise between different legitimate interpretive voices.

The point of this chapter has been to locate the place of interpretive conversation in collective decision-making processes. To Habermas, the impact of our interpretive conversations over our practices and principles has seemed limited because he makes a series of assumptions. First, he assumes that what he calls ethical discourse can suffice for collective will-formation only in homogeneous cultures whose members belong to a single tradition and can understand norms and history in similar ways. Second, he assumes that differences in the application of norms and principles can be resolved in application discourses that justify a single valid judgment of appropriateness. Finally, he assumes that interpretive discussions form part of a weak public sphere that can have no direct translation into law or policy.

The response to the first and second assumptions looks to our discussions of art and literature as forms of discussion that do not depend upon, and even avoid, a consensus on meaning. The response to the third assumption is perhaps more complicated. Nevertheless, it remains unclear why interpretive conversation should not directly translate into law and policy in two ways: first, as the recommendation that we look less for right answers to our disputes and more for forms of accommodation between different legitimate interpretations and, second, as a commitment to ensuring the space in which different interpretations can listen to and learn from one another.

In the next chapter of this book, I want to pursue the performative question that seems to be raised by McCarthy's idea of reflective participation. Can we think of ourselves as both actors in and, at the same time, merely interpretive observers of our common life? This same question is also suggested by an issue that Bernard Williams raises in *Ethics and the Limits of Philosophy*[40] as to whether ethical reflection can destroy knowledge. In Williams's view, participation in contemporary societies threatens to weaken our ability to act with conviction on our own norms and principles because that participation is reflective in the sense that we recognize that our norms and principles are not the only ones possible for any society. This problem can be recast to speak to the internal interpretive controversies of pluralistic and multicultural societies, the members of which recognize not only that other cultures employ other norms and principles but that members of their own society belong to different cultures and traditions and can understand the norms and principles of that society in different legitimate ways. How can we really act on or argue for our understanding of our principles, norms, and practices if we also acknowledge the existence of other legitimate understandings of them?

CHAPTER SEVEN

Tradition and Ethical Knowledge

For Habermas, an ethical knowledge of who we are and what our norms and values mean can lead to collectively binding decisions on what we ought to do only in homogeneous societies, the members of which share backgrounds and interpretive orientations. Moreover, the legitimacy of these decisions depends on procedures that guarantee equal participation and refer ultimately to forms of moral discourse that justify universal principles in the equal interest of all. For his part, Bernard Williams links ethical knowledge to what he calls the thick concepts of a tradition and asks how such thick concepts can continue to provide the conviction that would seem to be necessary for action in contemporary societies that recognize the existence of diverse traditions, all with action-orienting, thick concepts of their own. At the same time, Williams remains committed to the resources of our ethical knowledge and does not suppose that moral discourse can resolve the issue of action that is raised by the presence of competing ethical traditions.

In this chapter, I want to explore these issues and the conclusions Williams draws from his discussion of them as a way of further elaborating the place of interpretive conversation in public debate. First, however, I shall try to establish the link between tradition and ethical knowledge that Williams assumes by returning to Gadamer's account of prejudice and tradition since this account most firmly establishes the link. I shall then raise the issue that seems to follow from this account by looking at Austen's *Pride and Prejudice,* thereby providing a matching bookend to the account of Austen's *Sense and Sensibility* with which this book began. I shall start with Gadamer's analysis of the role prejudice and tradition play in the understanding of meaning and then consider the questions that arise for contemporary societies with regard to this role.

GADAMER'S ACCOUNT OF PREJUDICE AND TRADITION

Gadamer's account of prejudices includes at least four important aspects. First, he understands prejudices as assumptions or sets of assumptions that orient our initial take on the meaning of what we are trying to understand, whether that meaning is of a text, an action or event, or a social norm or practice. Prejudices reflect preliminary anticipations or preconceptions that form the context for understanding and allow the meaning of an object to be projected in a tentative way. We presume that a certain object is a book, for example, even before we open it. Our general expectation is that it will contain pages inside what we assume to be its covers and that these pages will be printed with a written text. We also bring more concrete expectations to the task of understanding, expectations as to the genre to which the book belongs, the topic it treats, and so on. Such expectations form the original ground for understanding meaning, a ground without which, Gadamer suggests, we could have no basis upon which to conduct our further investigation of what a text, practice, or the like means.[1]

Second, since prejudices represent simply the complex of expectations, presuppositions, and projections through which we first anticipate the meaning of what we are trying to understand, they are themselves neither valid nor invalid, neither positive nor negative. Rather, they are necessary orientations toward a meaning and are either further elaborated or replaced with alternative anticipations of meaning depending upon the way they work out in our attempts to understand. Indeed, the assumption that prejudices are always only misleading is, Gadamer insists, a prejudice of the Enlightenment—that is, a prejudice against prejudice. As he explains:

> Actually "prejudice" means a judgment that is rendered before all the elements that determine a situation have been finally examined. In German legal terminology a "prejudice is a provisional legal verdict before the final verdict is reached. For someone involved in a legal dispute, this kind of judgment . . . affects his chances adversely. . . . But this negative sense is only derivative. The negative consequence depends precisely on the positive validity, the value of the provisional decision as a prejudgment like that of any precedent."[2]

The idea of precedent leads to a third important aspect of the idea of prejudices, namely their relation to history and tradition.[3] The connection we make between the appearance of a book and the expectation of a written text is neither arbitrary nor idiosyncratic. Rather, it is one we share with others whose lives include the existence of books and one we and others base on our previous experiences with objects that have the appearance and feel of books. Books are cultural and historical artifacts. It is possible to anticipate that something is a book, then, only because we know what a book is, and it is possible to anticipate that it is a science fiction novel only because we are familiar with the general tradition of science fiction as well as the literary and cultural traditions out of which it emerges. Our anticipations of meaning arise out of history and experience, out of connections and ideas that have been proven to hold in the past, and out of orientations that issue from the cultures and traditions to which we belong. If one anticipates that a certain book is science fiction, this prejudice may or may not help ultimately to illuminate its meaning or point. Still, it is grounded in familiar structures of the sort we must rely upon in order to have any orientation toward what the book is at all.

A fourth important feature of Gadamer's account of prejudice involves their revision. Here he insists that revisions of our understanding of meaning depend on the possibility of appealing to other prejudices, to other concepts and presumptions that are still unquestioned, at least for the purposes of considering the understanding of meaning at issue. We cannot question all our assumptions at once without losing the very grounds on, or perspective from, which we might adjudicate them. Hence, Gadamer's criticism of the Enlightenment is that in its discrediting of prejudice and tradition it assumes that prejudices can only ever prove to be misleading and that traditions ought never be authoritative. But if the possibility of understanding something as something rests on the tentative orientations provided by prejudices, if these are revised against the background of other prejudices, and if this background of prejudices constitutes what we mean by a tradition, then tradition remains the ground of knowledge.

This connection that Gadamer establishes between prejudice, tradition, and an understanding of meaning is both confirmed and further elucidated, I think, by a text that might appear an unlikely witness: Austen's *Pride and Prejudice*.[4] At the same time, this text indicates the potential problem with the connection Gadamer makes. The society Austen describes is one that Williams would call a "hypertraditional" one, or, in other words, a self-enclosed society that, in contrast to more modern societies, does not view alternative ethical traditions or standards as even potential challenges to its own.[5] But if such a society confirms the link between prejudice, tradition, and understanding, it remains unclear what happens to this link in a modern society, at least insofar as it acknowledges the challenge of diverse traditions with different assumptions that orient different understandings of meaning.

Pride and Prejudice contains a puzzle: namely, how it is possible for Elizabeth Bennet to move as quickly as she does from her initial unproductive prejudices to a clearer understanding of herself and others. In the first part of the book, Elizabeth holds two firm views about Darcy, the man she eventually marries. First, she thinks that he has deprived Wickham of the living Darcy's father left to him because he is either jealous or spiteful. Second, she thinks that he has separated his friend Bingley from her sister, Jane Bennet, because he is overly concerned with issues of wealth and social standing, neither of which the Bennets possess in abundance. Elizabeth grounds these views in prejudices about Wickham's and Darcy's characters, prejudices that she derives from their respective outward demeanors. She believes Wickham's account of his dealings with Darcy because Wickham's "countenance, voice, and manner, had established him at once in the possession of every virtue."[6] In contrast, when Darcy asks Elizabeth to marry him, she replies that:

> "From the beginning, from the first moment, I may almost say, of my acquaintance with you, your manners impressing me with the fullest belief of your arrogance, your conceit and your selfish disdain for the feelings of others, were such as to form that ground of disapprobation on which succeeding events have built so immovable dislike; and I had not known you a month before I felt that you were the last man in the world whom I could ever be prevailed upon to marry."[7]

Yet a day later so immovable a dislike begins to remove itself. Darcy gives Elizabeth a letter that she begins to read, Austen writes, "with a strong prejudice against everything he might say."[8] A minute later she is less convinced of her assumptions, and two hours later she has "reconciled herself" to a total reversal not only of her beliefs about Darcy but about Wickham, the consequences of her mother's moral emptiness, and the proper measure of misplaced pride to be parceled out to Darcy and herself. "Pleased with the preference of one, and offended by the neglect of the other, on the very beginning of our acquaintance I have courted prepossession and ignorance, and driven reason away, where either were concerned."[9]

Assuming that this swift reversal cannot be attributed to Austen's inability to describe complex psychological processes, how might it be explained?[10] Elizabeth herself has trouble clarifying it for her father, who objects to her plan to marry Darcy because he has been convinced by her actions and remarks that she cannot love him. And when Jane asks her directly how she did come to love him, she can only joke that her change in attitude must have begun when she saw his "beautiful grounds at Pemberley."[11] Nor is the reversal adequately explained by recourse to Enlightenment conceptions of the capacity of reason and understanding to overcome the power of a misleading prejudice rooted in pride and hasty judgment. Darcy's letter claims that his actions with regard to Bingley had less to do with issues of wealth and standing than with the general vulgarity and materialism of the Bennet family. Moreover, whereas Wickham insists that Darcy simply chose not to honor his father's will, Darcy claims that he acceded to Wickham's desire to exchange the living for money and chose not to give Wickham more money or the living when he later asked for it. In addition, he notes the "general profligacy" and "extravagance" of Wickham's nature that led him to be unsuited for a life in the church and eager for money to support his lifestyle. Still, given the strength of Elizabeth's prejudices against Darcy, it remains unclear how she can even begin to credit these claims with any truth. If Elizabeth is as prejudiced in her perception of the world as Austen suggests she is, how does she ever replace her "prepossession" and "ignorance" with understanding?

To be sure, Elizabeth acknowledges that she can find no proof of the injustice of the claims Darcy makes. She acknowledges, for example, that she cannot recall observing one act of goodness, integrity, or benevolence on Wickham's part. Still, since she is prejudiced in favor of Wickham and against Darcy, why does she suddenly think she needs proof of the injustice of Darcy's claims rather than their justice? How is the light of reason supposed to break so successfully through her prejudices? Austen's account makes sense only insofar as it does not simply appeal to the connection between blind prepossession, pride, and hasty judgment. Rather, it must also appeal to a connection between understanding and what might be called the productive or enabling prejudices and prepossessions of a tradition,[12] a connection that indicates that, in this regard, *Pride and Prejudice* could as appropriately have been titled *Pride in Prejudice*.[13]

In Austen's novel, the impact of Darcy's letter on Elizabeth has less to do with its actual explanation of his actions than with the reminder it

offers Elizabeth of the "impropriety" and "indelicacy" of certain aspects
of Wickham's behavior. Although she was originally too inclined to think
well of him to notice, she now sees he should not have put himself forward
on the first evening he and Elizabeth spent together at her aunt's house.
Nor, since she was almost a complete stranger at the time, should he
have told her of Darcy's supposed misconduct toward him. To these fail-
ings in proper behavior, Elizabeth adds her recollection that Wickham
had eagerly spread his story of Darcy's misconduct after Darcy and the
Bingley party had left the area and despite his professed regard for Darcy's
father and therefore for the family's name. As Elizabeth remarks to herself, "he had then no reserves, no scruples in sinking Mr. Darcy's character though he had assured her that respect for the father would always
prevent his exposing the son." [14]

What is significant in these reflections is the way in which Elizabeth
is able to refer to standards of virtue and propriety that she regards as a
fixed and stable backdrop for revising her interpretations of individual
actions and behaviors.[15] At the end of his letter, Darcy refers Elizabeth
to his cousin, Colonel Fitzwilliam, as a witness for the truth at least of
his account of Wickham's attempt to run off with his sister to procure
her fortune. But such a witness is superfluous since Elizabeth is already
able to check the accuracy of Darcy's account by comparing her own observations of Wickham's behavior against firm assumptions of what that
behavior should have been. One does not divulge one's personal history
to someone with whom one is barely acquainted, and one does not spread
stories about another's character in that person's absence, particularly
when one owes the family to which the person belongs a debt of gratitude. Because Wickham does both, Elizabeth now knows how to understand his character and virtue. She knows how to understand it because
she can revise her first impressions of him by relying upon other authoritative assumptions within a tradition, assumptions that contain strict positions on the appropriate forms of action and behavior and the meaning of deviations from them.

Elizabeth's procedure here is a hermeneutically circular one in which
she attempts to come to an adequate understanding of Wickham, Darcy,
and herself by fitting her various impressions and beliefs into a coherent
whole. Her initial prejudices in favor of Wickham are not misleading, if
we follow Gadamer's analysis, simply because they are prejudices. Elizabeth has initially to understand Wickham in some way or other, and her
first favorable impressions of Mr. Bingley, for example, turn out to be
productive prejudices that enable her to appreciate his general amiabil-

ity. Still, her prejudices in favor of Wickham are contradicted not only by Darcy's view of him, a view she cannot completely discredit, but by Wickham's own abrupt loss of interest in her in favor of Miss King. Elizabeth at first tries to understand this loss of interest in consistency with her initial assumptions, as a product both of Wickham's prudence, given Elizabeth's own "want of fortune," and of his moderation since Miss King's fortune is only a modest one. But once she links his preference for Miss King with the attempt to smear Mr. Darcy's name, that preference appears to Elizabeth in a different light. "His attentions to Miss King were now the consequence of views solely and hatefully mercenary; and the mediocrity of her fortune proved no longer the moderation of his wishes, but his eagerness to grasp at anything." [16] What Elizabeth initially understood as Wickham's virtues, his attentiveness, approachability, and easy temperament, she now understands as part of a larger context that includes his fickleness and even desperation. Similarly, what she initially understood as Darcy's "arrogance . . . conceit . . . and selfish disdain for the feelings of others" become part of what she later tells her father is "no improper pride" [17] but rather a demeanor that is more concerned with rectitude than its appearance.

The ethical knowledge that Elizabeth possesses in virtue of belonging to a tradition of action and behavior that she does not question is clearest in her response to Lady Catherine de Bourgh. Lady Catherine confronts her with the rumor that Elizabeth is to marry Darcy, who is Lady Catherine's nephew, and asks her to declare that she will never do so. Not only is Elizabeth insufficiently wealthy in Lady Catherine's eyes, her mother's connections are questionable and her sister has run off with Wickham without being married to him. But Elizabeth replies with unwavering conviction both with regard to the criteria appropriate to her own actions and with regard to which portion of her private life she need reveal to anyone. Lady Catherine insists that marriage to Darcy is an unfeeling, selfish act on Elizabeth's part, one that will disgrace him "in the eyes of everybody," and she asks whether Elizabeth is really resolved "to have him" under these circumstances. Elizabeth responds "I am only resolved to act in that manner which will, in my own opinion, constitute my happiness, without reference to you, or to any person so wholly unconnected with me." When Lady Catherine claims that she thereby violates "the claims of duty, honour, and gratitude," she is even firmer in her conviction. "Neither duty, nor honour, nor gratitude have any possible claim on me in the present instance," she replies. "No principle of either would be violated." [18]

Elizabeth's ethical standards are secure. Lady Catherine insists that honor, decorum, and prudence require her to give Darcy up, that her connection to his family can only disgrace it, and even that proper gratitude and deference to Lady Catherine herself forbid the marriage. But Elizabeth knows what she owes to whom, who is entitled to what from her, and what Darcy or anyone really owes his or her family. She knows that one need not be imposed upon by the desires of those "wholly unconnected" to one by family or friendship. Moreover, she knows that duty requires deference rather to her own silly mother than to Lady Catherine, that honor is a question not just of social station but actions in accord with it and that, if gratitude is due anyone, it is due Darcy for his attentions to her in spite of her behavior toward him. She need not be grateful to Lady Catherine for her condescension to her, nor need she pretend that Lady Catherine's snobbery is a form of propriety. Whereas Lady Catherine's appeal to a tradition of action and behavior refers only to the most superficial conventions of status and privilege, Elizabeth is able to focus on the substance of the concepts of her tradition, concepts that include norms of honor, duty, deference, and social disgrace, as well as ideas about what it is and is not to be a gentleman.

But the certainty of Elizabeth's ethical knowledge raises two problems. First, as significant as what her tradition allows her to recognize is what it does not. It allows her to revise her original understanding of both Wickham and Darcy, to see through Lady Catherine's standards, and to come to a better understanding of herself and her happiness. Yet it does not allow her to question the justice of the social hierarchy in which her life is embedded or why her own options should be limited to the choices contained in various proposals of marriage. The form of life to which Elizabeth is bound is one that provides a framework within which she can develop sound interpretations of the meaning of the actions and behavior she encounters. But this framework also excludes what seem to be significant issues.

Second, Elizabeth's certainty seems obsolete. If the strength of her tradition and the unquestioned character of its assumptions allow her to overcome other misleading prejudices, it is not clear what lesson we might draw from this accomplishment. While Lady Catherine's appeal to tradition is simply an appeal to a superficial version of the same tradition to which Elizabeth appeals, the problem with certainty and ethical knowledge in contemporary society seems, at least in part, to involve the encounter with different traditions in which different groups appeal to equally substantive assumptions about action and behavior. Elizabeth's poise in pursuing her happiness in a way consistent with her principles is the result of the sure ethical knowledge that comes of participating in a tradition that has no doubts about itself. But what happens to the possibility of such knowledge and of sure action in a multicultural society in which individual traditions can no longer assume the unique legitimacy of their own assumptions and in which they must acknowledge the challenge of different traditions with substantive assumptions of their own? How are we to respond to the issues that divide us if these issues can be understood under different assumptions and in different ways depending upon the traditions to which we appeal?

Elizabeth knows what selfishness is and what it is not. She also knows how to counter what Lady Catherine thinks duty, honor, and gratitude require. But suppose Lady Catherine's concerns were less superficially linked to wealth and social status. Suppose she possessed alternative conceptions of selfishness, honor, duty, and gratitude that Elizabeth had to take seriously. Consider women in contemporary societies who are faced with similar conceptions and who no longer do seem to know which tradition is appropriate for adjudicating them. Do duty, honor, and gratitude require a surrogate mother to surrender custody of her child to the biological father, for example? Some certainly insist that she has at least a contractual duty to do so.[19] If, in addition, honor involves keeping the promises and contracts one has made, and if gratitude is due sponsoring parents because of the financial and emotional support they typically give the surrogate mother, then one might well decide that all three concepts of duty, honor, and gratitude do require a surrogate mother to surrender custody of her child. If we introduce a concept of selfishness that renders it part of a mother's duty and honor to sacrifice her good for the good of her child, then relinquishing a child to a father who is typically wealthier than the surrogate seems perhaps even more appropriate.

But, as we saw in Chapter Two, we also have recourse to different traditions with different values, ones that speak to the value and duties of motherhood and to the sanctity of the family as a sphere of life inaccessible to the demands of contracts and economics.[20] According to this tradition, duty, honor, and gratitude are defined in terms of family bonds, and if selfishness is an issue at all it pertains to those who would uphold a formal contract over a mother's love for her child. It seems that as members of contemporary societies we might appeal equally easily to either tradition in trying to resolve the issue. Moreover, whichever ideas about surrogate motherhood we adopt, it seems impossible to convince either ourselves or others of their exclusive validity. The conjunction of these two circumstances seems to lead to the impossibility of acting on the certainty of our own ethical knowledge. We find ourselves, instead, in a Hamletlike paralysis of overinterpretation: we can understand the issues surrounding surrogacy and motherhood under at least two sets of premises and assumptions, and the same seems to hold of other issues that we have examined in this book. In each case, we have explored at least two sets of interpretive positions and, moreover, claimed more than one is legitimate. But if we know we can understand practices, the issues they involve, and the principles they entail in different ways, how are we to argue for our interpretations or take any action with regard to them? What does it mean to overcome our possibly unproductive or misleading prejudices with regard to different issues in a context in which they are possibly unproductive or misleading only from one among a number of possible points of view? What does it mean to overcome prejudices and act on our understanding under circumstances in which we recognize that our traditions have become porous enough to include different sets of assumptions and orientations that make different claims on us?

Habermas insists that the limits of tradition-bound ethical under-standing in multicultural societies require us to engage in moral dis-courses through which we can justify moral principles while retaining a diversity of ethical opinions. But the problem suggested by a comparison of Elizabeth Bennet's ethical understanding with our own is not whether our societies can permit a diversity of ethical opinions. Nor is it even whether ethical discourse must be supplemented with moral discourse to reach legitimate results. Rather, the problem concerns the implica-tions of the diversity we have in our ethical understandings themselves. How are we to think of our own ethical opinions and orientations if we recognize that they are not the only legitimate ones? This problem is the one Williams explores.

THE LIMITS OF ETHICAL KNOWLEDGE

Williams employs a notion of thick concepts to make much the same point that Gadamer makes with prejudices, namely that our understand-ing at least of our human and social world is bound up with the orien-tations provided by our traditions. Thick concepts are concepts such as coward, brutality, and gratitude that combine fact and value by provid-ing for both the description of an action or character and its evalua-tion.[21] Description and evaluation cannot be pulled apart in thick con-cepts; their evaluative aspect cannot be stripped off the description to leave a simply neutral way of depicting facts of the social world. Rather, one understands the meaning of the facts in the social world by taking up the evaluative stance contained in the concept and knowing how to use the concept appropriately. Thick concepts thus form parts of traditions with other assumptions and evaluations. One can be a coward in different ways in different cultures, and the particular way in which one is a coward in a particular culture will depend upon the concepts to which cowardice is related—for instance, fear of battle in one and fear of intimacy in another—as well as the other concepts from which coward is distinguished. Similarly, one can have the proper pride that Darcy has only in cultures in which a distinction between proper and improper pride makes sense and where proper pride legitimately relates to family pedigree and the performance of the duties attendant upon it.

Thick concepts have two additional features as Williams conceives of them. First, they are action motivating. When we know the concept in terms of which to understand someone or something, we also know how to act with regard to that person or thing. Thus, Elizabeth knows how to act with regard to both Wickham and Darcy once she knows the thick concepts under which their characters are to be understood. Second, thick concepts admit of right and wrong applications and are thus "world-guided," as Williams puts the point.[22] Knowing what it means to attribute cowardice to someone and how cowardice is to be distinguished from diffidence and timidity depend upon the features of the social world to which these concepts belong. Similarly, knowing how pride is to be distinguished from both arrogance and disdain for the feelings of others "tracks the truth" in the sense that it adequately comprehends actual features of the tradition or social world to which the thick concepts belong.

Still, what happens to the possibility that thick concepts can orient action and track truth if our social world contains multiple traditions and competing sets or understandings of thick concepts? Can we count as knowledge the understanding of the thick concepts of a tradition that its members possess if we are also aware that different traditions have different thick concepts and understand shared concepts differently? I shall try to work out Williams's answer to this question by using Elizabeth Bennet's world as an example.

Under what Williams describes as an "objectivist" analysis,[23] Elizabeth cannot possess ethical knowledge. She does not possess any understanding of the principles of equality and women's rights that her tradition obscures. In addition, the understanding that she does develop of Wickham and Darcy can be questioned from outside the traditional framework she employs. Is it "really" legitimate, for instance, to contrast proper to improper pride? Why should one be proud of one's wealth, family pedigree, and social standing even if one's tradition connects wealth, family pedigree, and social standing to specific duties and obligations? And even if we equate pride with the self-respect that comes of fulfilling one's social role, what connection does either pride or self-respect legitimately have to the question of whether one should marry someone with a vulgar mother? Indeed, is Mrs. Bennet really vulgar outside of the confines of the world Austen creates? From an "objectivist" point of view, might she not rather be responding to an impossible situation in which she must marry off her five daughters if she is to provide for their futures at all? On an "objectivist" model, the assumptions and prejudices that are never questioned in *Pride and Prejudice* would serve as an indication that "an entire segment of the local discourse may be seen from outside as involving a mistake."[24] What counts as pride or vulgarity inside the tradition is revealed, from outside of it, to be simply mistaken. Hence, the knowledge that Elizabeth comes to have of both proper pride and vulgarity would not count as knowledge at all.

Still, Williams argues that to conceive of the ethical understanding of a tradition in an objectivist way is to equate ethical knowledge with scientific knowledge. In relation to Elizabeth's world, it would be to suppose, for example, that in coming to understand Darcy's pride as proper or her mother's character as not merely silly but vulgar, Elizabeth comes to understand incorrectly a characteristic another culture or our own understands correctly. This sort of objectivism does not need to be of a naively realist kind that supposes pride or vulgarity is something in the world about which we can have right or wrong accounts, much in the way that stars are features of the world about which we can have right or wrong explanations. Rather, all the objectivist model need imply is that in making claims for a proper sort of pride, for instance, Elizabeth fails to pursue their broader implications, especially those that would necessarily lead her to question the connection between pride and social standing. Williams admits that one legitimately might make such a claim with regard to the stars since we might "see primitive statements about the stars as having implications that can be contradicted by more sophisticated statements about the stars."[25] If one can make the same sort of distinction between primitive and sophisticated statements about pride or vulgarity, then one will be able correctly to locate the place of ethical knowledge. It will belong not to Elizabeth and her contemporaries, who do not see the implications of their claims, but rather to those with more sophisticated views of virtue and vice.

But Williams rejects the comparison between ethical and scientific knowledge on which this conclusion rests. From the perspective he offers, the judgments that Elizabeth makes about Darcy's pride or her mother's character could not count as statements about discoveries she has made with regard to the truth of an extratraditional concept of pride or with regard to extratraditional standards of action. Williams insists that we can say that we know something about phlogisten that our predecessors did not. Still, in his account it would be a mistake to say that someone who rejected the idea of proper pride in favor of a more Christian humility, for example, knew something about pride that Elizabeth did not. Rather, Elizabeth's concept of pride is one internal to the descriptions and evaluations of the tradition to which she belongs and cannot be stripped of its traditional context if it is to remain the concept it is. Hence, what she comes to understand of it remains internal to her tradition as well.

For Williams, the judgments Elizabeth ultimately makes about Darcy, Wickham, and herself would indicate that she has learned to deploy the thick concepts of her society in ways appropriate to the form of life she inhabits. Her judgments are part of her way of living, "a cultural artifact,"[26] and their adequacy depends upon the extent to which they cohere with other parts of that form of life. To the extent that Elizabeth raises questions about the adequacy of her judgments, she must do so from within that form of life, in terms of the other thick concepts or prejudices to which her ethical knowledge is connected. The development of Elizabeth's understanding in this regard is one that moves entirely within the compass of her tradition and as we have seen is made possible by it. But, on Williams's analysis this compass would not mean she does not have or come to possess knowledge. Rather, for Williams members of a tradition possess ethical knowledge just as long as they use their thick concepts carefully and refer to appropriate criteria in applying them.[27]

Yet if Williams rejects objectivism, at least as an adequate account of the possibility of ethical knowledge, he also rejects relativism and, indeed, denies that relativism is an intelligible theory at all. In the first place, relativism assumes that, when members of one tradition meet members of another and react to their customs, they are involved in some sort of "anthropological misunderstanding."[28] It assumes, in other words, that ethical reactions to the practices of others are precluded by the claim that all thick concepts are tradition bound and cannot be stripped of their context without losing their meaning. But this supposition does not follow from any connection between ethical knowledge and the thick concepts of a tradition; to the contrary, to the extent that a tradition possesses thick concepts it will necessarily react to another tradition in terms of them. In other words, it will understand the thick concepts of the other culture in terms of its own thick concepts or in terms of what Gadamer calls its own hermeneutic horizon.

Nor, in the second place, can we simply assume the existence of self-enclosed cultures that confront each other as self-enclosed cultures. As Williams points out, "social practices could never come forward with a certificate saying that they belonged to a genuinely different culture, so that they were guaranteed immunity to alien judgments and reactions." [29] Rather, to the extent that we belong to traditions and employ their thick concepts we will employ them to understand and evaluate all the practices we encounter, even those of other cultures, just because our thick concepts serve as the meanings that actions and practices have for us. To this extent, at least the aspiration of ethical thought seems to extend beyond the supposed boundaries of a given tradition. Our thick concepts of pride or selflessness do not typically include caveats attaching them only to us, even if we do recognize that others might understand them differently. As Williams puts this point, "even if there is no way in which divergent ethical beliefs can be brought to converge by independent inquiry or traditional argument . . . each outlook may still be making claims it intends to apply to the whole world, not just to that part of it that is its 'own' world." [30]

But if both objectivism and relativism are excluded, the issue to which relativism tries to supply the answer remains crucial. Williams defines that issue in two ways: as the impact of reflection on the certainty of ethical knowledge and as the recognition of nonobjectivity or the acknowledgment that the thick concepts that make up one tradition's ethical knowledge are not the only possible ones. If Elizabeth can be said to have ethical knowledge insofar as she learns to deploy the thick concepts of her tradition in ways appropriate to it, what does this definition of ethical knowledge mean for the members of multicultural societies? What does it mean for those who are aware that their own traditions and thick concepts are not unique and, indeed, may already be considerably "thinner" than Elizabeth's to the extent that they include the recognition of other ways of understanding the issues or practices in question? How are we to think about our understanding of the issue of surrogate mothering, for example, if we know that the thick concepts in terms of which we might understand it, those of duty, selflessness, motherhood, and honor, may not represent the thought of more than one tradition and that other traditions can understand these same concepts in different ways?

Nor is surrogate mothering the only issue in which differing ethical traditions with different understandings of thick concepts compete with one another within contemporary American life. In current controversies over abortion, we have seen that pro-life and pro-choice advocates differ in the concepts and traditions in terms of which they understand not only the practice of abortion itself but also the sanctity of life, personal liberty, the equality of men and women, the meaning of sexual intercourse, the place of motherhood, and the meaning of family. If we are aware of nonobjectivity, however, if we are aware that our thick concepts either differ from those of others or are already thin enough to include an appreciation of the different starting points from which their concepts emerge, how are we to act? We might simply try to enforce our concepts and understanding dogmatically, or, conversely, we might simply adapt to theirs. We might allow for abortion as a consequence of an understanding of freedom that emphasizes personal decision, or we might prohibit it as a form of murder. By the same token, we might enforce surrogacy contracts or outlaw them altogether, depending on which traditions and which understanding we adopt. Still, Williams's formulation of the problem is worth quoting at length:

> While it is true that nonobjectivity does not imply any relativistic attitude, there does seem something blank and unresponsive in merely stopping at that truth. If you are conscious of nonobjectivity, should that not properly affect the way in which you see the application or extent of your ethical outlook? If so, how? . . . If we become conscious of ethical variation and of the kinds of explanation it may receive, it is incredible that this consciousness should just leave everything where it was and not affect our ethical thought itself. We can go on, no doubt simply saying that we are right and everyone else is wrong (that is to say, on the nonobjectivist view, affirming our values and rejecting theirs), but if we have arrived at this stage of reflection, it seems a remarkably inadequate response.[31]

What, then, is an adequate response? How are we to think of our own ethical understanding of thick concepts once we acknowledge that this understanding is not the only possible one? Williams suggests a notion of confidence. In contemporary pluralistic and multicultural societies, an ethical certainty of the sort Elizabeth possesses may no longer be attainable; yet it might be replaced with a confidence that Williams defines as a sense that the life we are living is worth living. This sense does not issue only from the results of the sort of rational argumentation Habermas ascribes to moral discourses, although rational argument is part of what produces confidence. But Williams also looks to institutions, upbringing, and public discourse in general and concludes that "one question we have to answer is how people, or enough people, can come to possess a practical confidence that, particularly granted both the need for reflection and its pervasive presence in our world, will come from strength and not from the weakness of self-deception and dogmatism." [32]

Williams does not try to answer this question or indicate how confidence might help resolve issues such as surrogate mothering or abortion. Indeed, he sees confidence primarily as the appropriate attitude that a democratic culture might take toward cultures alien to it. In the remainder of this chapter, however, I want to take up his idea of confidence as the appropriate attitude that members of the diverse traditions within a pluralistic and multicultural society might take toward each other's orientations and understandings. Moreover, I want to suggest that one way to instill confidence might be to recognize the place it already has in our discussions of art and literature. For one way to characterize these understandings and discussions is to show that they already replace rational conviction with confidence and knowledge with understanding. To this extent, they might form part of the answer to the question of how members of multicultural societies can acquire the practical or ethical confidence Williams proposes.

CONFIDENCE AND INTERPRETATION

My account of Austen's *Pride and Prejudice* attends to issues of prejudice, knowledge, and self-knowledge because it addresses the text with a specific question—namely, how is Elizabeth Bennet's progression from blind prejudice to knowledge and self-knowledge possible? This question leads to further questions about the limits of a tradition-bound knowledge and the possibility of ethical knowledge in a society with competing traditions. To this extent, the question is situated within a particular hermeneutic horizon. It emerges from a particular context of expectations and assumptions that involve late twentieth-century suspicions about the force and limits of reason, as well as late twentieth-century issues about pluralism and multiculturalism.

That *Pride and Prejudice* offers an answer to the question of overcoming blind prejudices, however, does not entail that this question is one that Austen intended to answer. To the contrary, to suppose that

Austen's questions and our own converge is to assume that what a person intends to do or say is always transparent in his or her speech act, text, or action or that one's plans always coincide with the actual course of events. But if it is only by examining the resulting text, speech act, or action as we find it that we can reconstruct the question, then the question we reconstruct is one to which the text or action actually provides an answer, at least for us. It is not necessarily the question the author or agent may have initially intended to answer.[33]

But who is the we here? If the meaning of a text can be disassociated from its author's intentions, and if questions about knowledge and prejudice lead to one way of understanding Austen's *Pride and Prejudice,* they are clearly not the only questions one might address to the novel. Nor is this way the only one available to contemporary readers. Others might attend to the ways in which Austen undermines a particular patriarchal form of the novel[34] or to issues concerning the ethics of laughter.[35] Such attention will emphasize different aspects of the novel and reveal different dimensions of it. What the novel means to some of us because of the questions and interests we bring to it and the hermeneutic context in which we place it will differ from the hermeneutic context and questions others bring. The meaning we understand does not conform to the objective meaning of the text, then, but to the meaning of the text for us, given the interpretive context within which we find ourselves.

Still, if objectivism is ruled out in the literary domain, so is a relativism that would argue that, because meaning depends on the questions we ask, any questions and therefore any meaning must be legitimate. Rather, our understanding of texts and works of art remains guided by them in the way in which an appropriate use of thick concepts is world guided for Williams. Just as thick concepts of propriety and impropriety lead Elizabeth to a deeper understanding of Wickham, Darcy, and herself, the prejudices from which we proceed and the questions we ask of a text are validated to the extent that they help to reveal dimensions of the meaning of the text. One way to specify the content of this revelation is to employ the hermeneutic concept of a unity of whole and part. The claim here, as we have seen, is that only the premise that a text as a whole forms a coherent, unified meaning allows the sort of investigation into it and revision of initial inadequate interpretations that can illuminate it for us. Furthermore, despite theories such as deconstruction, even the claim that a text subverts its meaning presupposes an understanding of what that meaning, in its unity, could be.[36] Still, the argument against relativism in our understanding of texts is simply that we can distinguish between the various legitimate understandings of a text and those that fail to make sense of it at all.

Indeed, as we have also seen, we can distinguish between understandings of its unity that allow us to learn from a text and those that do not. Elizabeth's understanding of the thick concepts of duty, honor, gratitude, and the like is more adequate, in this sense, than Lady Catherine's, for example, because it not only gives a coherent sense to the thick concepts of her tradition but it grasps their point and is not attentive only to their surface appearance. Similarly, the more illuminating understandings of a text will be those that allow it to speak to concerns that are or can be shown by the interpretation to be real concerns for us. Of course, a given text may not have a point; attempts to show that it does will often possess a forced character, usually betrayed in the necessity the interpretation confronts of giving up some portion of the unity of part and whole.[37] Showing the point of a text does not require conscious efforts to modernize it or show its relevance. In the main, however, the understandings of a text that are most productive or helpful are those that succeed in showing that the meaning it has provides answers or provokes new questions about issues with which we are or can learn to be concerned. Texts that cannot ask or answer questions for us are thus dead in the sense that we can no longer find or inhabit the hermeneutic horizon that might awaken their meaning for us.

Both nonobjectivist and nonrelativist sides of this analysis of the understanding of textual meaning are important for elucidating the concept Williams introduces of a confidence in our ethical understanding. On the one hand, in interpreting texts we are already aware of what Williams calls nonobjectivity. We are aware that our interpretations are not the only possible ones, that interpreters with different concerns, different theoretical and practical commitments, and different historical and hermeneutic contexts can find very different meanings in the same text. On the other hand, we are also aware of the adequacy of our own interpretations as interpretations that awaken meaning, that allow perhaps new or different dimensions of the meaning of a text to emerge. Our textual interpretations are not ones about which we can have conviction as long as the concept of conviction implies an absolute trust in the exclusive correctness of our own views; nor are our interpretations ones that we think others could reject only on pain of irrationality. Rather, our textual interpretations are ones in which we appropriately have confidence as adequate, revealing, and illuminating interpretations insofar as they can tell us something about a text and, perhaps, even about ourselves. Our understanding of texts as well as works of art are ones in which we can have confidence, then, rather than conviction because we recognize that the understanding we have is both disclosive of meaning and nonexclusive.

The other side of this confidence in our own interpretations is an acknowledgment of the confidence others have in their interpretations. If we recognize the nonexclusive character of our understanding of meaning, then we must also recognize that other interpretations are capable of delivering important, nonexclusive insights of their own in which their proponents can appropriately have confidence. In the literary domain, we offer our interpretations as ones that illuminate the text in a way that we are confident others might appreciate. But we also assume that we can appreciate and even learn from their interpretations as well. Indeed, this assumption seems crucial to our interest in engaging in discussions of texts and works of art in the first place. We are not concerned to show the mistake in every possible interpretation other than our own; nor are we interested in ending discussion of specific texts and works of art once and for all. Rather, we assume that different vantage points, different connections, and different interests will continue to reveal new dimensions of a text or work of art in a never-ending way. Moreover, we assume that the strength of our own interpretation depends upon its openness to others, upon its ability to incorporate the insights it may have that are relevant to our own understanding, and upon its ability to situate these insights in relation to our own.

The idea of a confidence in our interpretations of texts and works of art transfers easily to the ethical understanding on which Williams focuses. In both cases, first of all, we can distinguish between legitimate and illegitimate interpretations of meaning without insisting that our legitimate interpretations are canonically correct. Second, in both cases we can allow for the possibility of other thick concepts and other legitimate interpretations. Thus, we recognize that Jane Austen's novels admit of different illuminating interpretations and that we can have confidence in our own understanding even as we appreciate that of others. Similarly, a principle linking pride, not to social standing, but to achievement is a principle in which we can have confidence even if we recognize alternative thick concepts in terms of which the idea of pride can be constructed. We can recognize that a principle respecting the sanctity of human life can be understood in terms that speak either to the creativity of nature or the investment of human beings in their own lives and the lives of those close to them. A principle of liberty can be understood to involve both the capacity for the autonomous decisions of individuals and the rights of self-determination of communities in establishing what they understand as the conditions for flourishing lives.

Third, we recognize that the strength of our interpretations depends upon their capacity to participate in an ongoing discussion and elaboration of meaning. In the case of diverging interpretations of a literary text, we acknowledge, appreciate, and even try to learn from an interpretation that differs from our own. We try to understand what it understands of the text that we may have missed, and we try to incorporate some of its insights into our own account. Were each side to proceed in this way in the case of interpreting our principles and practices, we might acknowledge that different sides can understand them in ways from which we all might learn.

If we add to these three similarities a commitment to avoid those interpretations that suppress the interpretive voices of others, then I think we can appropriately have as nondogmatic a confidence in our ethical understanding as we do in our understanding of texts. Indeed, the idea of a practical confidence in our understanding of the meaning of our principles works with McCarthy's conception of reflective participation to resolve what might be called the performative problem with interpretive conversation. We can put our own interpretations forward as ones that illuminate important aspects of our principles and practices without denying that others with a different orientation might illuminate important aspects as well. Indeed, if we are aware of nonobjectivity, dogmatically trying to impose our own particular interpretation as social policy seems not only "remarkably inadequate," as Williams writes with regard to our attitude towards our ethical understandings. It also reflects an attempt we have productively done without in the domain of art and literature.

To this extent, the discussions of art and literature in which we already commonly participate seem to provide a kind of quasi-institutional setting and a part of our common upbringing that lend themselves to answering the question Williams raises as to "how people, or enough people, can come to possess a practical confidence that, particularly granted both the need for reflection and its pervasive presence in our world, will come from strength and not from the weakness of self-deception and dogmatism." How does this practical confidence in our ethical understanding translate into decisions about which policies we should pursue as a collectivity? If conceptions of the rule of the majority typically look to the means for legitimately imposing or establishing one understanding of the issue in question as the proper one, then a practical confidence in our own particular ethical understanding might encourage us, instead, as both citizens and legislators to remain open to the ethical understandings of others and to try to incorporate what we can of each other's interpretations into our own. Moreover, again as both citizens and legislators, we might compromise on what we cannot incorporate, in the recognition that what is at stake is not knowledge but understanding, not conviction but confidence.

Two different traditions of thought compete in their understanding of the practice of abortion itself, the principles it involves, and the issues of sex, reproduction, and motherhood surrounding it.[38] Pro-life groups understand abortion as murder and, hence, as a violation of the principles of respect for the sanctity of life. Further, they understand sex as a sacred act, reproduction as the most basic point of human life, and motherhood as that place in any culture that speaks to its regard for the virtues of care and concern for others. Conversely, pro-choice groups understand abortion as a personal procreative decision based on a family's particular understanding of respect for the sanctity of life. In addition, they see sex as either sacred or not sacred, depending upon its connection to intimacy, reproduction as a life-option, and motherhood as a grave responsibility to be entered into, at best, under conditions that allow families to flourish. But it is unclear how either side might maintain the conviction that its interpretation of this complex of principles, values, and meanings is the only possible one. How might one say definitively what motherhood, for example, is once one is aware of the different forms it has taken both historically and culturally and the different forms it may take in the future? And while we might say that, at least for us, the ideal of motherhood speaks to a kind of selfless love and generosity, it also may legitimately seem to include the idea of a responsibility taken up freely and consciously. But why should we have to choose between one concept of motherhood and the other? Rather, each set of interpretations is one in which its proponents can have confidence as a legitimate understanding that illuminates some part of what abortion, respect for the sanctity of life, sex, reproduction, and motherhood mean even if it cannot illuminate all of what any mean and, indeed, even if no interpretation can illuminate all of what any mean. But if each set of interpretations is one in which its advocates can have confidence as opposed to conviction, then might we not look for legislative solutions to the controversy over abortion that try to accommodate both? Indeed, might we not try different sorts of legislative solutions in different states while assuring ourselves of their validity by examining or relying on the Supreme Court to examine their legitimacy as interpretations of our principles? I have suggested that such solutions accommodate our differences by finding ways to reduce the incidences of abortion while creating the social and economic conditions under which families can make autonomous and responsible choices. Still, whatever accommodations different legislatures might establish, what is crucial is that they base themselves on a recognition of legitimate differences.

Our different understandings of surrogate mothering seem to admit of a similar ethical confidence. Carmel Shalev argues that if we conceive of surrogate mothering in terms of norms involving the freedom of contract, we are led to demand specific compliance of surrogacy contracts even in cases in which the surrogate mother finds it difficult to relinquish the child she has conceived and to whom she has given birth.[39] To allow surrogate mothers to change their minds and renege on the contracts they have made freely and consciously is, according to Shalev, to deny women both autonomy and rationality. The policy assumes that women cannot be trusted to act responsibly, to understand the consequences of their actions, or to think clearly and with foresight. Hence, it revokes any thought of women's equality with men and associates women with the age-old stereotype of emotional immaturity.

Yet this interpretation of surrogate mothering is not the only one that makes sense to us. We can also understand surrogacy as an exploitation of poor women for the benefit of economically better-off couples. In this case, we will understand the demand for specific compliance as further exploitation. Poorer women sell their procreative capacities in relatively selfless attempts to help their own families and infertile couples. When they cannot help but treat the babies to which they give birth as family, they are required to sacrifice their own happiness and what they conceive of as their own babies' well-being to satisfy the demands of an economic marketplace that has intruded into all spheres of life, even those of love and intimacy. On this interpretation of surrogacy, either the practice is inhumane and ought to be prohibited or, at the very least, its norms should mirror those of adoption rather than commerce.

Given these different rubrics and traditions in terms of which we might confidently understand surrogate mothering—those of family versus marketplace and love versus commerce—how can we come to any conclusion as to whether it amounts to an extension of contract law or an extension of adoption law? If we combine Williams's suggestions with the form our literary discussions already take, then we might say that while we maintain our commitment to our own understanding of the practice, we recognize the nonobjective or nonexclusive character of that understanding and refuse to rule out the possible legitimacy of other interpretations. Hence, we might acknowledge that both sides in the debate understand the practice of surrogacy as a coherent whole; nor does either try to minimize the significance of the issues involved, those of autonomy, rationality, equality, love, and family. But this circumstance seems to indicate that we might try to accommodate both interpretations of the practice. Hence, state legislatures might develop policies on surrogate mothering that allow women to decide not to relinquish custody of their babies once they have given birth and as long as they make their decision within a short period of time. At the same time, such policies might take seriously the contract into which the surrogate and sponsoring couple have entered and allow for the father's custody rights as well as those of the mother. Answers to the issue of surrogate mothering might then involve flexible policies that lead to various forms of joint custody in cases in which the birth mother cannot give up custody of her child.

We have suggested similar accommodations in the cases of affirmative action and pornography. These suggestions stem, again, from the recognition that in multicultural and pluralistic societies our understanding of the principles we share warrants confidence rather than conviction and thus has more in common with our interpretations of texts and works of art than it does with a moral absolutism. At stake is neither scientific knowledge nor unjustified opinion but, instead, legitimate understandings of the meaning of our principles and ideals. While not every interpretation of their meaning will be legitimate, more than one may be. Our confidence in our own interpretations comes from our ability to show their legitimacy as productive illuminations of the issues at stake. At the same time, this confidence is one that can admit and even learn from the possible illumination that other approaches offer as well. This sort of confidence leads away from dogmatism and to an openness that is willing to incorporate different voices in our discussions of meaning and that encourages forms of accommodation.

CHAPTER EIGHT

Conclusion

Clearly, there are contested social issues in American public life other than those I have looked at in this book. Physician-assisted suicide, the right to bear arms, capital punishment, and same-sex marriage are some of the controversies that currently concern Americans, while human cloning and genetic engineering hover on the horizon. Still, the issues that I have examined here suffice, I think, to illuminate three considerations we might employ, and ask our legislators to employ, in looking at different voices in current and future discussions.

First, we might try to articulate and include in our discussions different plausible understandings of the practices, principles, and concepts at issue. This approach is the one I adopted in trying to open up the debate over surrogate mothering to different possibilities for what we can understand or count as a family. I interpreted part of the meaning of family to involve its unintentional dimension or the way in which relationships between parents and children supersede their expectations and intentions. But this unintentional dimension seems to cast doubt on attempts to legislate through either contract law or philosophy what are to count as legitimate family relationships. Rather, biological, adoptive, surrogate, and foster parents might all have important and legitimate relationships to a child whose custody is contested. Barring neglect, abandonment, and abuse, it is unclear why courts should limit the extent of the family or families in which a child may already be involved and why a legal decision should determine which among the different existing family relationships is legitimate. There are certainly ways of understanding what a family is other than that of stressing its unintentional dimension. Still, if this interpretation is compelling in grasping some part of what a family is, then why might not courts and legislatures expand the conception of legitimate family relationships to include the relations a child might have to all the adults to whom he or she has substantive ties, whether these ties issue from a genetic connection that a surrogate mother takes seriously or the intensive care and nurturing that an adoptive or foster family offers?

This approach seems to have obvious implications for the issue of same-sex marriage, for if family relationships exceed legal and contractual attempts to define legitimacy, the same would seem to hold of the intimate relationships that lead to marriage. Part of the meaning of marriage involves its "public recognition of a private commitment."[1] But, again, it seems odd for courts and legislatures to decide in advance which commitments can be legitimate and which cannot. Just as we have the families we have whether we intended them or not, we have the commitments of love and support we have whether we intended to fall in love with a man or a woman.

Of course, many Americans understand marriage just as a long-term commitment specifically between one man and one woman. In light of an interpretive or hermeneutic approach to our shared principles and practices, however, the idea that courts and legislatures might install this understanding as the only possible definition of marriage seems not only dogmatic but unnecessarily intrusive on a domain tailor-made for legitimate differences. In addition, it appears to be a consequence of the same fear for social institutions that led the Feversham Committee to condemn artificial insemination by donor as a threat to marriage, the family, and the peerage itself.[2] Yet just as the complex relationships that issue from artificial insemination by donor as well as from adoption, surrogate mothering, and even from divorce and remarriage allow us to open up our conception of family, the forms of love that can arise between individuals, whether of the same sex or not, allow us to expand our idea of marriage beyond those life commitments currently sanctioned by the state. Again, as in the case of family relationships, opening marriage up to the different forms it can take does not require us to accept the legitimacy of commitments that issue from physical or mental abuse or intimidation or those that involve the consent of minor children. But an understanding of family and marriage that includes loving, consensual relationships and commitments between members of the same sex obviously need include none of these disqualifications; nor is it clear, therefore, why the public expression of a same-sex commitment in the form of marriage should not receive the public support that other public expressions of commitment between members of the opposite sex receive.

An inclusive approach that tries to help articulate new or quieter voices in our debates over social issues is also the approach I took to the debate over affirmative action in trying to resuscitate an understanding of the meaning of the principle of equal opportunity that has been somewhat obscured by our exclusive attention to ideals of neutrality, on the one hand, and ideals of diversity, on the other. According to this third understanding, the principle of equal opportunity includes not only neutrality in admissions and hiring decisions but the participation of all citizens in the practices and institutions of their society. To the extent that affirmative action polices undermine conceptions of merit and fairness, their critics can justifiably object to them. Yet are neutrality and the participation of all necessarily opposed to one another? If federal and state governments complement affirmative action policies with remedial programs, support for public education and training programs as well as support for families and neighborhoods, it is not clear that we cannot accommodate both principles of neutrality and those of participation, where the participation of all in the practices and institutions of the society necessarily includes both their ability to perform the tasks required of them and their diversity.

Suppose we took this inclusive approach to our debates over the meaning of a right to keep and bear arms as codified in the Second Amendment. While the amendment has usually been understood to present a problem for advocates of restrictive gun control laws, its meaning is also notoriously complex and can support alternative readings. The amendment states that "a well-regulated militia being necessary to the security of a free state, the right of the people to keep and bear arms shall not be infringed."[3] Depending on whether one emphasizes the first or second part of the amendment, one can understand it to justify either a communal right to bear arms or an individual right to keep them. On one reading, the amendment simply prohibits Congress from forbidding states to maintain militias. On another reading, it guarantees the right of every law-abiding citizen of the United States to own and use guns as long as he or she does so in a law-abiding way.

Significantly, both sides in this debate look to the context of the eighteenth century to support their respective interpretations. Thus, in an essay entitled, "The Ideological Origins of the Second Amendment," Robert E. Shalhope justifies an individualistic interpretation of the law by appealing to the civic republican tradition of Niccolo Machiavelli. According to this tradition, a right to bear arms is essential to individual liberty in both economic and political senses. The individual citizen must be able to hunt, to protect himself, to defend against foreign invasion, and to mount a credible opposition to the possible corruption of government. As taken up by English and American writers, Shalhope contends, the civic republican tradition served to focus the right to bear arms on the necessary capacity for responsible citizens to defend themselves against governmental tyranny. Indeed, proponents of the right consistently distinguished between the independent, self-reliant, arms-bearing American citizen and his oppressed, disarmed European cousin.[4]

On this reading, it is important that when James Madison offered the amendments that compose the Bill of Rights he proposed that they be inserted directly into the body of the Constitution in article 1, section 9. Shalhope insists that in so doing:

> He did not separate the right to bear arms from the other rights designed to protect the individual; he did not suggest placing it in Section 8 . . . which dealt specifically with arming and organizing the militia. When he prepared notes for an address supporting the amendments, Madison reminded himself "They relate first to private rights." And when he consulted with Edmund Pendleton, he emphasized that "the amendments may be employed to quiet the fears of many, by supplying these further grounds for private rights."[5]

Of course, even if Madison did understand the Second Amendment as a private and individual right, his interpretation can have no privileged status unless we identify the meaning of a text or action with its author's or agent's intentions. Meanings, as families do, supersede our intentions, and they do so for similar reasons: because they are complex and because they become parts of structures, perspectives, and relationships beyond our control. For his part, Lawrence Delbar Cress appeals to the same civic republican tradition as Shalhope does but uses it to defend the opposite view of the right to bear arms as a communal right meant to support an armed citizenry. Indeed, Cress claims that it is crucial to distinguish between an armed citizenry and an armed population. In the context of the eighteenth century, the right to bear arms applied to the civic responsibility of citizens and, more specifically, it applied to "propertied yeoman" who were to form part of a well-regulated militia led by a community's "most prominent citizens." As Cress writes,

> When discussions during the early national period turned to the preservation of liberty, then classical assumptions about the citizen's responsibility to bear arms in the interest of the common good quickly came to the fore. "For a people who are free, and who mean to remain so," Jefferson reminded Congress in 1808 in language that summarized the republican principles embodied in the Second Amendment, "a well-organized and armed militia is their best security." No one argued that the individual had a right to bear arms outside the framework of the established militia structure.[6]

Still, if Madison had no privileged insight into the meaning of the Second Amendment, neither did Jefferson. Nor is it clear that either understanding is one that twentieth-century Americans can possess without significant modifications. Shalhope tries to dismiss the communal understanding of the Second Amendment by insisting that the glorification of the role of militia in the American Revolution and the reference to militias in general as bulwarks against governmental tyranny were already bits of nostalgia for late-eighteenth century Americans. But for contemporary Americans the individualist conception seems equally nostalgic insofar as it involves the idea of the self-reliant American hunting for his own food and conquering the West. Moreover, how are individuals meant to defend themselves with their rifles against a supposedly tyrannical government if it has the force of a modern army and its weapons behind it?

How might we expand our conceptions of legitimate understandings of the Second Amendment then? Suppose we connect the amendment not only to notions of an individual prerogative but also to ideas of a communal duty that emerge from the alternative reading of the civic republic tradition. Then why not impose all and any regulations on the sale and ownership of firearms that can enhance the stability of communities while upholding a right to keep and bear arms, duly regulated in the same way that other rights are regulated? Why not experiment with different combinations of regulations and support the needs of law enforcement in trying to reduce accidents and incidents of murder? The Supreme Court has historically upheld the rights of states to regulate the ownership and use of guns, and, if the states and U.S. Congress have, at least until recently, been reluctant to impose restrictive regulations on mentally competent, law-abiding adults, this reluctance seems to issue more from the political and economic influence of the so-called gun lobby than from concerted attempts to understand what the Second Amendment means.

Yet we might also question whether either individualist or communal interpretations of the Second Amendment are legitimate insofar as neither seems able to transcend the gap between the twentieth-century and eighteenth-century context in which it may have had its only point. On the one hand, I have argued against the idea that legitimate understandings of texts or text-analogues must "modernize" their meaning in explicit attempts to render them relevant to modern audiences. On the other hand, the possibility remains that certain texts and text-analogues are simply dead to us in the sense that we can no longer see their point. This eventuality is one I have mentioned only briefly as a possibility of interpretation. While the burden of understanding lies on the interpreter to try to make sense out of what he or she is attempting to understand, not all meaning need ultimately be intelligible. And if any meaning the Second Amendment possesses is inextricably connected to eighteenth-century conceptions of individualism and citizenship, is it entirely clear what the amendment still has to say, at least to us? Issues surrounding gun control in the United States today often center on the alleged right "to blow away potential assailants." [7] To this extent, the issue is framed in terms of the question of whether or not individuals should have access to the guns of their choosing without governmental restrictions on what kinds of guns should be available to them. Still, is this issue connected in any plausible way to the Second Amendment? Is it legitimate to interpret this amendment in terms of an individual's right "to blow away potential assailants"? Perhaps it is. Still, introducing the question into our debates might help to expand all our understandings of both the Second Amendment and the principles that are supposed to lie behind it.

A second consideration we might employ in looking at different voices in our current and future discussions involves reflecting on what each side in them can learn from the others. This question is the one we explored in examining what we have learned and can continue to learn from each other in the debate over abortion. In this case, the extent of what we might learn stretches beyond possible meanings of a respect for the sanctity of human life to encompass ideas about liberty and equality, acceptance and control, and care and responsibility. Yet what we have learned and can continue to learn from each other in this debate would seem to have obvious implications for our debates over physician-assisted suicide or euthanasia. Indeed, this issue often mirrors that of abortion in its formulation as a "clash of absolutes" pitting the right to life against the principle of autonomy or self-determination. Those who are against any form of euthanasia argue that it involves the deliberate ending of a human life and is therefore murder. Those who argue for the right to physician-assisted suicide argue, in contrast, that the right to self-determination includes the right to die in a way that is consistent with one's own ideas of dignity and honor. As in the case of the debate over abortion, however, the various sides in the debate share principles of the sanctity of life and the right to self-determination. Again, they simply interpret them differently and do so along the lines one would expect from the debate over abortion.

Thus, Ronald Dworkin suggests that one claim central to many arguments against physician-assisted suicide includes an understanding of the sanctity of life that says that one ought not intervene in human life to end it, either at or before its start, with abortion, or at or before its end with euthanasia. On this view, life is a gift of God or a miracle of nature that attests to a nonhuman investment in human life. Indeed, some religious conceptions view human life as belonging to God rather than to the individual; hence, it can be taken only by God. Even under less strict conceptions of a divine or natural investment in human life "any human intervention—injecting a lethal drug into someone dying of a painful cancer or withdrawing life support from a person in a persistent vegetative state—cheats nature, and if the natural investment . . . dominates the sanctity of life, then euthanasia always insults that value." [8]

Opposed to this conception of the sanctity of life, however, is one that looks not to the natural investment in a human life but to the human investment. On this analysis, it may respect the value of human life not to extend it when the interests, pursuits, and life projects that made it valuable to the individual who invested in it are made impossible by crippling pain and disease. Indeed, for those who think that physician-assisted suicide should be legally available, that which insults the value of life is precisely the refusal to honor the wishes of those who want to die, the refusal to assist them in an easy death, and the insistence on extending their biological life beyond all honor and dignity through the use of breathing machines, feeding tubes, and the like.

Dworkin points out that even those who understand the sanctity of life in terms of a divine or natural investment can intelligibly object to a life unnaturally extended by machines and modern medicine.[9] Moreover, because of the different understandings different people can have of the sanctity of life, he insists that the same principles guaranteeing the free exercise of religion that allow for abortion also allow for ending a life when its continuation violates its holder's conception of its value. But as does our debate over abortion, our debate over physician-assisted suicide extends beyond the understandings that Dworkin explores of the way in which principles involving the sanctity of life comport with death. In addition, it includes conceptions of autonomy, equality, and the role of acceptance and control in the conduct of life. Thus, principles of autonomy and self-determination are linked for some to the right to determine the conditions under which one will cling to life, on the one hand, or expect to be eased into death, on the other. For others, they are linked to a community's right to decide how it is to cope with death and old age as policy matters. From this second perspective, even if a right to physician-assisted suicide is a matter of self-determination, it is a matter of self-determination applying to states or community-based forms of decision, not to individuals. Similarly, for some, the prospect of physician-assisted suicide raises important threats to equality in offering physicians an unprecedented power. Old and ill patients can be pressured to let go of life before they are ready in order not to create a burden on their relatives or expense for their health plan. For others, the threat to equality comes not from the unequal power relations between doctors and patients but, first, from the absence of laws, guidelines, and regulations that can protect the old and the sick from their doctors and relatives and, second, from social conditions that render them burdens in the first place. Moreover, considerations of equality, on this view, require giving the old and sick equal say in decisions about their lives, including decisions about ending them.

Finally, our differences over euthanasia seem to engage existential attitudes about life that are similar to those we found in our divisions over abortion. For some, the good life is one planned and controlled as far as possible and planned even with regard to death; for others, the good life involves acceptance and gratitude; an interest in control signals a life seriously deaf to the vicissitudes of living and dying. But if we can learn from each other to take seriously the considerations our different understandings offer of euthanasia, what sort of accommodations or compromises are possible? One answer involves promoting the same policies I suggested as possible resolutions to the issue of abortion. In the first place, we might work to establish those legal, social, and financial conditions that would allow old or ill patients the independence that would guard them from choosing death to avoid being a burden on others or, indeed, under coercion from others. This condition mirrors the request in the case of abortion that communities provide financial and psychological support in the care and nurturing of children. In the same way, we might accommodate the interpretations of those who oppose physician-assisted suicide by providing for social support for the care of the old and the sick. We might also focus on improving hospice care to minimize, as far as possible, the pain and fear of dying. And, finally, courts and legislatures might support euthanasia under these conditions as the personal choice of some, given their understanding of the dignity and meaning of human life, even if it is not the understanding of all.

How might these or somewhat similar proposals play out in another case that seems to engage principles of life, liberty or autonomy, and equality, that of capital punishment? Can we learn from and accommodate each others' different understandings of principles and meanings in this case as well? Current discussions of capital punishment include questions about the rights of victims versus the rights of criminals, as well as questions about what a respect for the sanctity of human life means.[10] Does it exhibit appropriate respect for the lives of victims to allow those who have murdered them in particularly heinous ways to continue to live? Does it exhibit appropriate respect for human life in general for the state to kill some of its citizens years after they may have committed the crime with which they are charged, years in which they may have changed in significant ways? What about questions of liberty and equality? If death rows across the country are filled with more blacks than whites, is this an issue of equality or fairness? Or is the meaning of equality here more appropriately applied to the way in which a murderer robs his victim of any equal chance to live his or her life or pursue his or her life projects? Are these matters of finding the single appropriate principle to apply to the particular case, as Habermas and Günther argue? Or is the issue one, again, of fundamental differences in interpretations of the principles to which both sides in the debate adhere? If we differ in our understandings of equality, liberty, and the sacred quality of human life, is any accommodation possible here?

At the very least, if we are to allow that capital punishment is consistent with some legitimate understandings of the sanctity of life, liberty, and equality, accommodating different understandings would seem to require just the sort of lengthy appeals process that most states in the United States currently conduct, as well as much better and perhaps more expensive legal representation for defendants than most states currently afford. At the same time, capital punishment presents a problem for a politics that takes interpretive conversation seriously, for, if any practice silences and suppresses interpretive voices, it would seem to be a government's ability to enforce a death penalty. Can judges and juries be so certain of their interpretation of events that they are willing to kill those they think have murdered others in appalling ways?

A third consideration we might employ in looking at the different voices in our public debates concerns the danger of ideological interpretations that serve to degrade rather than to educate us. In this regard, I have claimed that we need not take seriously interpretations of our practices and principles that include in their content the silencing and suppression of other legitimate interpretive voices. The debate over abortion and the feminist debate over pornography served to raise this issue and to emphasize an important condition on the openness of hermeneutic conversation. If that conversation is to retain the potential to inform and to educate us while helping to develop our understandings of ourselves and our principles, then it must also try to guard against the influence of money, power, and ideology. This ideal of free speech is the lesson that antipornography feminism has to teach us, I think, even if we reject its claims about the ideological content of pornography itself. Moreover, it is a lesson we might take into account in considering objections to same-sex marriage and apply to our debates over gun control, in which the money and political clout of some groups seem to fill up a disproportionate amount of the available space for public debate.

In assessing particular claims to the distorting influence of money, power, and ideology, however, it is important to add at least two provisos to the conditions of free speech. First, we might acknowledge that charges of ideological distortion can themselves be ways of suppressing or failing to hear legitimate interpretive voices. Second, if a particular interpretation of our principles or practices does appear to silence other interpretations, we still need to conduct careful empirical research to confirm or reject the charge. Indeed, if we find that pornography or some other practice does silence the interpretive voices of women or of some other group by throwing systematic disturbances into the arena in which we try to communicate with one another, it remains a separate question whether state-sanctioned censorship is the best way to ensure the openness of our hermeneutic conversations. Nonetheless, if we take the openness of hermeneutic conversation as our goal, many of the issues surrounding the ideal of free speech seem easier to resolve. The goal is to open our public debates to the full range of legitimate interpretive voices. Doing so is crucial to the capacity of our public debates to educate and enrich us once we understand our own contributions, not as dogmatic renditions of the truth, but illuminating interpretations of meaning. To the extent that money, power, and ideology skew or curtail the range of legitimate interpretive voices, they are a threat to the strength and development of own interpretive voices. Hence, restricting their influence is not a restriction on the free speech rights of the rich and powerful as much as a securing of the space for interpretive discussion.

The proposals for compromise and accommodation that I have articulated in this book have been offered to courts, legislatures, feminists, and other citizens. Still, I have been more concerned simply to open our public debates to the range of legitimate voices within them and to ask whether the best response to these voices is to select some over others as somehow more legitimate or less interpretive. A hermeneutic acknowledgment of our legitimate interpretive differences cannot itself claim insight into the one correct understanding of our norms, principles, or practices. Nor can it offer either a single appropriate application of them or a single appropriate means of accommodating or compromising between our understandings of them. Indeed, a hermeneutic conception of our public debates might lead us, instead, to appreciate the possibility of different legitimate compromises and accommodations arrived at in different states and communities with the salutary result that all can learn from the solutions or partial solutions each state and community has found to the understanding of principles we continue to share. A hermeneutic conception of our public debates can also add its voice to them. Moreover, it can provide reassurance that if we acknowledge a range of legitimate interpretations we can still have confidence in our own understanding, a confidence that issues from the way we think that understanding contributes important and illuminating perspectives to the issue under consideration.

Still, to suppose that our interpretations can contribute to an ongoing debate, that they can raise important issues and elucidate valuable insights, is not to suppose that they are canonically correct. Hence, we can no longer have the ethical certainty and conviction that Jane Austen's heroines seem inevitably to attain. We can no longer speak with their precision or act with their elegance and may stutter and digress instead, acting in ways that are perplexing even to us. We may, for example, support a right to abortion, on the one hand, and worry about a right to physician-assisted suicide, on the other. Or we might be pulled in two different directions on the question of abortion itself because we understand the way in which the principles of equality and respect for the sanctity of life ground both a pro-life and a pro-choice position on abortion. Still, if we react in these ways, we might also remember that part of what we consider the mark of a sensitive reading of a text or work of art is its ability to appreciate the different ways in which it can be understood. Such readings do not simply dismiss or ignore alternative readings but rather cast their own light on the text or work of art and seek to situate that light in the reflection of others.

For the most part, we have given up the idea in our literary and artistic debates that only one understanding of a single work can be correct, and instead we have come to appreciate the variability of interpretive perspective, the inexhaustibility of the nuances and dimensions of textual meaning, and the ways in which contemporary concerns can illuminate even ancient texts. Were we to treat text-analogues such as the principles and practices we share in similar ways, we might resolve just as many issues as we do now through majority fiat, partisan conflict, and infusions of money, but we might also do so without the residual bitterness these strategies occasion. Indeed, it is perhaps misleading to think that majorities, money, and partisan conflict succeed in resolving our controversies. Despite laws, judicial decisions, and commercial campaigns, our public debates seem to continue. Were all sides to approach them hermeneutically, with an appreciation of legitimate differences, they might be able to accept policies and decisions with which they disagree as the outcome of legitimate interpretations. Hence, they might also be able to appreciate them as interpretations in which their advocates themselves can have only confidence but not a conviction it will take war or money to overcome. In other words, where there is a need to make decisions with which we disagree, we can recognize both that our own position is just an interpretation and that so is the interpretation at the heart of the decision with which we disagree. Hence, we need not approach that decision as wrong-headed or criminal but as the outcome of a legitimate interpretation that we can work to supplement and rework. Indeed, we can work to supplement and rework it with those others who regard the decision as appropriate but appreciate its merely interpretive basis. It is hard to see how such an interpretive approach can lead to the acrimony with which our public debates are currently conducted.

At the same time, to suggest that debates over social issues are closer to our debates over art and literature than they are to clashes of absolutes is not to aestheticize them, if by aestheticizing them we mean that the principles and issues they concern are only artifacts and do not matter. The presumption here is rather that Americans share principles that matter to them so deeply that they must continue to try to understand them in the varying situations in which they find themselves and with the varying concerns they possess. Still, they must try to understand them in a multicultural society in which they cannot suppose that only their understanding can be right. Were we to start from the assumption, instead, that no understanding can be canonically correct and try to attend to all the legitimate voices our debates include, then we might also reinforce institutional support for an unconstrained continuing conversation about what our principles and ideals can mean. Moreover, we might view various compromises and accommodations between legitimate voices as our best way of proceeding in a multicultural society in which confidence replaces conviction and duly constrained interpretations replace the knowledge of righteousness.

Notes

NOTES TO PREFACE

1. Amy Gutmann and Dennis Thompson, *Democracy and Disagreement* (Cambridge, Mass.: Harvard University Press, 1996), 346.

2. This term is taken from Stanley Fish's *Is There a Text in This Class?: The Authority of Interpretive Communities* (Cambridge, Mass.: Harvard University Press, 1980). I am not supposing Fish would endorse my use of the term, however.

3. See Martha Nussbaum, *Poetic Justice* (Boston: Beacon Press, 1995).

NOTES TO CHAPTER ONE

1. For a general analysis that understands our current disputes as moral disagreements and is therefore concerned with the place of moral disagreement in American political life, see Amy Gutmann and Dennis Thompson, *Democracy and Disagreement* (Cambridge, Mass.: Harvard University Press, 1996).

2. Lawrence Tribe, *Abortion: The Clash of Absolutes* (New York: W. W. Norton, 1990), 3.

3. Ibid., 224–25.

4. Ibid., 230–31.

5. See Kristin Luker, *Abortion and the Politics of Motherhood* (Berkeley: University of California Press, 1984). Also see Chapter Four, below.

6. Tribe, *Abortion*, 237.

7. It might seem odd to suggest this interpretive pluralism as a model for literary discussion just at the point at which some English departments are erupting into battle over what one side criticizes as political correctness and the other as conservatism. (See, for example, John M. Ellis, *Literature Lost: Social Agendas and the Corruption of the Humanities* [New Haven: Yale University Press,

1997].) Nor have all literary critics been tolerant of the interpretations of others. But if discussions of literature and works of art are adopting the attitudes of much of our discussions of social issues, that one and only one side can be right about meaning, then this book goes in the opposite direction. That queer theory allows for new and illuminating interpretations of the novels of Henry James is a cause for celebration, not dogmatic reaction. At the same time, such celebration does not mean that we cannot also be enlightened by more traditional approaches to his texts.

8. See Hans-Georg Gadamer, *Truth and Method*, trans. Joel Weinsheimer and Donald G. Marshall, 2d rev. ed. (New York: Crossroads Press, 1992), 302.

9. Columbia Pictures, 1995.

10. See Richard Rorty, *Consequences of Pragmatism* (Minneapolis: University of Minnesota Press, 1982).

11. See Kent Greenawalt, "Interpretation and Judgment," *Yale Journal of Law and Humanities* 9 (1997): 423–24, and my "Reply to Greenawalt," pp. 437–38 in the same issue.

12. Gadamer, *Truth and Method*, 296.

13. Ibid., 306.

14. See E. D. Hirsch, *Validity in Interpretation* (New Haven: Yale University Press, 1967), 31.

15. See Tony Tanner, introduction to Jane Austen, *Sense and Sensibility* (1811) (New York: Penguin Books, 1978), 7 and 15–22. See George Haggerty, "The Sacrifice of Privacy in *Sense and Sensibility*," *Tulsa Studies in Women's Literature* 7 (1988): 221–37.

16. Tanner, introduction to Austen, *Sense and Sensibility*, 15. To supplement this interpretation, we might note that it is Marianne's very sincerity and unwillingness to mask her feelings that attracts the man she eventually marries and that this man might be thought to possess far more substance than Edward, whose appeal seems, from some perspectives, limited to his ethical propriety. It may be for this reason that Thompson's film version adds a beginning sequence at Norland Park to give Edward more depth, evidently because he is so slight a character as written in the novel, at least for contemporary readers. But Marianne's eventual husband, Colonel Brandon, has both ethical propriety and a kind of depth of experience and sorrow that makes him more credible, at least to us, as someone Marianne or Elinor might love.

17. Haggerty, "Sacrifice of Privacy in *Sense and Sensibility*," 222.

18. Ibid., 234.

19. Gadamer, *Truth and Method*, p. 298.

20. Ibid., 291.

21. Ibid.

22. Ibid., 294.

23. Ibid.

24. Ibid.

25. Ibid., 457. Also see Hans-Georg Gadamer, *Dialogue and Dialectic: Eight Hermeneutical Studies on Plato*, trans. P. Christopher Smith (New Haven: Yale University Press, 1980), 146.

26. See Arthur Danto, *Analytical Philosophy of History* (Cambridge: Cambridge University Press, 1965), 17.

27. *Truth and Method,* 307–12.

28. See, for example, John Rawls, *Political Liberalism* (New York: Columbia University Press, 1992), and Michael Walzer, *Spheres of Justice* (New York: Basic Books, 1987). See also my *Justice and Interpretation* (Cambridge, Mass.: MIT Press, 1993).

29. Jürgen Habermas, *Between Facts and Norms: Contributions to a Discourse Theory of Law,* trans. William Rehg (Cambridge, Mass.: MIT Press, 1996), 307.

NOTES TO CHAPTER TWO

1. See Carmel Shalev, *Birth Power: The Case for Surrogacy* (New Haven: Yale University Press, 1989), 12.

2. See Cass R. Sunstein, "Neutrality in Constitutional Law (with Special Reference to Pornography, Abortion, and Surrogacy)," *Columbia Law Review* 92 (1992): 4, and Elizabeth S. Anderson, "Is Women's Labor a Commodity?" *Philosophy and Public Affairs* 19 (1990).

3. See, for example, Anderson, "Is Women's Labor a Commodity?"

4. See Shalev, *Birth Power,* esp. chapters 4 and 7.

5. Phyllis Chesler, *Sacred Bond: The Legacy of Baby M* (New York: Times Books, 1988), appendix A (pp. 169–73).

6. Ibid., appendix G (198–99).

7. Ibid., 208.

8. See A. M. C. M. Schellen, *Artificial Insemination in the Human* (New York: Elsevier, 1957), 245ff., and *Law and Ethics of A.I.D. and Embryo Transfer,* Cibe Foundation Symposium 17 (North Holland: Elsevier, 1973), 45ff.

9. Shalev, *Birth Power,* 27–28.

10. Ibid., 22.

11. Cited in Gena Corea, *The Mother Machine* (New York: Harper and Row, 1985), 47. Also see *Law and Ethics of A.I.D. and Embryo Transfer,* 48.

12. Schellen, *Artificial Insemination in the Human,* chapter 9.

13. Ibid., 150–54.

14. Cited in Shalev, *Birth Power,* 67.

15. Schellen, *Artificial Insemination in the Human,* 284. Even in 1976, "any display of interest" in the operation "by an unmarried woman" is called "evidence of psychological distress." Also see Shalev, *Birth Power,* 67.

16. Schellen, *Artificial Insemination in the Human,* 254.

17. The New York State Task Force on surrogate mothering argued that it "is not possible for women to give informed consent to the surrender of a child prior to the child's conception and birth." But it denied that this view rested on assumptions about women in particular. "The inability to predict and project a response to profound experiences that have not yet unfolded is shared by men and women alike" (quoted in Amy Gutmann and Dennis Thompson, *Democracy and Disagreement* [Cambridge, Mass.: Harvard University Press, 1996], 244).

Still, the task force assumes that childbirth necessarily counts as a profound experience for women and that surrogacy contracts should therefore be prohibited.

18. Quoted in Martha Field, *Surrogate Motherhood: The Legal and Human Issues* (Cambridge, Mass.: Harvard University Press, 1980), 20.

19. Chesler, *Sacred Bond*, appendix D (p. 185).

20. Ibid., esp. chapter 5, "A Pound of Flesh: Surrogacy, Adoption, and Contracts." See also Margaret Moorman, *Waiting to Forget: A Mother Opens the Door to Her Secret Past* (New York: W. W. Norton, 1996).

21. Carol Gilligan, *In a Different Voice: Psychological Theory and Women's Development* (Cambridge, Mass.: Harvard University Press, 1982).

22. See Nancy Chodorow, *The Reproduction of Mothering: Psychoanalysis and the Sociology of Gender* (Berkeley: University of California Press, 1978).

23. Gilligan, *In a Different Voice*, 26–28.

24. Ibid., 30.

25. Ibid., 127.

26. Mary Lyndon Shanley, "'Surrogate Mothering' and Women's Freedom: A Critique of Contracts for Human Reproduction," *Signs: Journal of Women in Culture and Society* 18 (1993): 633.

27. Anderson, "Is Women's Labor a Commodity?" 82. See also Elizabeth Anderson, *Value in Ethics and Economics* (Cambridge, Mass.: Harvard University Press, 1993), 168–89.

28. Barbara Katz Rothman, *Recreating Motherhood: Ideology and Technology in a Patriarchal Society* (New York: W. W. Norton, 1989), 242.

29. Thomas H. Murray, *The Worth of a Child* (Berkeley: University of California Press, 1996), 36.

30. Shalev, *Birth Power*, 127.

31. Ibid., 135–36.

32. Ibid., 98.

33. Compare Thomas Murray: "The emphasis . . . on control and choice does not fit well with our understanding of families. Good families are characterized more by acceptance than control. Furthermore, families are the preeminent realm of unchosen obligations. We may choose our spouses (although a persuasive argument could be made that for most of us this choice bears scarce resemblance to the model of rational, autonomous, carefully considered decision making). We may choose to have a child but . . . we do not choose to have this particular child, with its interests, moods, and manners. And as offspring, we certainly did not choose our parents" (*Worth of a Child*, 31). Murray thinks that this lack of control tells against surrogacy arrangements primarily because they try to control genetics. I think the lack of control that is part of belonging to a family only tells against our being able to control the path and consequences of any such fundamental arrangements, including child birth by traditional means.

34. Anderson, "Is Women's Labor a Commodity?" 75; Anderson, *Value in Ethics and Economics*, 170.

35. Anderson argues that, despite the majority of surrogates who relinquish their children to the sponsoring couple, giving the child up is typically difficult. The fact that most surrogates do not try to keep their children shows only that

they have been manipulated or intimidated by surrogate mothering agencies (see *Value in Ethics and Economics,* 185–87).

36. Anderson, "Is Women's Labor a Commodity?" 77.

37. See *New York Times,* February 17, 1990, 1.

38. Also see Shanley, "'Surrogate Mothering,'" 630.

39. See *New York Times,* August 29, 1993, 28.

40. See also Elizabeth Bartholet, *Family Bonds: Adoption and the Politics of Parenting* (Boston: Houghton Mifflin, 1993), especially chapters 3 and 4.

41. See, Lucinda Franks, "Annals of Law: The War for Baby Clausen," *New Yorker,* March 22, 1993, 56–73.

42. In the case of Baby Jessica, as in the somewhat similar case of Baby Richard, neither father had surrendered his parental rights. (See "High Court Call: Father's Right or Child's Interest?" *New York Times,* July 17, 1994.) Moreover, at least in the case of Baby Jessica the father moved swiftly to try to gain custody of the child as soon as he discovered its existence. A father who did not move swiftly in similar cases might be said to have abandoned his child and hence to have given implicit consent to its adoption. In the case of Baby Richard, however, why might his best interests not have resided in remaining with his adoptive parents with whom he had lived for almost four years while assuring that his biological father, who pursued a relation with him, had a significant part in his life?

43. Jürgen Habermas, *The Theory of Communicative Action,* vol. 2: *Lifeworld and System: A Critique of Functionalist Reason,* trans. Thomas McCarthy (Boston: Beacon Press, 1984), 361–73.

NOTES TO CHAPTER THREE

1. See Nicolaus Mills, "Introduction: To Look Like America," in Nicolaus Mills, ed., *Debating Affirmative Action: Race, Gender, Ethnicity and the Politics of Inclusion* (New York: Delta Books, 1994), 6.

2. Herman Belz, *Equality Transformed* (New Brunswick, N.J.: Transaction Publishers, 1991), 1–2.

3. Lino Graglia, "Title VII of the Civil Rights Act of 1964: From Prohibiting to Requiring Racial Discrimination in Employment," in Mills, ed., *Debating Affirmative Action,* 105.

4. *Bolling v Sharpe,* 347 US 497 (1954). See also the appendix to Richard Kluger, *Simple Justice* (New York: Random House, Vintage Books, 1977), 786.

5. Quoted in Ronald Dworkin, "How to Read the Civil Rights Act," in *A Matter of Principle* (Cambridge, Mass.: Harvard University Press, 1985), 316.

6. Belz, *Equality Transformed,* 9.

7. Mills, "Introduction: To Look Like America," 9.

8. Ibid, 11.

9. Ibid, 14.

10. Ibid, 12; Belz, *Equality Transformed,* 51–52.

11. Belz, *Equality Transformed,* 54.

12. Graglia, "Title VII of the Civil Rights Act of 1964," 107.

13. Belz, *Equality Transformed,* 136.

14. Ibid., 149.

15. Ibid., 154.

16. Graglia, "Title VII of the Civil Rights Act of 1964," 108.

17. Belz, *Equality Transformed,* 165.

18. Ibid., 234.

19. Ibid., 11.

20. Kluger, *Simple Justice,* 259.

21. Ibid., 275–76.

22. Ibid., 260.

23. *Sweatt v Painter,* 339 US 629 (1950).

24. Ibid.

25. *McLaurin v Oklahoma State Regents for Higher Education,* 399 US 637 (1950), quoted in Kluger, *Simple Justice,* 283.

26. *Brown v Board of Education of Topeka,* 347 US 483 (1954), quoted in Kluger, *Simple Justice,* 781–82.

27. *Brown v Board of Education of Topeka,* 349 US 487 (1955), cited in Jill Norgen and Serena Nanda, *American Cultural Pluralism and the Law* (New York: Praeger, 1988), 48.

28. Kluger, *Simple Justice,* 767.

29. Graglia, "Title VII of the Civil Rights Act of 1964," 106.

30. For an analysis of the way the Supreme Court withdrew from its integrationist tendencies in school desegregation cases after the *Swann* decision, see Donald E. Lively, *The Constitution and Race* (New York: Praeger, 1992), 118–30.

31. Dworkin, "How to Read the Civil Rights Act," 324.

32. Ibid., 319. 443 US 254 (1979) dissenting.

33. 443 US 204 (1979), quoted in Belz, *Equality Transformed,* 163.

34. Lyndon Johnson, "To Fulfill These Rights," speech delivered at Howard University, June 1965, quoted in Mills, "Introduction: To Look Like America," 7.

35. Shelby Steele, "A Negative Vote on Affirmative Action," in Mills, *Debating Affirmative Action,* 41.

36. See Stephen Carter, *Reflections of an Affirmative Action Baby* (New York: Basic Books, 1991), 12–17.

37. As a student at Harvard, Jerry Watts asked the law school dean why his friend, a member of Phi Beta Kappa, was not admitted into Harvard Law School although black students with lower GPAs were. The dean talked about the need for well-rounded candidates and then "mentioned that about 60% of the white students admitted . . . had lower GPA's than my friend. 'Why,' he said, 'don't you ask about them?'" "Symposium on Affirmative Action," *Dissent* 42 (1995): 476.

38. Charles Murray, "Affirmative Racism," in Mills, ed., *Debating Affirmative Action,* 199.

39. Ibid., 199.

40. Ibid., 202.

41. Ibid., 203.

42. Ibid., 204.

43. Ibid.

44. Ibid., 206–7.

45. See Brett Pulley, "A Reverse Discrimination Suit Upends Two Teachers' Lives," *New York Times*, August 3, 1997, 1.

46. Murray, "Affirmative Racism," 196.

47. Carter, *Reflections of an Affirmative Action Baby*, 71.

48. Ibid., 82–83.

49. Ibid., 50.

50. Murray, "Affirmative Racism," 206.

51. See, for example, Iris Marion Young, *Justice and the Politics of Difference* (Princeton: Princeton University Press, 1990), chapter 6.

52. See Chang-Lien Tien, "Diversity and Excellence in Higher Education," in Mills, ed., *Debating Affirmative Action*, 237–46.

53. See Cornel West, "The New Cultural Politics of Difference," in *Keeping Faith: Philosophy and Race in America* (New York: Routledge, 1993), 17. It is not clear that Young's analysis in *Justice and the Politics of Difference* presupposes this homogenization.

54. This account of the place of the ideal of diversity in affirmative action policies may seem to be at odds with the general thrust of this book, which is precisely to open up our public debates to the full range of legitimate interpretations of our principles and practices. More in keeping with this idea would seem to be Iris Young's argument, according to which affirmative action policies are necessary "neither to compensate for past discrimination nor to make up for supposed deficiencies of formerly excluded groups. Instead, the primary purpose of affirmative action is to mitigate the influence of current biases and blindnesses of institutions and decisionmakers" (*Justice and the Politics of Difference*, 198). Clearly, one of the virtues of affirmative action is to have helped to open up our public debates to a myriad of interpretations and perspectives on our history, as well as on our principles and practices. Moreover, this expansion of our public debates has served to mitigate some of our "biases and blindnesses."

The problem with a justification of affirmative action that looks to diversity, then, is not that diversity is not important and not that we should not look for ways to open up our public debates to the variety of legitimate voices that may be silenced or presently too quiet to hear. Still, while affirmative action policies are consistent with an integrationist understanding of the principle of equal opportunity, it remains unclear how the ideal of diversity is consistent with it. Hiring, promotion, and admissions decisions that look to race or gender, as well as to criteria involving merit and qualification, are consistent with the ideal of equal opportunity because the participation of these groups is affected by the continuing effects and actions of discrimination. But the participation of legitimate voices in our public debate does not require merit or qualification. It requires only the possibility of contributing. Hence, the relevant institutional structures would seem to involve institutions of free speech and the like, which I consider in Chapters Five and Six.

55. See "Symposium on Affirmative Action," 469–70.

56. Cornel West, *Race Matters* (Boston: Beacon Press, 1993), 52.

57. Randall Kennedy "Persuasion and Distrust: The Affirmative Action De-

bate," in Mills, ed., *Debating Affirmative Action,* 52. Or, as Virginia Held defines
the pertinent question, "given continuing discrimination, is it better for women
and minority members to face the slurs and innuendoes from the position of having a job or a promotion or a degree, or to face comparable slurs and innuendoes about a lack of competence or merit from the position of not having the job
or the promotion or the degree?" ("Symposium on Affirmative Action," 467).

58. Carter, *Reflections of an Affirmative Action Baby,* 89–90.

59. Ibid., 86.

60. Ibid., 95.

61. See Joanne Barkan, "Symposium on Affirmative Action," 462.

NOTES TO CHAPTER FOUR

1. Lawrence Tribe, *Abortion: The Clash of Absolutes* (New York: W. W. Norton, 1990), 3.

2. Ibid., 3. Also see Chapter One above.

3. Ronald Dworkin, *Life's Dominion: An Argument about Abortion, Euthanasia, and Individual Freedom* (New York: Alfred A. Knopf, 1993).

4. Ibid., 11.

5. Ibid., 12.

6. Ibid., 16–17.

7. Ibid., 18.

8. Ibid., 14–15.

9. See Chapter One. Thomas H. Murray's analysis of a derivative or what he
calls a "top-down" pro-life position points to the possibility that it contains another internal conflict. Many pro-life advocates consider the practice and extent
of abortion in the United States to be the equivalent of the Nazis' genocide of the
Jews. But, if they do, Murray argues that they must, for consistency's sake and
if they would have supported violence against those who ran the death camps,
also support fanatics who bomb abortion clinics or kill doctors who perform
abortions. Or, if they do not support violence in the abortion case, they would
have had to oppose violence even against those death camp operators. It seems
likely that many pro-life advocates, in contrast, would have supported violence
against Nazis and do not support the killing of those who perform abortions.
Hence, it is not clear that the problem with abortion for them is directly tied to
fetal personhood. For Murray, as for Dworkin, in any case, top-down arguments about personhood are a dead-end in the debate. See Thomas H. Murray,
The Worth of a Child (Berkeley: University of California Press, 1996), 151–57.

10. Dworkin, *Life's Dominion,* 28.

11. Ibid., 15.

12. Ibid., 163.

13. *United States v Seeger,* 380 US 163 (1965). The opinion continues: "the
idea of God has taken hold in many forms. Mention of only two—Hinduism
and Buddhism—illustrates the fluidity and evanescent scope of the concept."

14. Dworkin, *Life's Dominion,* 163.

15. Ibid., 149.

16. Kristin Luker, *Abortion and the Politics of Motherhood* (Berkeley: Uni-

versity of California Press, 1984), and Faye Ginsburg, *Contested Lives: The Abortion Debate in an American Community* (Berkeley: University of California Press, 1984).

17. Luker, *Abortion and the Politics of Motherhood*, 195; Ginsburg, *Contested Lives*, 172–193.

18. Luker, *Abortion and the Politics of Motherhood*, 197.

19. Ibid., 168.

20. Ibid., 167–68.

21. Ibid., 198.

22. Ginsburg, *Contested Lives*, 127–29.

23. I have extrapolated here from the findings Luker reports in *Abortion and the Politics of Motherhood*, 159–63.

24. Ginsburg, *Contested Lives*, 185.

25. Luker, *Abortion and the Politics of Motherhood*, 178.

26. See ibid., 176–78.

27. Ibid., 181; See also the remarks of a pro-choice activist in Ginsburg, *Contested Lives*, 153: "In my experience, people who have made the choice to have an abortion made it because they want a strong family."

28. Luker, *Abortion and the Politics of Motherhood*, 182.

29. See Chapter Two.

30. Luker, *Abortion and the Politics of Motherhood*, 176.

31. Ibid., 158.

32. Ibid., 191.

33. Also see Laurie Shrage, *Moral Dilemmas of Feminism: Prostitution, Adultery, and Abortion* (New York: Routledge, 1994), chapter 3.

34. Ronald Dworkin, "How Law Is Like Literature," in *A Matter of Principle* (Cambridge, Mass.: Harvard University Press, 1985), 149. Also see my *Justice and Interpretation* (Cambridge, Mass.: MIT Press, 1993), chapter 4.

35. See Ronald Dworkin, *Law's Empire* (Cambridge, Mass.: Harvard University Press, 1986), 230ff.

36. Ibid., 150.

37. Luker, *Abortion and the Politics of Motherhood*, 159.

38. See, for example, Kathleen McDonnell, *Not an Easy Choice: A Feminist Re-Examines Abortion* (Boston: South End Press, 1984), 46–47.

39. Also interesting in this regard is the Japanese practice called *mizuko kuyo*, which involves a memorial service in which the death of a fetus is acknowledged. As June O'Connor writes, "*mizuko kuyo* enables the woman who has lost or terminated her offspring to process her feelings ritually, in a home or temple religious ceremony, at the same time that it provides the larger community—husband, children and siblings, extended family, and others—an opportunity to mourn the loss of the fetus and to reflect on the ways in which they suffer or benefit from this loss" ("Ritual Recognition of Abortion: Japanese Buddhist Practices and American Jewish and Christian Proposals," paper presented to the American Academy of Religion, November 22, 1993). See Tribe's account in *Abortion: The Clash of Absolutes*, 61.

40. See, in particular, Elizabeth Bartholet, *Family Bonds: Adoption and the Politics of Parenting* (Boston: Houghton Mifflin, 1993).

41. Many pro-life advocates seem already to admit this point. Thus, in *Life Itself: Abortion in the American Mind* (New York: W. W. Norton, 1990), 153–54, Roger Rosenblatt quotes Marlys Popma, president of the Iowa Right to Life Committee: "The pro-life movement had better, doggone better, be ready to help in crisis pregnancies. To help, we are going to have to regear our focus. It is going to have to be geared toward dealing compassionately with that girl in crisis pregnancy. Am I going to be willing to take her child or her into my home and am I going to be willing, are we going to be willing in the Right to Life movement to initiate and help in programs where these girls can continue their education? Where they don't necessarily have to get stuck on a welfare roll because they are children having children?"

42. A more general problem in this regard is how we can act on or maintain our conviction of the validity of our understanding of our principles if we know it to be only one possible interpretation of them. I shall take up this "performative" problem at greater length in Chapter Seven in conjunction with Bernard Williams's account of the problem of ethical knowledge in multicultural societies.

43. See Rosenblatt, *Life Itself: Abortion in the American Mind*, 8, 43, and 135.

44. Ibid., 6. Rosenblatt's book demonstrates all of these virtues.

45. See also Nancy (Ann) Davis, "The Abortion Debate: The Search for Common Ground Part I," *Ethics* 103 (1993): 538.

46. See Chapter Three.

47. Cass Sunstein, "Neutrality in Constitutional Law (with Special Reference to Pornography, Abortion, and Surrogacy," *Columbia Law Review* 92 (1992): 1–52.

48. Ibid., 32.

49. *DeShaney v Winnebago County Department of Social Services*, 489 US 189, 195 (1989). See Sunstein, "Neutrality in Constitutional Law," 41 n. 148.

50. Sunstein, "Neutrality in Constitutional Law," 34.

51. Ibid., 32.

52. Eileen L. McDonagh, *Breaking the Abortion Deadlock* (Oxford: Oxford University Press, 1996), 11.

53. Compare the views of women's roles and selfishness in the debate over surrogate mothering (Chapter Two).

54. Sunstein, "Neutrality in Constitutional Law," 36.

55. Amy Gutmann and Dennis Thompson, *Democracy and Disagreement* (Cambridge, Mass.: Harvard University Press, 1996), 375 n. 21.

56. I am grateful to Michael Walzer for help with this argument.

NOTES TO CHAPTER FIVE

1. See Harry Kalven Jr., *A Worthy Tradition: The Freedom of Speech in America*, ed. Jamie Kalven (New York: Harper and Row, 1988), chapter 3.

2. These terms characterize the test for obscenity as formulated by the decision in *Miller v California* (413 US 24 [1973]); cited in Kalven, *Worthy Tradition*, 49–50.

3. See, for example, Andrea Dworkin, *Pornography: Men Possessing Women* (New York: Penguin Books, 1989), xxxiii, and Catherine MacKinnon, *Only Words* (Cambridge, Mass.: Harvard University Press, 1993), 22.

4. See Nadine Strossen, *Defending Pornography: Free Speech, Sex, and the Fight for Women's Rights* (New York: Scribner, 1995), 250–56, for studies that show no correlation between pornography and increased harm to women, and see Susan M. Easton, *The Problem of Pornography: Regulation and the Right to Free Speech* (New York: Routledge, 1995), 10–31, for studies that indicate the opposite.

5. I am using the idea of sexual authenticity to cover both the claim anti-pornography feminists make that certain expressions of sexuality are ideologically distorted and the claim free speech feminists make that pornography encourages the blossoming of new sexual identities.

6. *United States v Schwimmer,* 279 US 644 (1929) dissenting, quoted in Strossen, *Defending Pornography,* 39.

7. *Whitney v California* 274 US 357 (1927) concurring, quoted in Strossen, *Defending Pornography,* 48.

8. Ibid.

9. Jennifer Hornsby, "Speech Acts and Pornography," in Susan Dwyer, ed., *The Problem of Pornography* (Belmont, Calif.: Wadsworth, 1994), 220–32.

10. Ibid., 225.

11. Quoted from *The Sunday Times,* December 12, 1982, in Hornsby, "Speech Acts and Pornography," 226.

12. *The Times,* June 10, 1993, quoted in Hornsby, "Speech Acts and Pornography," 232 n. 6. MacKinnon tells another horror story: "In the prosecution by Trish Crawford of South Carolina against her husband for marital rape, a thirty-minute videotape he took of the assault was shown. In it, Mr. Crawford has intercourse with her and penetrates her with objects while her hands and legs are tied with rope and her mouth is gagged and eyes blinded with duct tape. He was acquitted on a consent defense. . . . The defendant testified he did not think his wife was serious when she said 'no'" (*Only Words,* 114 n. 3). For a treatment of the issues pornography raises with regard to Gadamer's hermeneutics, see my "Legitimate Prejudices," *Laval théologique and philosophique* 53 (1997): 89–103.

13. See Cass R. Sunstein, "Neutrality in Constitutional Law (with Special Reference to Pornography, Abortion, and Surrogacy)," *Columbia Law Review* 92 (1992): 22–25.

14. Easton, *Problem of Pornography,* 55–56.

15. See Sunstein, "Neutrality in Constitutional Law," 28.

16. Ibid.

17. See MacKinnon, *Only Words,* 79.

18. See Sunstein, "Neutrality in Constitutional Law."

19. *Buckley v Valeo,* 424, US 1, 48–49 (1976), cited in Sunstein, "Neutrality in Constitutional Law," 10.

20. MacKinnon, *Only Words,* 78.

21. See Kalven, *Worthy Tradition,* 445–47.

22. *Red Lion Broadcasting v FCC,* 395 US 367 (1969).

23. *Kleindiest v Mandel,* 408 US 753 (1972).

24. *Stanley v Georgia,* 394 US 557 (1969). See Kalven, *Worthy Tradition,* 45–46.

25. *Abrams v United States,* 250 US 630 (1919). Quoted in Kalven, *Worthy Tradition,* 145.

26. In Ronald Dworkin, "Do We Have a Right to Pornography?" in *A Matter of Principle* (Cambridge, Mass.: Harvard University Press, 1985).

27. See Rae Langton, "Whose Right? Ronald Dworkin, Women, and Pornographers," in Dwyer, ed., *Problem of Pornography,* 102.

28. Dworkin, "Do We Have a Right to Pornography?" 360.

29. Ibid., 364.

30. Ibid., 353.

31. Ibid., 364.

32. Feinberg makes a different use of this suggestion than Langton. See Joel Feinberg, *Offense to Others* (New York: Oxford University Press, 1985), 151, and Langton, "Whose Right?" 105.

33. MacKinnon, *Only Words,* 12.

34. Ibid., 13.

35. Ibid., 7

36. Strossen, *Defending Pornography,* 60.

37. Ibid., 39.

38. Also see Chapter Three.

39. Strossen, *Defending Pornography,* 149.

40. Christine Wenz, "In Our Heads," *Stranger,* July 5–11, 1993, quoted in Strossen, *Defending Pornography,* 150.

41. See Georg Lukacs, *History and Class Consciousness* (Cambridge, Mass.: MIT Press, 1972), 83–110.

42. Lisa Duggen, Nan D. Hunter, and Carole S. Vance, "False Premises: Feminist Anti-Pornography Legislation," in *Caught Looking,* 82, quoted in Strossen, *Defending Pornography,* 175–76.

43. See Ellen Willis, "Feminism, Moralism, and Pornography," in Dwyer, ed., *Problem of Pornography,* 170–76.

44. Myrna Kotesh, "Second Thoughts," in *Women against Censorship,* 37, quoted in Strossen, *Defending Pornography,* 175.

45. Strossen documents instances of MacKinnon's refusal to debate anti-antipornography feminists. MacKinnon's excuse seems to be that the form of such debates plays into "the pimps' . . . strategy for legitimizing a slave trade in women" (see Strossen, *Defending Pornography,* 85).

46. MacKinnon, *Only Words,* 25.

47. Strossen, *Defending Pornography,* 40.

48. This third conception is the one Alexander Meiklejohn promotes in *Political Freedom: The Constitutional Powers of the People* (New York: Harper, 1960). The formulation of the three ideas of the meaning of the principle of free speech that I am using comes from Paul G. Stern's note, "A Pluralistic Reading of the First Amendment and Its Relation to Public Discourse," *Yale Law Journal* 99 (1990): 926–27.

49. See Jürgen Habermas, *Moral Consciousness and Communicative Action* (Cambridge, Mass.: MIT Press, 1990).

50. 163 US 537 (1896).

51. See Strossen, *Defending Pornography,* 200.

52. MacKinnon, *Only Words,* 91–92.

53. Strossen, *Defending Pornography,* 204.

54. See ibid., 229–33.

55. See, for example, Jürgen Habermas, "Morality and Ethical Life," in *Moral Consciousness and Communicative Action,* trans. Christian Lenhardt and Shierry Weber Nicholsen (Cambridge Mass.: MIT Press, 1990), 197.

NOTES TO CHAPTER SIX

1. Also see Amy Gutmann and Dennis Thompson, *Democracy and Disagreement* (Cambridge, Mass.: Harvard University Press, 1996).

2. See Jürgen Habermas, *Between Facts and Norms,* trans. William Rehg (Cambridge, Mass.: MIT Press, 1996), 96–97.

3. Ibid., 159.

4. Jürgen Habermas, "On the Pragmatic, the Ethical, and the Moral Employments of Practical Reason," in Habermas, *Justification and Application,* trans. Ciaran P. Cronin, (Cambridge, Mass.: MIT Press, 1994), 3.

5. Ibid., 4.

6. Ibid., 6.

7. Ibid., 16.

8. Habermas, *Between Facts and Norms,* 160.

9. Ibid., 162.

10. Ibid., 164.

11. Ibid., 165.

12. Ibid.

13. Ibid.

14. See Steven Vogel, *Against Nature: The Concept of Nature in Critical Theory* (Albany: State University of New York Press, 1996).

15. See Charles Taylor and Amy Gutmann, *Multiculturalism and "The Politics of Recognition"* (Princeton: Princeton University Press, 1992), 51–61.

16. Habermas, *Between Facts and Norms,* 167.

17. Ibid., 163.

18. Ibid., 282.

19. Ibid., 108.

20. Ibid., 281.

21. John Rawls's use of public reason is somewhat similar. On the one hand, Rawls recognizes the interpretive element of our disagreements over important issues. Hence, among the sources of such disagreement he lists the vagueness of our concepts, a vagueness that "means we must rely on judgment and interpretation (and on judgments about interpretations) within some range (not sharply specifiable) where reasonable persons may differ" (*Political Liberalism* [New York: Columbia University Press, 1993], 56). Moreover, he claims that:

> To some extent . . . the way we assess evidence and weigh moral and political values is shaped by our total experience, our whole course of life up to now; and our total experiences must always differ. Thus, in a modern society with its numerous offices and positions, its ethnic variety, citizens' total experiences are disparate enough for their judgments to diverge, at least to some degree, on many if not most cases of any significant complexity. (57)

On the other hand, as Habermas does, Rawls associates interpretive disagreement with disagreements between different private views and different comprehensive doctrines, disagreements that lead reasonable people to "endorse some form of liberty of conscience and freedom of thought" (61). In the political sphere, in contrast, public reason requires recourse only to publicly agreed-upon principles and political values. Of course, where Habermas appeals to a political discourse that ties ethical and pragmatic discourses to moral discourse, Rawls limits political discourse to public political values and banishes both comprehensive moral and ethical views to the private sphere. Still, both solutions seem to overlook an important sort of public discussion, namely interpretive discussion of how we differ in our understanding of our fundamental principles and political values.

22. Habermas, "Remarks on Discourse Ethics," 60.

23. See Chapter Four above and Ronald Dworkin, *Life's Dominion: An Argument about Abortion, Euthanasia, and Individual Freedom* (New York: Alfred A. Knopf, 1993).

24. See Chapter Four above.

25. Jürgen Habermas, *The Theory of Communicative Action,* trans. Thomas McCarthy (Boston: Beacon Press, 1984), 25.

26. See Habermas, *Between Facts and Norms,* 232–33.

27. Klaus Günther, *The Sense of Appropriateness: Application Discourse in Morality and Law,* trans. John Farrell (Albany: State University of New York Press, 1993).

28. Habermas, *Between Facts and Norms,* 217. See also "Remarks on Discourse Ethics," 38.

29. Habermas, *Between Facts and Norms,* 218.

30. Ibid. See also Günther, *Sense of Appropriateness,* 229–38.

31. Habermas, *Between Facts and Norms,* 229.

32. Ibid., 229.

33. Ibid., 307.

34. Ibid., 307–8.

35. Ibid., 167.

36. Ibid., 179.

37. Thomas McCarthy, "Practical Discourse: On the Relation of Morality to Politics," in Craig Calhoun, ed., *Habermas and the Public Sphere* (Cambridge, Mass.: MIT Press, 1992), 66.

38. Ibid., 65.

39. Ibid., 67.

40. Bernard Williams, *Ethics and the Limits of Philosophy* (Cambridge, Mass.: Harvard University Press, 1985).

NOTES TO CHAPTER SEVEN

1. Hans-Georg Gadamer, *Truth and Method,* trans. Joel Weinsheimer and Donald G. Marshall, 2d rev. ed. (New York: Continuum, 1994).

2. Ibid., 270. Also see my *Gadamer: Hermeneutics, Tradition, and Reason* (Stanford: Stanford University Press, 1987), 75–82.

3. Gadamer, *Truth and Method,* 277–85.

4. Jane Austen, *Pride and Prejudice* (New York: Bantam Classic Edition, 1981).

5. Bernard Williams, *Ethics and the Limits of Philosophy* (Cambridge, Mass.: Harvard University Press, 1985), 142.

6. Austen, *Pride and Prejudice,* 154.

7. Ibid., 145.

8. Ibid., 153.

9. Ibid., 156.

10. That Austen can describe such processes seems fairly well established by her other work. See, for example, George Haggerty's account of her attempts to find a suitable language for expressing them in "'The Sacrifice of Privacy' in *Sense and Sensibility,*" *Tulsa Studies in Women's Literature* 7 (1988):230–33.

11. Austen, *Pride and Prejudice,* 280.

12. Also see Gadamer, *Truth and Method,* 279.

13. This is the title given by the editors to my review of Gadamer's *Truth and Method* in *New Society* (1988).

14. Austen, *Pride and Prejudice,* 155.

15. Austen may be trying to establish this tradition, a tradition emphasizing virtue instead of wealth, in writing *Pride and Prejudice.* The point I am making, however, is that Elizabeth Bennet can rely upon the former tradition in trying to sort through her confusion and that only by relying upon some such tradition of action and behavior can she sort through it at all. I am grateful to the participants in the *Journal of the History of Ideas* conference on "Tradition," in New Brunswick, New Jersey, in November 1997 for help with this point.

16. Austen, *Pride and Prejudice,* 155.

17. Ibid., 282.

18. Ibid., 268.

19. See Chapter Two above and Carmel Shalev, *Birth Power: The Case for Surrogacy* (New Haven: Yale University Press, 1989).

20. See, for example, Elizabeth Anderson, *Value in Ethics and Economics* (Cambridge, Mass.: Harvard University Press, 1993), 168–89.

21. Williams, *Ethics and the Limits of Philosophy,* 140.

22. Ibid., 141.

23. Ibid., 147.

24. Ibid., 145.

25. Ibid., 147.

26. Ibid.

27. Ibid., 143–44.

28. Ibid., 158.

29. Ibid.

30. Ibid., 159.

31. Ibid., 149–60.

32. Ibid., 171.

33. See Gadamer, *Truth and Method*, 373. Also see Chapter One.

34. See George Haggerty, *Unnatural Affections: Women and Fiction in the Later Eighteenth Century* (Bloomington: Indiana University Press, 1998).

35. See Edward Copeland and Juliet McMaster, eds., *The Cambridge Companion to Jane Austen* (Cambridge: Cambridge University Press, 1997).

36. See Diane P. Michelfelder and Richard E. Palmer, *Dialogue and Deconstruction: The Gadamer–Derrida Debate* (Albany: State University of New York Press, 1989). Also see Chapter One above.

37. Dworkin thus insists that his criteria of fit and best light stand and fall together. See "How Law Is Like Literature," in *A Matter of Principle* (Cambridge, Mass.: Harvard University Press, 1985). See also Chapter Four above.

38. See Chapter Four above and, for example, Kristin Luker, *Abortion and the Politics of Motherhood* (Berkeley: University of California Press, 1984).

39. See Shalev, *Birth Power.*

NOTES TO CHAPTER EIGHT

1. Andrew Sullivan, *Virtually Normal: An Argument about Homosexuality* (New York: Alfred A. Knopf, 1995), 179.

2. See Chapter Two above.

3. U.S. Constitution, amendment 2, quoted in Robert Emmet Long, ed., *Gun Control* (New York: H. W. Wilson, 1989), 8.

4. Robert E. Shalhope, "The Ideological Origins of the Second Amendment," in Long, ed., *Gun Control,* 15–17.

5. "The Second Amendment and the Right to Bear Arms: An Exchange," in Long, ed., *Gun Control,* 51.

6. Lawrence Delbar Cress, "An Armed Community: The Original Meaning of the Right to Bear Arms," in Long, ed., *Gun Control,* 46.

7. Naomi Wolf, *Fire with Fire: The New Female Power and How It Will Change the Twenty-First Century* (New York: Random House, 1993), 216. See also Nancy Zeiss Stange, "Arms and the Woman: A Feminist Reappraisal," in David B. Kopel, ed., *Guns: Who Should Have Them* (New York: Prometheus Books, 1995), 15.

8. Ronald Dworkin, *Life's Dominion: An Argument about Abortion, Euthanasia, and Individual Freedom* (New York: Alfred A. Knopf, 1993), 214.

9. Ibid., 215.

10. Our current discussion of the death penalty does not seem to be focused on the question of deterrence. In a 1986 Gallup pole, 73 percent of those who supported capital punishment said they would continue to do so even if it could be shown that it had no deterrent effect. Similarly, 71 percent of those who opposed capital punishment said they would do so even if it could be shown that it did have a deterrent effect. See Raymond Paternoster, *Capital Punishment in America* (New York: Lexington Books, 1991), 246.

Index

Text: 10/13 Sabon
Display: Sabon
Composition: G & S Typesetters, Inc.
Printing and binding: Thomson-Shore